Hocąk Teaching Materials
Volume 2

Texts with Analysis and Translation
and an Audio-CD of Original Hocąk Texts

North American Native Peoples, Past and Present

Raymond Demallie and Douglas Parks, editors

Hocąk Teaching Materials
Volume 2

Texts with Analysis and Translation
and an Audio-CD of Original Hocąk Texts

EDITORS

Iren Hartmann
Christian Marschke

HOCĄK ASSISTANTS

Bill O'Brien†
Chloris Lowe Sr.
Corina Lonetree
Carolyn White Eagle
Ed Lonetree
Cecil Garvin
Richard Mann

Cover photograph by Sylvio Tüpke.

Published by State University of New York Press, Albany

Printed in the United States of America

For information, contact State University of New York Press, Albany, NY
www.sunypress.edu

Library of Congress Cataloging-in-Publication Data

Hocąk teaching materials. Vol. 2 : Texts with Analysis and Translation, and an Audio-CD of original Hocąk Texts / editors iren Hartmann, Christian Marschke.
p. cm.
ISBN 978-1-4384-3335-6 (alk. paper) – ISBN 978-1-4384-3336-3 (pbk. : alk. paper) 1. Winnebago language–Grammar. 2. Winnebago language–Phonetics. 3. Winnebago language–Spoken Winnebago. 4. Indians of North America–Languages. I. Hartmann, Iren. II. Marschke, Christian.
PM2591.H64 2010
497'.526–dc22

2010000814

10 9 8 7 6 5 4 3 2 1

Contents

Preface

The Hocąk texts presented in this volume have been recorded, documented and prepared for publication in the research project "Documentation of the Hocąk language" conducted at the University of Erfurt, Germany during the years 2003–2008 and funded by Volkswagen Foundation in its program "Documentation of endangered languages" (DoBeS). The original plan was to publish one volume of Hocąk teaching materials consisting of a learners dictionary, some elements of grammar, and just one analyzed text, Child Teaching (Text #4 in this volume). But since these are teaching (and learning) materials, we have decided to provide the prospective learner with more actual language material from our "oral library" in a separate volume.

This volume is therefore the second part of a two volume edition and complements a concurrent publication of the project:

Helmbrecht, Johannes & Lehmann, Christian (eds.) 2010, *Hocąk Teaching Materials. Volume I. Elements of Grammar. Learner's Dictionary.* Albany: SUNY Press.

Volume 1 not only provides the basic Hocąk vocabulary but also explains some important elements of Hocąk grammar. These explanations are crucial for the full comprehension of the grammatical glosses used in this volume's analyzed texts. Thus, we strongly recommend obtaining and using both volumes in order to make full use of these teaching materials.

We would like to take the opportunity to thank all the Hocąk speakers who agreed to have their stories published in this volume. We are very grateful for all their help, patience, and kindness. We particularly want to thank Chloris Lowe Sr. who kindly prepared and provided the artwork illustrating the Child teaching story and of course Cecil Garvin who helped us not only by providing a story, but also by proofreading our transcriptions and making sure we weren't missing any words from the original stories.

We hope that these materials will contribute to the Hocąk Nation's efforts to preserve and revitalize their ancestors' language.

Erfurt/Leipzig, February 2010 Iren Hartmann and Christian Marschke

1 Introduction

The purpose of the texts presented here is to show the learner how the words and grammatical information given in Volume 1 are used in actual speech. All texts are provided with a precise grammatical analysis and a word-by-word as well as a free translation. Despite the detailed analysis this material is not meant to serve academic purposes, but rather as a reference tool for the learner (or the teacher) of the Hocąk language.

The enclosed Audio-CD contains recordings of all texts made for documentary purposes in the afore mentioned research project. Language documentation is largely dedicated to preserving "natural" spoken language. Just as for the main part of our text corpus, this holds true for all texts presented here. Thus, most of the recordings are not of studio quality. Despite the sometimes not so perfect quality the language learner is advised not only to read the texts, but also to listen to the audios in order to get an impression of how the words are pronounced.

To some extend text #4 (Child teaching, see §5) is an exception to this: The text itself is of oral origin – as are all Hocąk texts, since the Hocąk language has never been a written language, until most recently. "Nįįkjąk hookárakų́ Teaching His Child" was originally recorded by Amelia Susmann by the end of the 1930s and was eventually included in her PhD dissertation (1943:134-47) submitted at Columbia University[1]. Unfortunately, the original recording has been lost. The audio track provided on the CD contains a recording of Bill O'Brien reading this text. The content of the original text as it is presented in Susmann (1943) has not been modified. However, the text has been processed according to modern linguistic standards. That is, the text received a word-by-word translation and grammatical glosses. The orthographic representation was adapted to the learner's orthography as described and used in the dictionary. Furthermore, the translation has been checked with contemporary speakers of Hocąk. The speaker in the recording read the entire text very carefully and slowly articulated each word separately without merging or contracting any of them (this normally happens in rapid speech and can be heard in many of the other recordings). Thus, the form of the text given here separates words and indicates primary stress exactly on the syllable where Bill O'Brien pronounced main stress. This explains the differences in writing and stress marking in our representation of the Susmann text. All other texts are represented here as closely to the way they were told as possible. Parenthesis may indicate a speaker's hesitiation or false starts.

Presentation of the text

The presentation of the texts requires some explanation. Every text is represented in two different ways: (i) as an analyzed version (§X.1) and (ii) as the plain text version (§X.2 for the Hocąk text and §X.3 for the English translation). In its first representation, each sentence comprises four lines that are easily distinguished by their different colors and font sizes. The first line contains the Hocąk sentence in the learner's Hocąk orthography. The second line segments the sentence into words and grammatical parts and the third line assigns to each word or grammatical part exactly one English meaning or one grammatical gloss. For instance, sentence #3 of the Connection text (text #6, see §7) begins like this:

[1] Susmann, Amelia 1943. *The Accentual System of Winnebago*. Unpubl. PhD dissertation. New York: Columbia University.

Line	Content	Example
#1	Original sentence in Hocąk learner's orthography	BO: hąą CG: Hagoreižą 'eejašge hakirira, ...
#2	Words and their grammatical parts	BO: hąą CG: Hagoreižą 'eeja-šge ha-kiri-ra ...
#3	Their English meaning	BO: yes CG: sometime there-also 1E.A-arrive.back.here-DEF
#4	A free translation	BO: Yes. CG: At one time when I came back there, ...

The last word in the first line (#1) *hakirira* consists of three parts, the verb stem *kiri* 'arrive back here', the pronominal form *ha-* '1E.A' (meaning 'I') and the definite article *-ra* 'DEF'. All three parts are separated by a hyphen in line two. The English meaning and the grammatical glosses are aligned in the third line exactly in the same order and are also separated by a hyphen. The fourth line contains the free English translation of the sentence. This is also an example for a dialogic sequence, of which many can be found throughout our texts. If two or more speakers are talking to each other, their initials are used to indicate who is speaking.

The plain text versions are for the advanced learner who no longer needs the grammatical segmentation. The entire Hocąk texts as well as their free English translations are rendered separately without any further grammatical analysis. All sentences are numbered so that reference can be made to the grammatically analyzed versions, if needed.

2 A bear appears (Bill O'Brien) (CD 1 track 1)

2.1 Text with analysis and translation

1. BO: Jaagušge hihekjenegųnį, hegų wažą
BO: jaagu-šge hihe-kjene-gųnį hegų wažą
BO: what-also say\1E.A-FUT-DUB that.way something

jaanįkrašąną ha'e haagi hegų.
jaanįk-ra-šąną ha'e_haa-gi hegų
be.drunk/foolish(OBJ.3SG)-DEF-only talk.about\1E.A-TOP that.way

BO: I wonder what am I going to say, I'll only talk about foolish things.

2. Wažą jaanįkrašąną ha'e haagi, hegų kiira.
wažą jaanįk-ra-šąną ha'e_haa-gi hegų kira
something be.drunk/foolish(OBJ.3SG)-DEF-only talk.about\1E.A-TOP that.way only

I'll talk about foolish things only, that's all.

3. Jaagurašge hižą hotaknągųnį?
jaagu-ra-šge hižą hotak-nąą-gųnį
what-DEF-also one tell\1E.A-POT-DUB

I wonder what I can tell about?

4. Hegų...
hegų
that.way

Well...

5. CL: Hegų wažąñą hižą hotaki, hegų warukos
CL: hegų wažą-ra hižą hotak-gi hegų waarukos
CL: that.way something-DEF one tell\1E.A-TOP that.way police

hįįguajiraną.
hį-hagu-ha-jii-ire-ną
1E.U-fetch-COLL-arrive.here-SBJ.3PL-POT

CL: When I tell something the police may come and get me.

6. BO: Neecąą hanįrukosire.
BO: nee-cąą ha<nį>rukos-ire
BO: 2EMPH-instead <2.U>hold-SBJ.3PL

BO: Then they arrest you instead.

7.

CL:	Hąhą,	'ee	nąąk'ų...
CL:	hąhą	`ee	nąąk-`ų
CL:	yes	3EMPH	POS.NTL.PL-SIM

CL: Yes, while they do that...

8.

BO:	Hagoreižą	wii howešgųnį	'eeja	hahiwira,	haastįk
BO:	hagoreižą	wii_howešgųnį	`eeja	ha-hii-wi-ra	haastįk
BO:	sometime	north	there	1E.A-arrive.there-PL-DEF	blueberry

hagihį	hahiwi,	hąįnįgają	hegų	hogihi	'eeja	hegų
ha-gihi	ha-hii-wi	hąįnį-gają	hegų	ho-gihi	`eeja	hegų
1E.A-pick	1E.A-arrive.there-PL	morning-SEQ	that.way	APPL.INESS-pick	there	that.way

caawawigają,	hija	hahiwį.
caa<ha>we-wi-gają	hija	ha-hii-wį
<1E.A>approach-PL-SEQ	there	1E.A-arrive.there-PL

BO: At one time we went up north, we went there to pick blueberries, in the morning we headed to the picking spot, we arrived there.

9.

Cooka	'eera	hireanąga	hįnį	haara,	Hank	T
cooka	`ee-ra	hireanąga	hįnį	haa-ra	Hank	T
grandfather	have.kin\1E.A-DEF	along.with	older.brother	have.kin\1E.A-DEF	Hank	T

Rave,	hegų	'eeja	wagihinąąkšąną,	hegų	hokisaknįįsge
Rave	hegų	`eeja	wa-gihi-nąąk-šąną	hegų	hokisak-nįįsge
Rave	that.way	there	OBJ.3PL-pick-POS.NTL.PL-DECL	that.way	middle-VAGUE

'eeja	paac	hižą	mįįnąkšąną.
`eeja	paac	hižą	mįįnąk-šąną
there	woods	one	sit-DECL

My grandfather and my older brother Hank T Rave (they) were sitting there picking, and in the sort of the middle there was a little grove of trees there (sitting).

10.

Hegų	xųnųįkšąną	hegų,	hegų	hogįgįx	žee	'eeja
hegų	xųnų-įk-šąną	hegų	hegų	hogįgįx	žee	`eeja
that.way	be.small(OBJ.3PL)-DIM-DECL	that.way	that.way	go.around	that	there

haastįk	gihinąąkšąną.
haastįk	gihi-nąąk-šąną
blueberry	pick-POS.NTL.PL-DECL

It (the grove) was small, and all around there they were picking blueberries.

11. Hegų 'ųų hanįhaire, tee woiraki hųųc seep
hegų 'ųų ha-nįhe-ire tee woiraki hųųc seep
that.way do/make COLL-be/PROG-SBJ.3PL this suddenly bear be.black(OBJ.3SG)

hižą 'eeja huu.
hižą 'eeja huu
one there come.here(SBJ.3SG)

And they continued to pick and then all of a sudden a black bear came.

12. Hegų cooka 'eera hireanąga Hank Tga, hąąke hija
hegų cooka 'ee-ra hireanąga Hank T-ga hąąke hija
that.way grandfather have.kin\1E.A-DEF along.with Hank T-PROP NEG.IN there

howesįwįñąnį.
howesįwį-ire-nį
notice-SBJ.3PL-NEG.FIN

My grandfather and Hank T did not notice it.

13. Hegų jaagu paacnąka hogįgix hegų 'eeja
hegų jaagu paac-nąka hogįgix hegų 'eeja
that.way what woods-POS.NTL:DIST go.around that.way there

wagihinąąkgają, gaagų haraire.
wa-gihi-nąąk-gają gaagų ha-ree-ire
OBJ.3PL-pick-POS.NTL.PL-SEQ this.way COLL-go.there-SBJ.3PL

Well, they were still picking making their way around that little patch of trees, they moved further that way.

14. Saanįk 'eeja hahiiregają, hegų hinųbike hųųcjeega
saanįk 'eeja ha-hii-ire-gają hegų hinųbike hųųc-jeega
side there 1E.A-arrive.there-SBJ.3PL-SEQ that.way both.of.them bear-POS.VERT:DIST

haja kąnąkirešgųnį.
haja kąnąk ire-šgųnį
see place-SBJ.3PL-DUB

When they got to the other side, they must have both seen the bear.

15. Hua! Hegų haastįk reexra hegų xįnįhe hiireną.
hua hegų haastįk reex-ra hegų xįnįhe hii-ire-ną
INTJ that.way blueberry pail-DEF that.way knock.off/scatter make/CAUS-SBJ.3PL-DECL

Whoa! Then the blueberry pails, they just scattered them all over the place.

16. Howe 'eegi gi'asxete 'ųįñe.
howe 'eegi gi'as-xete 'ųų-ire
go.about and.then run.away-be.big do/make-SBJ.3PL

They made a great run-away.

17.

Hegų	hakirihakarairenạ,	šgųnį.
hegų	ha-kiri-ha-kere-ire-nạ	šgųnį
that.way	COLL-arrive.back.here-COLL-go.back.there-SBJ.3PL-DECL	DUB

Well, they just came by, I guess.

18.

Heejạga,	hopįnįįsge	'eeja	hagiregajạ,	Hank
heejạga	ho-pįį-nįįsge	'eeja	ha-gii-ire-gajạ	Hank
now	APPL.INESS-be.good-VAGUE	there	COLL-arrive.back.there-SBJ.3PL-SEQ	Hank

Tga	wookarakjeenạ,	hegų.
T-ga	wa-ho<ka>rak-jee-nạ	hegų
T-PROP	OBJ.3PL-<POSS.RFL>tell-POS.VERT-DECL	that.way

And when they got back to kind of good ground Hank T was telling about himself.

19.

"Hegų	gi'asxete	ha'ųwira,	hegų	waicekįgšge
hegų	gi'as-xete	ha-'ųų-wi-ra	hegų	wa<hį>cek-jį
that.way	run.away-be.big	1E.A-do/make-PL-DEF	that.way	<1E.U>be.young-INTS

waa'ųąježe,	waįsisikįkšge	waa'ųąježe
wa<ha>'ų-ha-jee-že	wa<hį>sisik-įk-šge	wa<ha>'ų-ha-jee-že
<1E.A>do/be-1E.A-POS.VERT-QUOT	<1E.U>be.agile-DIM-also	<1E.A>do/be-1E.A-POS.VERT-QUOT

yaakiregajạ,	tee	wąknųįkjaane	jiire.
hii<ha-kii>re-gajạ	tee	wąąknųįk-jaane	jiire
<1E.A-RFL>think-SEQ	this	old.man-POS.VERT:PROX	go.by(SBJ.3SG)

"We made a big run-away, well, I thought of myself that I was young and fast on foot, here, this old man came by.

20.

Cooka	'eera	hegų	'ee	hajiakiri
cooka	'ee-ra	hegų	'ee	ha-jii-ha-kiri
grandfather	have.kin\1E.A-DEF	that.way	3EMPH	1E.A-arrive.here-1E.A-arrive.back.here

hoginąkšąną.
hoginąk-šąną
go.via(SBJ.3SG)-DECL

My grandfather came running right on by.

21.

Nąįjiskirinạ,	hegų."
nąą<hį>jis-kiri-nạ	hegų
<1E.U>outrun(SBJ.3SG)-arrive.back.here-DECL	that.way

He outran me."

22.

Heesge	'eewešgųnį.
heesge	'ee-wee-šgųnį
that's.why	say-talk-DUB

That's what he said.

23.

Tee	'eeja	heesge	'eewen.
tee	'eeja	heesge	'ee-wee-ną
this	there	that's.why	say-talk-DECL

That's what he said there.

24.

Hegų	kiirašge	yaaperessąną.
hegų	kiira-šge	hi<ha>peres-šąną
that.way	only-also	<1E.A>know-DECL

That's all I know.

2.2 The complete Hocąk text without analysis

[1]BO: Jaagušge hihekjenegųnį, hegų wažą jaanįkrašąną ha'e haagi hegų. [2]Wažą jaanįkrašąną ha'e haagi, hegų kiira. [3]Jaagurašge hižą hotaknągųnį? [4]Hegų... [5]CL: Hegų wažąňą hižą hotaki, hegų warukos hįįguajiraną. [6]BO: Neecąą hanįrukosire. [7]CL: Hąhą, 'ee nąąk'ų... [8]BO: Hagoreižą wii howešgųnį 'eeja hahiwira, haastįk hagihį hahiwi, hąįnįgają hegų hogihi 'eeja hegų caawawigają, hija hahiwį. [9]Cooka 'eera hireanąga hįnį haara, Hank T Rave, hegų 'eeja wagihinąąkšąną, hegų hokisaknįįsge 'eeja paac hižą mįįnąkšąną. [10]Hegų xųnųįkšąną hegų, hegų hogįgįx žee 'eeja haastįk gihinąąkšąną. [11]Hegų 'ųų hanįhaire, tee woiraki hųųc seep hižą 'eeja huu. [12]Hegų cooka 'eera hireanąga Hank Tga, hąąke hija howesįwįňąnį. [13]Hegų jaagu paacnąka hogįgįx hegų 'eeja wagihinąąkgają, gaagų haraire. [14]Saanįk 'eeja hahiiregają, hegų hinųbike hųųcjeega haja kąnąkirešgųnį. [15]Hua! Hegų haastįk reexra hegų xįnįhe hiireną. [16]Howe 'eegi gi'asxete 'ųįňe. [17]Hegų hakirihakaraireną, šgųnį. [18]Heejąga, hopįnįįsge 'eeja hagiregają, Hank Tga wookarakjeeną, hegų. [19]"Hegų gi'asxete ha'ųwira, hegų waicekįgšge waa'ųąježe, waįsisikįkšge waa'ųąježe yaakiregają, tee wąknųįkjaane jiire. [20]Cooka 'eera hegų 'ee hajiakiri hoginąkšąną. [21]Nąįjiskirią, hegų." [22]Heesge 'eewešgųnį. [23]Tee 'eeja heesge 'eewen. [24]Hegų kiirašge yaaperesšąną.

2.3 The complete English translation

[1]BO: I wonder what am I going to say, I'll only talk about foolish things. [2]I'll talk about foolish things only, that's all. [3]I wonder what I can tell about? [4]Well... [5]CL: When I tell something the police may come and get me. [6]BO: Then they arrest you instead. [7]CL: Yes, while they do that... [8]BO: At one time we went up north, we went there to pick blueberries, in the morning we headed to the picking spot, we arrived there. [9]My grandfather and my older brother Hank T Rave (they) were sitting there picking, and in the sort of the middle there was a little grove of trees there (sitting). [10]It (the grove) was small, and all around there they were picking blueberries. [11]And they continued to pick and then all of a sudden a black bear came. [12]My grandfather and Hank T did not notice it. [13]Well, they were still picking making their way around that little patch of trees, they moved further that way. [14]When they got to the other side, they must have both seen the bear. [15]Whoa! Then the blueberry pails, they just scattered them all over the place. [16]They made a great run-away. [17]Well, they just came by, I guess. [18]And when they got back to kind of good ground Hank T was telling about himself. [19]"We made a big run-away, well, I thought of myself that I was young and fast on foot, here, this old man came by. [20]My grandfather came running right on by. [21]He outran me." [22]That's what he said. [23]That's what he said there. [24]That's all I know.

3 Bill O'Brien & Hollywood (Bill O'Brien) (CD 1 track 2)

3.1 Text with analysis and translation

1.

Hąhą'ą,	mąąnąpeeja	yaahinąpregi,	Disneyland	'airenį,	'eeja	watenį.
hąhą'ą	mąąnąąpe-'eeja	hi<ha>hinąp-regi	Disneyland	'ee-ire-nį	'eeja	wate-nį
yes	military-there	<1E.A>go.outside-SIM/LOC	Disneyland	say-SBJ.3PL-DECL	there	work\1E.A-DECL

When I got out of the military service, I worked in Disneyland, as they call it.

2.

Žee	'eeja	wąąkšik	ciinąkįk	hižą	'ųįňegi,	'eeja	paašiwi	'anąga	nąąwąwianąga	(žeegų)	žeegų	haawišųnų.
žee	'eeja	wąąkšik	ciinąk-įk	hižą	'ųų-ire-gi	'eeja	paaši-wi	'anąga	nąą<ha>wą-wi-'anąga	(žeegų)	žeegų	haa-wi-šųnų
that	there	Indian/person	village-DIM	one	do/make-SBJ.3PL-TOP	there	dance\1E.A-PL	and	<1E.A>sing-PL-and	(thus)	thus	make/CAUS\1E.A-PL-HAB

And there they made a small Indian village there, we danced and we sang and that is what we used to do.

3.

Hegų	'eejaxjį	wii	taanįhąxjį	hija	wate.
hegų	'eejaxjį	wii	taanį-hą-xjį	hija	wate-nį
that.way	about.there	month	three-times-INTS	there	work\1E.A-DECL

Well, I had worked there for about three months.

4.

Hagoreižą	Uncle	Walt	yaagawišųnų,	Walt	Disneyga,	hagoreižą	hija	hajiire,	wąąkra	nųųp	hakižu	jii.
hagoreižą	Uncle	Walt	hi<ha>ge-wi-šųnų	Walt	Disney-ga	hagoreižą	hija	ha-jii-ire	wąąk-ra	nųųp	hakižu	jii
sometime	Uncle	Walt	<1E.A>say.to-PL-HAB	Walt	Disney-PROP	sometime	there	COLL-arrive.here-SBJ.3PL	man-DEF	two	be.together	arrive.here(SBJ.3SG)

Then at one time, Uncle Walt as we used to call him, Walt Disney, at one time they came there, he came along together with two men.

5.

Nįge	paaśıhajawiga	'eeja,	(hą)ho	hegų	howe	hiperes	kįįjee	hegų,	wąąknąąkašąną	raašra
nįge	paaši-ha-jee-wi-ga	'eeja	hąho	hegų	howe	hiperes	kįį-jee	hegų	wąąk-nąąka-šąną	raaš-ra
somewhere	dance\1E.A-1E.A-POS.VERT-PL-CONT	there	INTJ	that.way	go.about	know(SBJ.3SG)	make.self-POS.VERT	that.way	man-POS.NTL.PL:DIST-only	name-DEF

hųųgirakwianąąga	wawoįgirakwianąągašge,	žee	žeesge
ho<hį-gi>rak-wi-'anąąga	wa-ho<hį-gi>rak-wi-'anąąga-šge	žee	žeesge
<1E.U-APPL.BEN>tell-PL-and	OBJ.3PL-<1E.U-APPL.BEN>tell-PL-and-also	that	thus

hiiną.
hii-ną
make/CAUS(SBJ.3SG)-DECL

The place where we danced, he knew his way around there, he only introduced those two other men to us, that's what he did.

6.

Hegų	(rušjąįňe	hegų)	rušjąįňegają	hegų	'ee
hegų	(rušją-ire	hegų)	rušją-ire-gają	hegų	'ee
that.way	(quit-SBJ.3PL	that.way)	quit-SBJ.3PL-SEQ	that.way	3EMPH

howahuu,	hacįįja	ha'ųhajera	hegų	'ee
howe-huu	hacįįja	ha-'ųų-ha-jee-ra	hegų	'ee
go.about-come.here	where	1E.A-be-1E.A-POS.VERT-DEF	that.way	3EMPH

howahuu,	'ee	howaahuire	hitanįke,	"hią!"
howe-hahu	'ee	howe-ha-huu-ire	hitanįke	hią
go.about-approach(SBJ.3SG)	this	go.about-COLL-come.here-SBJ.3PL	all.three.of.them	INTJ

weeną,	hegų	te'e	Rawhide	'airegi,	tee	director	hireanąąga
weeną	hegų	te'e	Rawhide	'ee-ire-gi	tee	director	hireanąąga
spring	that.way	this	Rawhide	say-SBJ.3PL-TOP	this	director	along.with

producerra	wa'ųnąąkšąną.
producer-ra	wa'ų-nąąk-šąną
producer-DEF	do/be-POS.NTL.PL-DECL

Then when they finished, he came to where I was, where I was at, that's where he came, all three of them came towards me, "hey!" he said, this spring the movie called Rawhide they were the director and the producer for it.

7.

Wa'ųajawiną.
wa'ų-ha-jee-wi-ną
do/be-COLL-POS.VERT-PL-DECL

That's who they were.

8.

"Honįkit'e	roogųįňeną."
ho<nį>kit'e	roogų-ire-ną
<2.U>talk.to	want-SBJ.3PL-DECL

"They want to talk to you."

9.

"Hąą,"	wawiage.
hąą	wa-hi<ha>ge
yes	OBJ.3PL-<1E.A>say.to

"Okay," I told them.

10. 'Eesge waireną, "hąą, wąąk serec waanįwiną,
'eesge wee-ire-ną hąą wąąk serec ho<ha>nį-wi-ną
that's.why talk-SBJ.3PL-DECL yes man be.long <1E.A>look.for/hunt-PL-DECL

š'ųųrajega hegų heejaixjį hižą raagųwįną.
š-'ųų-ra-jee-ga hegų heejaixjį hižą roo<ha>gų-wį-ną
2.A-do/make-2.A-POS.VERT-CONT that.way that.far one <1E.A>want-PL-DECL

They said "yes, we're looking for a tall man, we want someone who is as tall as you are.

11. Haramehį huhera, hokiwagax hixgąxgą ha'ų
haramįhe huhe-ra hokiwagax hixgąxgą ha-'ųų
week be.coming.here-DEF picture move.around 1E.A-do/make

hajitekjanawi," 'eeną.
ha-jiite-kjane-wi 'ee-ną
1E.A-begin\1E.A-FUT-PL say(SBJ.3SG)-DECL

Next week we're going to start making a movie," he said.

12. "Roonįgųwiną."
roo<nįį>gų-wi-ną
<1&2>want-PL-DECL

"We want you."

13. "Hąą, heesganąną," yaageną.
hąą heesge-nąą-ną hi<ha>ge-ną
yes be.thus-POT-DECL <1E.A>say.to(OBJ.3SG)-DECL

"Yes, it can be," I said to him.

14. Žee, žee ceek hokiwagax hixgąxgą, kagašge 'eesge
žee žee ceek hokiwagax hixgąxgą kaga-šge 'eesge
that that first/new picture move.around NEG.IN.never-also that's.why

haanįšųnųną, žee žeesge wažą ceek ha'ų.
haa-nį-šųnų-ną žee žeesge wažą ceek ha-'ųų
make/CAUS\1E.A-NEG.FIN-HAB-DECL that thus something first/new 1E.A-do/make

It was a new movie, I had never done these before, I did something new.

15. Hegų 'eeja hotiirera heregają hegų 'eepa hegų
hegų 'eeja ho-tiire-ra here-gają hegų 'eepa hegų
that.way there APPL.INESS-move-DEF be-SEQ that.way from.that.point that.way

hokiwagax hixgąxgą 'ųųrašąną ha'ų, žeesge 'eeja
hokiwagax hixgąxgą 'ųų-ra-šąną ha-'ųų žeesge 'eeja
picture move.around do/make-DEF-only 1E.A-do/make thus there

watešųnų.
wate-šųnų
work\1E.A-HAB

That's where everything started, from then on, that's what I did, I only did moving pictures, that's where I used to work.

16.

Hegų	hahi	ha'ųhaja'ų	hegų	mąą	kerepąnątaanį
hegų	hahi	ha-'ųų-ha-jee-'ųų	hegų	mąą	kerepąnątaanį
that.way	there	1E.A-do/make-1E.A-POS.VERT-SIM	that.way	year	thirty

'anąga	nįgešge	mąą	kerepąnąjoopahą	heesge
'anąga	nįgešge	mąą	kerepąnąjoop-ahą	heesge
and	or	year	fourty-times	that's.why

haanįheną.
haa-ha-nįhe-ną
make/CAUS\1E.A-1E.A-be/PROG-DECL

When I was doing this, 30 years and perhaps 40 years I was there.

17.

Hegų	hagoreižą	hiš'aakįk	hatešgųnį,	hegų	'eeja	woorera
hegų	hagoreižą	hį-š'aak-įk	hate-šgųnį	hegų	'eeja	woore-ra
that.way	sometime	1E.U-be.old-DIM	become\1E.A-DUB	that.way	there	work-DEF

hegų	ğereįk	here.
hegų	ğere-įk	here
that.way	be.slow(OBJ.3SG)-DIM	be

Then one day I got a little old, I suppose, the work got a little slow.

18.

Hegų	hagairaxjįšąnąšge	watešunų.
hegų	hagaira-xjį-šąną-šge	wate-šųnų
that.way	sometimes-INTS-only-also	work\1E.A-HAB

Only once in a while I used to work.

19.

Nųnįge	ha'ųšųnųregi	hegų,	šųųkhamįnąkra	hireanąga
nųnįge	ha-'ųų-šųnų-regi	hegų	šųųkhamįnąk-ra	hireanąga
nevertheless	1E.A-do/make-HAB-SIM/LOC	that.way	ride.horseback-DEF	along.with

hegų	wakigucrašąną	hegų,	jaagu	hijąhį	jagu	wąąkšik
hegų	wa<kii>guc-ra-šąną	hegų	jaagu	hijąhį	jagu	wąąkšik
that.way	<RCP>shoot-DEF-only	that.way	what	be.different	and.so	Indian/person

hįwagaxiregają	hegų,	wąąkšikįka	hegų	goišip
hį-wa<ga>gax-ire-gają	hegų	wąąkšik-įk-ga	hegų	goišip
1E.U-<RDP>write-SBJ.3PL-SEQ	that.way	Indian/person-DIM-PROP	that.way	always

waaxu	harus,	hegų	nįįšge	hegų	nee	wįįnera	hegų
waaxu	harus	hegų	nįįšge	hegų	nee	wįįne-ra	hegų
be.tough	go.through	that.way	also	that.way	1EMPH	be\1E.A-DEF	that.way

hegų	teejąkišge	t'ee	wįįňe.
hegų	teejąki-šge	t'ee	hį-hii-ire
that.way	a.little.while-also	die	1E.U-make/CAUS-SBJ.3PL

Still I used to do horseback-riding and shooting at each other... what else... when they drew me as an Indian, the Indians always get the toughest end, and as for myself, every little while they killed me.

20.

'Eejaxjį	joobahąnįįsge	kiirašge	nį'ąp.
'eejaxjį	joop-ahą-nįįsge	kiira-šge	nį'ąp
about.there	four-times-VAGUE	only-also	be.alive

Just about four times I stayed alive.

21.

Hokiwagax	hixgąxgąnąąkrašge	ke	hįt'anį.
hokiwagax	hixgąxgą-nąąk-ra-šge	hąąke	hį-t'ee-nį
picture	move.around-POS.NTL.PL-DEF-also	NEG.IN	1E.U-die-NEG.FIN

I didn't die in these movies.

22.

Joopahąnįįsge	kiirašge,	hąąke	t'ee	wįįňąnį.
joop-ahą-nįįsge	kiira-šge	hąąke	t'ee	hį-hii-ire-nį
four-times-VAGUE	only-also	NEG.IN	die	1E.U-make/CAUS-SBJ.3PL-NEG.FIN

Only four times they didn't kill me.

23.

Hirotara	hanąąc	hegų	t'ee	wįįňegają.
hirota-ra	hanąąc	hegų	t'ee	hį-hii-ire-gają
rest-DEF	all	that.way	die	1E.U-make/CAUS-SBJ.3PL-SEQ

All the rest of the time they killed me.

24.

Hegų	žeesge	haanįhešųnųną,	hegų
hegų	žeesge	haa-ha-nįhe-šųnų-ną	hegų
that.way	thus	make/CAUS\1E.A-1E.A-be/PROG-HAB-DECL	that.way

hįtajiiirega	hegų	hitajihirega	jagu
hį-taa-jii-ire-ga	hegų	hį-taa-jii-ire-ga	hegų
1E.U-ask.for-arrive.here-SBJ.3PL-CONT	that.way	1E.U-ask.for-arrive.here-SBJ.3PL-CONT	that.way

hija	taahegają.
hija	taahe-gają
there	be.going.there\1E.A-SEQ

Well, that's what I was doing, when they sent for me, when they sent for me, I went there.

25.	Hegų	heesge	hiira	gipįesge	hiranąą'įšųnų.
	hegų	heeesge	hii-ra	gipįesge	hiraną<ha>'į-šųnų
	that.way	that's.why	make/CAUS(SBJ.3SG)-DEF	be.enjoyable	<1E.A>think.of-HAB

Doing that was wonderful, I used to think.

26.	Waxja	hiranąą'į.
	waxja	hiraną<ha>'į
	be.fun(ny)	<1E.A>think.of

I thought it was fun.

27.	Hegų	goišip	wajcek	hanįhežeeži,	hire
	hegų	goišip	wa<hį>cek	ha-nįhe-žeeži	hire
	that.way	always	<1E.U>be.young	1E.A-be/PROG-OPT	think-OBJ.3PL
	wahiiną.				
	wa-hii-ną				
	make/CAUS(SBJ.3SG)-DECL				

I want to stay young all the time, it makes one think.

28.	'Eejaxjį	hegų	wajcek	hajegi,	hegų
	'eejaxjį	hegų	wa<hį>cek	ha-jee-gi	hegų
	about.there	that.way	<1E.U>be.young	1E.A-POS.VERT-TOP	that.way
	ha'ųhajaną.				
	ha-'ųų-ha-jee-nąą				
	1E.A-do/make-1E.A-POS.VERT-POT				

If I was still young I would still be doing it that way.

29.	Hegų	š'aakra	hegų	wažąňą	hanąąc	horužinįįsgajeegają.
	hegų	š'aak-ra	hegų	wažą-ra	hanąąc	horuži-nįįsge-jee-gają
	that.way	be.old-DEF	that.way	something-DEF	all	dim-VAGUE-POS.VERT-SEQ

When you're old everything gets sort of dimmer.

30.	Žeešąną	hegų	ceek honųwąk	'eeja,	hakųnųnįšunų.
	žee-šąną	hegų	ceek_honųwąk	'eeja	ha-kųnųnį-šųnų
	that-only	that.way	at.first.start	there	1E.A-miss-HAB

That alone in the beginning, I used to miss it.

31.	Hąą,	žeenąga	hihe.
	hąą	žeenąga	hihe
	yes	this.time	say\1E.A

Well, that is all I'm saying.

3.2 The complete Hocąk text without analysis

[1]Hąhą'ą, mąąnąpeeja yaahinąpregi, Disneyland 'airenų, 'eeja watenų. [2]Žee 'eeja wąąkšik ciinąkįk hižą 'ųįňegi, 'eeja paašiwi 'anąga nąąwąwianąga (žeegų) žeegų haawišųnų. [3]Hegų 'eejaxjį wii taanįhąxjį hija wate. [4]Hagoreižą Uncle Walt yaagawišųnų, Walt Disneyga, hagoreižą hija hajiire, wąąkra nųųp hakižu jii. [5]Nįge paašihajawiga 'eeja, (hą)ho hegų howe hiperes kįįjee hegų, wąąknąąkašąną raašra hųųgirakwianąga wawoįgirakwianągašge, žee žeesge hiiną. [6]Hegų (rušjąįňe hegų) rušjąįňegają hegų 'ee howahuu, hacįįja ha'ųhajera hegų 'ee howahuu, 'ee howaahuire hitanįke, "hią!" weeną, hegų te'e Rawhide 'airegi, tee director hireanąga producerra wa'ųnąąkšąną. [7]Wa'ųajawiną. [8]"Honįkit'e roogųįňeną." [9]"Hąą," wawiage. [10]'Eesge waireną, "hąą, wąąk serec waanįwiną, š'ųųrajega hegų heejaixjį hižą raagųwįną. [11]Haramehį huhera, hokiwagax hixgąxgą ha'ų hajitekjanawi," 'eeną. [12]"Roonįgųwiną." [13]"Hąą, heesganąną," yaageną. [14]Žee, žee ceek hokiwagax hixgąxgą, kagašge 'eesge haanįšųnųną, žee žeesge wažą ceek ha'ų. [15]Hegų 'eeja hotiirera heregają hegų 'eepa hegų hokiwagax hixgąxgą 'ųųrašąną ha'ų, žeesge 'eeja watešųnų. [16]Hegų hahi ha'ųhaja'ų hegų mąą kerepąnątaanį 'anąga nįgešge mąą kerepąnąjoopahą heesge haanįheną. [17]Hegų hagoreižą hiš'aakįk hatešgųnį, hegų 'eeja woorera hegų ğereįk here. [18]Hegų hagairaxjįšąnąšge watešunų. [19]Nųnįge ha'ųšųnųregi hegų, šųųkhamįnąkra hireanąga hegų wakigucrašąną hegų, jaagu hijąhį jagu wąąkšik hįwagaxiregają hegų, wąąkšikįka hegų goišip waaxu harus, hegų nįįšge hegų nee wįįnera hegų hegų teejąkišge t'ee wįįňe. [20]'Eejaxjį joobahąnįįsge kiirašge nį'ąp. [21]Hokiwagax hixgąxgąnąąkrašge ke hįt'anį. [22]Joopahąnįįsge kiirašge, hąąke t'ee wįįňanį. [23]Hirotara hanąąc hegų t'ee wįįňegają. [24]Hegų žeesge haanįhešųnųną, hegų hįtajiiirega hegų hitajihirega jagu hija taahegają. [25]Hegų heesge hiira gipįesge hiranąą'įšųnų. [26]Waxja hiranąą'į. [27]Hegų goišip wajcek hanįhežeeži, hire wahiiną. [28]'Eejaxjį hegų wajcek hajegi, hegų ha'ųhajaną. [29]Hegų š'aakra hegų wažąňą hanąąc horužinįįsgajeegają. [30]Žeešąną hegų ceek honųwąk 'eeja, hakųnųnįšunų. [31]Hąą, žeenąga hihe.

3.3 The complete English translation

[1]When I got out of the military service, I worked in Disneyland, as they call it. [2]And there they made a small Indian village there, we danced and we sang and that is what we used to do. [3]Well, I had worked there for about three months. [4]Then at one time, Uncle Walt as we used to call him, Walt Disney, at one time they came there, he came along together with two men. [5]The place where we danced, he knew his way around there, he only introduced those two other men to us, that's what he did. [6]Then when they finished, he came to where I was, where I was at, that's where he came, all three of them came towards me, "hey!" he said, this spring the movie called Rawhide they were the director and the producer for it. [7]That's who they were. [8]"They want to talk to you." [9]"Okay," I told them. [10]They said "yes, we're looking for a tall man, we want someone who is as tall as you are. [11]Next week we're going to start making a movie," he said. [12]"We want you." [13]"Yes, it can be," I said to him. [14]It was a new movie, I had never done these before, I did something new. [15]That's where everything started, from then on, that's what I did, I only did moving pictures, that's where I used to work. [16]When I was doing this, 30 years and perhaps 40 years I was there. [17]Then one day I got a little old, I suppose, the work got a little slow. [18]Only once in a while I used to work. [19]Still I used to do horseback-riding and shooting at each other... what else... when they drew me as an Indian, the Indians always get the toughest end, and as for myself, every little while they killed me. [20]Just about four times I stayed alive. [21]I didn't die in these movies. [22]Only four times they didn't kill me. [23]All the rest of the time they killed me. [24]Well, that's what I was doing, when they sent for me, when they sent for me, I went there. [25]Doing that was wonderful, I used to think. [26]I thought it was fun. [27]I want to stay young all the time, it makes one think. [28]If I was still young I would still be doing it that way. [29]When you're old everything gets sort of dimmer. [30]That alone in the beginning, I used to miss it. [31]Well, that is all I'm saying.

4 The moccasin game – a picture description (Bill O'Brien) (CD 1 track 3)

4.1 Text with analysis and translation

1.

Tee	'eegi	hokiwagaxnąąre	waguje gikok	šgaac	hikorohonąąkšąną.
tee	'eegi	hokiwagax-nąąre	waguje_gikok	šgaac	hikoroho-nąąk-šąną
this	and.then	picture-POS.NTL:PROX	moccasin.game	play	get.ready-POS.NTL.PL-DECL

Here in this picture, they are getting ready to play the moccasin game.

2.

Hacąjaira	wa'ųnąąki.
hacąjaira	wa'ų-nąąk-gi
wherever	do/be-POS.NTL.PL-TOP

Wherever they are.

3.

(nąąkeregišge)	Nąąkeejašge	ciiporokešge	nąkwi.
(nąąke-regi-šge)	nąąke-'eeja-šge	ciiporoke-šge	nąk-wi
(back-SIM/LOC-also)	back-there-also	wigwam-also	POS.NTL-PL

Also behind them there are wigwams.

4.

'Eeja	wažąižąšge	higišiknąkšąną.
'eeja	wažą-įžą-šge	higišik-nąk-šąną
there	something-one-also	hang-POS.NTL-DECL

Also, there is something hanging there.

5.

(wa'į̨iža̧)	Wa'į̨iža̧	wa'ų̨na̧kna̧je.
(wa'į-iža̧)	wa'į-iža̧	wa'ų-na̧k=na̧je
(blanket/shawl-one)	blanket/shawl-one	do/be-POS.NTL=ASSUMP

It appears to be a blanket/shawl.

6.

Wa'į̨iža̧.
wa'į-iža̧
blanket/shawl-one

A blanket.

7.

Tee	waguje gikok	šgaacirekjanegi,	joopihikjanawi,	wa̧a̧kra	haruwa̧k	šgaacirekjaneana̧ga.
tee	waguje_gikok	šgaac-ire-kjane-gi	joopiwi-kjane-wi	wa̧a̧k-ra	haruwa̧k	šgaac-ire-kjane-'ana̧ga
this	moccasin.game	play-SBJ.3PL-FUT-TOP	four-FUT-PL	man-DEF	eight	play-SBJ.3PL-FUT-and

If they are going to play moccasin, there's going to be four, eight men are going to play.

8.

Joopihi	hikį̨kį̨irekjane.
joopiwi	hikį̨kį-ire-kjane
four	have.as.team.mate-SBJ.3PL-FUT

Four are going to team up.

9.

'Aa'aki	mį̨į̨na̧kireana̧ga.
'aa'aki	mį̨į̨na̧k-ire-'ana̧ga
on.opposite.sides	sit-SBJ.3PL-and

They sit opposite each other.

10.

(tee)	Hiža̧	hožukjanegi,	reex haruporokna̧gre	že'e	hi'ų̨ana̧ga	(žee	na̧a̧wa̧)	wana̧giwa̧kjane.
(tee)	hiža̧	hožu-kjane-gi	reex_haruporok-na̧gre	že'e	hi'ų-'ana̧ga	(žee	na̧a̧wa̧)	wa-na̧a̧<gi>wa̧-kjane
(this)	one	put.into(SBJ.3SG&OBJ.3SG)-FUT-TOP	drum-POS.NTL:PROX	that	use(SBJ.3SG&OBJ.3SG)-and	(that	sing)	OBJ.3PL-<APPL.BEN>sing(SBJ.3SG)-FUT

The one that's going to load (the moccasin), this drum is going to be used and he (one of them) will sing for them.

11.

Saanįk	'ee	(hožura)	hožuirekjanenąjexjį.
saanįk	'ee	(hožu-ra)	hožu-ire-kjane=nąje-xjį
side	this	(put.into-DEF)	put.into(OBJ.3SG)-SBJ.3PL-FUT=ASSUMP-INTS

That side, it appears, they are going to load it.

12.

Wagujerašge	'eegi	nąąk.
waguje-ra-šge	'eegi	nąąk
moccasin-DEF-also	here	POS.NTL.PL

The moccasins are here.

13.

Wąąknąągre	hižąšge	wookąnąk	hižą	hokąnąknągre,
wąąk-nąągre	hižą-šge	wookąnąk	hižą	hokąnąk-nągre
man-POS.NTL.PL:PROX	one-also	hat	one	wear.on.head-POS.NTL:PROX

žeešge	nee	hitek	haa.
žee-šge	nee	hitek	haa
that-also	1EMPH	maternal.uncle	have.kin(OBJ.3SG)\1E.A

Of these men, the one who is wearing the hat, he is my uncle.

14.

Hegų	'eegi	woomįšireanąga,	wiigisarax	hižąšge
hegų	'eegi	wa-homįš-ire-'anąga	wa-hi-gisarax	hižą-šge
that.way	and.then	OBJ.3PL-spread.out-SBJ.3PL-and	OBJ.3PL-APPL.INST-rattle	one-also

hanįire	nąga,	wiimąrak	hižąšge	hanįireanąga,	te'e	že'e
hanį-ire	'anąga	wiimąrak	hižą-šge	hanį-ire-'anąga	te'e	že'e
have.NTL-SBJ.3PL	and	pointer	one-also	have.NTL-SBJ.3PL-and	this	that

'ųųsge	woorucgairekjane.
'ųųsge	wa-horucga-ire-kjane
something:HESIT	OBJ.3PL-feel.around.for-SBJ.3PL-FUT

They've spread something (a blanket) on the ground, they even have a rattle, they also have a pointer, with this (the pointer) they are going to probe (under the moccasins).

15.

Wagujenąągre	'eeja	mąąs	poroporo	hižąšge
waguje-nąągre	'eeja	mąąs	poroporo	hižą-šge
moccasin-POS.NTL.PL:PROX	there	metal	be.round	one-also

hi'ųirešųnų.
hi'ų-ire-šųnų
use(OBJ.3SG)-SBJ.3PL-HAB

These moccasins, there they also used to use a round metal ball.

16.

(tee	'eeja)	Tee	'eeja	hižą	kųųhąija	hižą	hokąnąkra
(tee	'eeja)	tee	'eeja	hižą	kųųhą-ija	hižą	ho-kąnąk-ra
(this	there)	this	there	one	underneath-there	one	APPL.INESS-place-DEF

teegi	wažuirešųnų.
teegi	wa-žuu-ire-šųnų
right.here	OBJ.3PL-put-SBJ.3PL-HAB

When someone puts one underneath there, they put them here.

17.

Kųųhąija	nųųxąwą	kąnąkire	wağįğį	poroporoįknąka,
kųųhą-ija	nųųxąwą	kąnąk-ire	wağįğį	poroporo-įk-nąka
underneath-there	hide	place(OBJ.3SG)-SBJ.3PL	ball	be.round-DIM-POS.NTL:DIST

joopiwi	wagujera.
joopiwi	waguje-ra
four	moccasin-DEF

They hide that little round ball underneath, four moccasins.

18.

Mąąs	poroporoįknąka	hegų	kųųhąija	wagujenąąka
mąąs	poroporo-įk-nąka	hegų	kųųhą-ija	waguje-nąąka
metal	be.round-DIM-POS.NTL:DIST	that.way	underneath-there	moccasin-POS.NTL.PL:DIST

kųųhąija	hižą	'eeja	nųųxąwą	hožuirekjane.
kųųhą-ija	hižą	'eeja	nųųxąwą	hožu-ire-kjane
underneath-there	one	there	hide	put.into-SBJ.3PL-FUT

That little metal ball is going to be underneath one of these moccasins, they are going to hide it there.

19.

Te'e	(hi'e)	hi'e	nąą'įirekjane,	hi'eirekjeesge,	nįgeešge
te'e	(hi'e)	hi'e	nąą'į-ire-kjane	hi'e-ire-kje-heesge	nįgeešge
this	(find)	find	try-SBJ.3PL-FUT	find(OBJ.3SG)-SBJ.3PL-OBL.IN-OBL.FIN	or

kii'oireanąga,	nįgeešge	'oirekjane.
kii-'oo-ire-'anąga	nįgeešge	'oo-ire-kjane
RFL-hit.target-SBJ.3PL-and	or	hit.target-SBJ.3PL-FUT

This side will try to find it, they have to find it, or else, they could shoot themselves, or they will shoot it.

20.

Kii'oirega,	horocą	guucirega,	hąąke
kii-'oo-ire-ga	ho-roocą	guuc-ire-ga	hąąke
RFL-hit.target-SBJ.3PL-CONT	APPL.INESS-be.straight	shoot-SBJ.3PL-CONT	NEG.IN

hi'eiranį,	hąąke	'eejanįąki,	kii'o	wa'ųire.
hi'e-ire-nį	hąąke	'eeja-nį-'ąk-gi	kii-'oo	wa'ų-ire
find-SBJ.3PL-NEG.FIN	NEG.IN	there-NEG.FIN-POS.HOR-TOP	RFL-hit.target	do/be-SBJ.3PL

When they shoot themselves, if they shoot it straight on and they don't find it, it's not under there, they've shot themselves.

21.

Žee	'eeja	te'e	joop	hiruwe hiirekjane,	tee	'eeja	joop	hiruwe
žee	'eeja	te'e	joop	hiruwe_hii-ire-kjane	tee	'eeja	joop	hiruwe
that	there	this	four	pay.off-SBJ.3PL-FUT	this	there	four	pay

wagigirekjane.
wa-gigi-ire-kjane
OBJ.3PL-let/cause-SBJ.3PL-FUT

This side, they're going to pay four, they're going to pay them four.

22.

Hegų	žige	higicgairekjane.
hegų	žige	higicga-ire-kjane
that.way	again	attempt-SBJ.3PL-FUT

They are going to try again.

23.

Hicągeere	'ųnąąk'ų	hi'eiregi,	horocąišge
hicągeere	'ųų-nąąk-'ų	hi'e-ire-gi	ho-roocą-išge
with.difficulty	do/make-POS.NTL.PL-SIM	find(OBJ.3SG)-SBJ.3PL-TOP	APPL.INESS-be.straight-also

guuciregi,	horocą	guucireanąga	hi'eiregi,
guuc-ire-gi	ho-roocą	guuc-ire-'anąga	hi'e-ire-gi
shoot-SBJ.3PL-TOP	APPL.INESS-be.straight	shoot(OBJ.3SG)-SBJ.3PL-and	find-SBJ.3PL-TOP

te'e	joop	hiruwe	wagigirekjene.
te'e	joop	hiruwe	wa-gigi-ire-kjene
this	four	pay	OBJ.3PL-let/cause-SBJ.3PL-FUT

When they finally find it as they're doing it, they might have shot it straight on, if they shoot straight on and find it, they will pay this side four.

24.

Hąąke	horocą	'oiranįgi,	tee
hąąke	ho-roocą	'oo-ire-nį-gi	tee
NEG.IN	APPL.INESS-be.straight	hit.target-SBJ.3PL-NEG.FIN-TOP	this

waruğąire	waiğąiregi	hijopejanąki,
wa-ruğą-ire-ga	wa-giğą-ire-gi	hi-joop-'eeja-nąk-gi
OBJ.3PL-uncover-SBJ.3PL-CONT	OBJ.3PL-flip.over-SBJ.3PL-TOP	ORD-four-there-POS.NTL-TOP

taanį	ruğąirekjane.
taanį	ruğą-ire-kjane
three	uncover-SBJ.3PL-FUT

If they didn't shoot straight on, when they uncover them and flip them over, and if it's in the fourth one, they will have uncovered (the other) three.

25.

Hijopejanąki	te'e	woohikjane.
hi-joop-'eeja-nąk-gi	te'e	wa-hohi-kjane
ORD-four-there-POS.NTL-TOP	this	OBJ.3PL-defeat(SBJ.3SG)-FUT

If it's under the fourth, this (side) is going to win.

26.

'Eeja	te'e	'eeja	nųųp	hiruwe	wagigirekjane.
'eeja	te'e	'eeja	nųųp	hiruwe	wa-gigi-ire-kjane
there	this	there	two	pay	OBJ.3PL-let/cause-SBJ.3PL-FUT

So they're going to pay this (side) two.

27.

Nįšgaga	'ee	hožuirekjane,	'eejanąka.
nįšgaga	tee	hožu-ire-kjane,	'eeja-nąka
this.time	this	put.into-SBJ.3PL-FUT	there-POS.NTL:DIST

So now they get to load (the moccasins), there.

28.

Wagujera	waišeirekjane.
waguje-ra	wa-giše-ire-kjane
moccasin-DEF	OBJ.3PL-take.away-SBJ.3PL-FUT

They're going to take away the shoes.

29.

Nįšgaga	'ee	hožuirenąga	'ee	nąąwąirekjane.
nįšgaga	'ee	hožu-ire-nąga	'ee	nąąwą-ire-kjane
this.time	3EMPH	put.into-SBJ.3PL-and	3EMPH	sing-SBJ.3PL-FUT

This side is going to load now, and they're going to sing.

30.

Reex haruporokjaane	(tapping).
reex_haruporok-jaane	(tapping)
drum-POS.VERT:PROX	(tapping)

This drum (tapping on the table imitating the sound of the drum).

31.

'Eegi	žeegų	hiirekjane.
'eegi	žeegų	hii-ire-kjane
and.then	thus	make/CAUS-SBJ.3PL-FUT

That's what they're going to do.

32.

Žige	(nųųxąwą)	te'e	nųųxąwą	t'ųųpireanąga	nįšgaga	te'e	hi'eną'įirekjane,	wağįğįįknąka.
žige	(nųųxąwą)	te'e	nųųxąwą	t'ųųp-ire-'anąga	nįšgaga	te'e	hi'e-nąą'į-ire-kjane	wağįğį-įk-nąka
again	(hide)	this	hide	put.down(OBJ.3SG)-SBJ.3PL-and	this.time	this	find-try-SBJ.3PL-FUT	ball-DIM-POS.NTL:DIST

This (side) will hide it now, and this (side) is going to try and find that little ball.

33. Hegų hąąpserecšge, hąąheserecšge šgaaciresųnų hagaira, hegų.
hegų hąąp-serec-šge hąąhe-serec-šge šgaac-ire-šųnų hagaira, hegų
that.way day-be.long-also night-be.long-also play-SBJ.3PL-HAB sometimes that.way

Sometimes they'd play all day and even all night long.

34. Hegų 'ųnąąk'ų, wiimąraknąagre, 'eegi jaagušge
hegų 'ųų-nąąk-'ų wiimąrak-nąągre 'eegi jaagu-šge
that.way do/make-POS.NTL.PL-SIM pointer-POS.NTL.PL:PROX and.then what-also

wawigairera, "wiroikarapšge" 'airegųnį
wa-hige-ire-ra wa-hi-ho-gikarap-šge 'ee-ire-gųnį
OBJ.3PL-say.to-SBJ.3PL-DEF OBJ.3PL-APPL.INST-APPL.INESS-count-also say-SBJ.3PL-DUB

yaare.
hii<ha>re
<1E.A>think

In the process, what are these called now, I think they used to call them "counters."

35. Jaagušge 'aircra?
jaagu-šge 'ee-ire-ra
what-also say-SBJ.3PL-DEF

What did they say?

36. Nųųpiwi.
nųųpiwi
two

There were two of them (the counters).

37. Hirokikerešge wahiirešųnų hota, wiimąrak nįįsge;
hiro<kii>kere-šge wa-hii-ire-šųnų hota wiimąrak nįįsge
<RCP>connect-also OBJ.3PL-make/CAUS-SBJ.3PL-HAB some pointer kind.of

ceek honųwąk 'eeja hegų hąąke wažą cąąt'įnį.
ceek_honųwąk 'eeja hegų hąąke wažą cąąt'į-nį
at.first.start there that.way NEG.IN something be.perceivable-NEG.FIN

They used to connect those two together, some of them, as sort of markers; at first there is nothing to be seen.

38. Hižą te'e wawohigi, te'egi hižą hawają
hižą te'e wa-hohi-gi te'e-gi hižą hawają
one this OBJ.3PL-defeat(SBJ.3SG)-TOP this-TOP one push

kąnąkirega, hawają t'ųųpire.
kąnąk-ire-ga hawają t'ųųp-ire-ga
place-SBJ.3PL-CONT push put.down-SBJ.3PL-CONT

If one has won, they would lean it up, and then push it into position.

39.

Wiimąraknąka	hižąkiira	teegi	himąrakikjane.
wiimąrak-nąka	hižą-kiira	teegi	himąrak-i-kjane
pointer-POS.NTL:DIST	one-only	right.here	point.at(SBJ.3SG)-0-FUT

There is only one going to be pointing this way (out of these two).

40.

Hegų	šgaac	hanįhairegi	žige	te'e	wohiregi,
hegų	šgaac	ha-nįhe-ire-gi	žige	te'e	wa-hohi-ire-nį
that.way	play	COLL-be/PROG-SBJ.3PL-TOP	again	this	OBJ.3PL-defeat-SBJ.3PL-DECL

(nųųpnąka)	winųųpra	hija	jįįpirekjane.
(nųųp-nąka)	wi-nųųp-ra	hija	jįįp-ire-kjane
(two-POS.NTL:DIST)	ORD-two-DEF	there	lie.down(OBJ.3SG)-SBJ.3PL-FUT

And when they're playing, if this side wins again, the second stick will be placed along side.

41.

Hąąhą,	'eeja	žige	wawohiregi,	'eeja	hožejąra	herekjene.
hąąhą	'eeja	žige	wa-hohi-ire-gi	'eeja	hožeją-ra	here-kjene
yes	there	again	OBJ.3PL-defeat-SBJ.3PL-TOP	there	end-DEF	be-FUT

And after that if they win again that'll be the end.

42.

'Eegi	jaagu	hikiguciregi,	hegų	žee	hikiguciresųnų,	šųųkxetešge.
'eegi	jaagu	hikiguc-ire-gi	hegų	žee	hikiguc-ire-šųnų	šųųkxete-šge
and.then	what	bet-SBJ.3PL-TOP	that.way	that	bet-SBJ.3PL-HAB	horse-also

Whatever they bet with each other, they did, even horses.

43.

Hikigucireanąga	hegų	wažą	jaagu	žuurašge	hikigucireanąga,
hikiguc-ire-'anąga	hegų	wažą	jaagu	žuura-šge	hikiguc-ire-'anąga
bet-SBJ.3PL-and	that.way	something	what	money-also	bet-SBJ.3PL-and

koreesgešge	hinųkšge	hikigucireanąga	hegų.
koreesge-šge	hinųk-šge	hikiguc-ire-'anąga	hegų
maybe-also	woman-also	bet-SBJ.3PL-and	that.way

When they gambled with whatever, including money, maybe even women.

44.

(wawohi)	Tee	wawohigi,	hąą,	že'e
(wa-wohi)	tee	wa-hohi-gi	hąą	že'e
(OBJ.3PL-defeat)	this	OBJ.3PL-defeat(SBJ.3SG)-TOP	yes	that

wažąnąąka	hanąąc	'ee	waanįirekjene.
wažą-nąąka	hanąąc	'ee	wa-hanį-ire-kjene
something-POS.NTL.PL:DIST	all	3EMPH	OBJ.3PL-have.NTL-SBJ.3PL-FUT

If this side wins, yes, all those things belongs to them.

45.

“Hąą,	nįįkarakje	raagųwi,”	tee	’airekjene.
hąą	nįį-karakje	roo<ha>gų-wi	tee	’ee-ire-kjene
yes	1&2-take.revenge	<1E.A>want-PL	this	say-SBJ.3PL-FUT

“We’d like to challenge you,” this (side) will say.

46.

“Žige	hįšgacikjawi.”
žige	hį-šgaac-i-kje-wi
again	1PL.A-play-0-FUT-PL

“Let’s play again.”

47.

’Eesge,	hegų	žige	šgaac	hajiharaire.
’eesge	hegų	žige	šgaac	ha-jii<ha>re-ire
that’s.why	that.way	again	play	COLL-<COLL>begin-SBJ.3PL

That’s why they started to play again.

48.

Jaagu	hirakiguc,	koreesgešge	hegų	’ųųsge,	jaagu
jaagu	hi<ra>kiguc	koreesge-šge	hegų	’ųųsge	jaagu
what	<2.A>bet	maybe-also	that.way	something:HESIT	what

hikigucirera	žige	wiikigucirekjene.
hikiguc-ire-ra	žige	wahi-hikiguc-ire-kjene
bet-SBJ.3PL-DEF	again	OBJ.3PL-APPL.INST-bet-SBJ.3PL-FUT

Whatever you’re gambling with, they will gamble with it again.

49.

Tiinąągre	jaagu	’ee	wawohirera	wažą
tee-nąągre	jaagu	’ee	wa-hohi-ire-ra	wažą
this-POS.NTL.PL:PROX	what	3EMPH	OBJ.3PL-defeat-SBJ.3PL-DEF	something

hijąhįcą	wawikigucire,	koreesge	šųųkxeteraišge.
hijąhį-cąą	wa-hi-hikiguc-ire	koreesge	šųųkxete-ra-išge
be.different-instead	OBJ.3PL-APPL.INST-bet-SBJ.3PL	maybe	horse-DEF-also

These ones, whatever they won, they will gamble with something else, perhaps even a horse.

50.

Jaagu	horohąra	šųųkxetera	joop,	hakewexjįšge	hanįirešųnų.
jaagu	horohąra	šųųkxete-ra	joop	hakewe-xjį-šge	hanį-ire-šųnų
what	most.of	horse-DEF	four	six-INTS-also	have.NTL-SBJ.3PL-HAB

Most of them used to have four to six horses.

51.

Hegų	žige	šųųkxete	hikigucireanąga,	žuurašge	žige	hikigucireanąga.
hegų	žige	šųųkxete	hikiguc-ire-’anąga	žuura-šge	žige	hikiguc-ire-’anąga
that.way	again	horse	bet-SBJ.3PL-and	money-also	again	bet-SBJ.3PL-and

And then they would bet for horses again, and they would bet money again.

52.

Hegų	'eeja	'ųų	'eegi	te'e	wawohigi,
hegų	‘eeja	‘ųų	‘eegi	te‘e	wa-hohi-gi
that.way	there	do/make	and.then	this	OBJ.3PL-defeat(SBJ.3SG)-TOP

wažąnąągre	hanąąc	wakurusire,	hegų
wažą-nąągre	hanąąc	wa-kurus-ire	hegų
something-POS.NTL.PL:PROX	all	OBJ.3PL-take.back-SBJ.3PL	that.way

wawohirera.
wa-hohi-ire-ra
OBJ.3PL-defeat-SBJ.3PL-DEF

Thus they play and if this side wins this time, they take back all these things, they win.

53.

Heesgege	kii'ų	hošgac	hižą	hereže	'aire.
heesge-ge	kii‘ų	ho-šgaac	hižą	here-že	‘ee-ire
that's.why-CAUSAL	gamble	APPL.INESS-play	one	be-QUOT	say-SBJ.3PL

That's why it's called a gambling game, that's what they say.

54.

Hįha,	hegų	kiira	hihe.
hįha	hegų	kiira	hihe
INTERJ	that.way	only	say\1E.A

That's all I am saying.

4.2 The complete Hocąk text without analysis

[1]Tee 'eegi hokiwagaxnągre waguje gikok šgaac hikorohonąąkšąną. [2]Hacąjaira wa'ųnąąki. [3](nąąkeregišge) Nąąkeejašge ciiporokešge nąkwi. [4]'Eeja wažąižąšge higišiknąkšąną. [5](wa'į̨žą) Wa'į̨žą wa'ųnąknąje. [6]Wa'į̨žą. [7]Tee waguje gikok šgaacirekjanegi, joop-ihikjanawi, wąąkra haruwąk šgaacirekjaneanąga. [8]Joopihi hikį̨kįirekjane. [9]'Aa'aki mį̨nąkireanąga. [10](tee) Hižą hožukjanegi, reex haruporoknągre že'e hi'ųanąga (žee nąąwą) wanągiwąkjane. [11]Saanįk 'ee (hožura) hožuirekjanenąjexjį. [12]Wagujerašge 'eegi nąąk. [13]Wąąknąągre hižąšge wookąnąk hižą hokąnąknągre, žeešge nee hitek haa. [14]Hegų 'eegi woomįšireanąga, wiigisarax hižąšge hanįire nąga, wiimąrak hižąšge hanįireanąga, te'e že'e 'ųųsge woorucgairekjane. [15]Wagujenąągre 'eeja mąąs poroporo hižąšge hi'ųirešųnų. [16](tee 'eeja) Tee 'eeja hižą kųųhąija hižą hokąnąkra teegi wažuirešųnų. [17]Kųųhąija nųųxąwą kąnąkire wağį̨ğį̨ poroporojknąka, joopiwi wagujera. [18]Mąąs poroporojknąka hegų kųųhąija wagujenąąka kųųhąija hižą 'eeja nųųxąwą hožuirekjane. [19]Te'e (hi'e) hi'e nąą'į̨irekjane, hi'eirekjeesge, nįgeešge kii'oireanąga, nįgeešge 'oirekjane. [20]Kii'oirega, horocą guucirega, hąąke hi'eiranį, hąąke 'eejanįąki, kii'o wa'ųire. [21]Žee 'eeja te'e joop hiruwe hiirek-jane, tee 'eeja joop hiruwe wagigirekjane. [22]Hegų žige higicgairekjane. [23]Hicągeere 'ųnąąk'ų hi'eiregi, horocąišge guuciregi, horocą guucireanąga hi'eiregi, te'e joop hiruwe wagigirekjene. [24]Hąąke horocą 'oiranįgi, tee waruğąire waiğąiregi hijopejanąki, taanį ruğąirekjane. [25]Hijopejanąki te'e woohikjane. [26]'Eeja te'e 'eeja nųųp hiruwe wagigirek-jane. [27]Nį̨šgaga 'ee hožuirekjane, 'eejanąka. [28]Wagujera waišeirekjane. [29]Nį̨šgaga 'ee hožuirenąga 'ee nąąwąirekjane. [30]Reex haruporokjaane (tapping). [31]'Eegi žeegų hi-irekjane. [32]Žige (nųųxąwą) te'e nųųxąwą t'ųųpireanąga nį̨šgaga te'e hi'eną'į̨irekjane, wağį̨ğį̨iknąka. [33]Hegų hąąpserecšge, hąąheserecšge šgaacirešųnų hagaira, hegų. [34]Hegų 'ųnąąk'ų, wiimąraknągre, 'eegi jaagušge wawigairera, "wiroikarapšge" 'airegųnį yaare. [35]Jaagušge 'airera? [36]Nųųpiwi. [37]Hirokikerešge wahiirešųnų hota, wiimąrak nį̨isge; ceek honųwąk 'eeja hegų hąąke wažą cąąt'įnį. [38]Hižą te'e wawohigi, te'egi hižą hawają kąnąkirega, hawają t'ųųpire. [39]Wiimąraknąka hižąkiira teegi himąrakikjane. [40]Hegų šgaac hanįhairegi žige te'e wohiregi, (nųųpnąka) winųųpra hija jį̨ipirekjane. [41]Hąąhą, 'eeja žige wawohiregi, 'eeja hožejąra herekjene. [42]'Eegi jaagu hikiguciregi, hegų žee hikigucirešųnų, šųųkxetešge. [43]Hikigucireanąga hegų wažą jaagu žuurašge hikigucireanąga, koreesgešge hinųkšge hikigucireanąga hegų. [44](wawohi) Tee wawohigi, hąą, že'e wažąnąąka hanąąc 'ee waanįirekjene. [45]"Hąą, nį̨ikarakje raagųwi," tee 'airekjene. [46]"Žige hį̨šgacikjawi." [47]'Eesge, hegų žige šgaac hajiharaire. [48]Jaagu hirakiguc, koreesgešge hegų 'ųųsge, jaagu hikigucir-era žige wiikigucirekjene. [49]Tiinąągre jaagu 'ee wawohirera wažą hijąhicą wawikigucire, ko reesge šųųkxeteraišge. [50]Jaagu horohąra šųųkxetera joop, hakewexjį̨šge hanįirešųnų. [51]Hegų žige šųųkxete hikigucireanąga, žuurašge žige hikigucireanąga. [52]Hegų 'eeja 'ųų 'eegi te'e wawohigi, wažąnąągre hanąąc wakurusire, hegų wawohirera. [53]Heesgege kii'ų hošgac hižą hereže 'aire. [54]Hį̨ha, hegų kiira hihe.

4.3 The complete English translation

[1]Here in this picture, they are getting ready to play the moccasin game. [2]Wherever they are. [3]Also behind them there are wigwams. [4]Also, there is something hanging there. [5]It appears to be a blanket/shawl. [6]A blanket. [7]If they are going to play moccasin, there's going to be four, eight men are going to play. [8]Four are going to team up. [9]They sit opposite each other. [10]The one that's going to load (the moccasin), this drum is going to be used and he (one of them) will sing for them. [11]That side, it appears, they are going to load it. [12]The moccasins are here. [13]Of these men, the one who is wearing the hat, he is my uncle. [14]They've spread something (a blanket) on the ground, they even have a rattle, they also have a pointer, with this (the pointer) they are going to probe (under the moccasins). [15]These moccasins, there they also used to use a round metal ball. [16]When someone puts one underneath there, they put them here. [17]They hide that little round ball underneath, four moccasins. [18]That little metal ball is going to be underneath one of these moccasins, they are going to hide it there. [19]This side will try to find it, they have to find it, or else, they could shoot themselves, or they will shoot it. [20]When they shoot themselves, if they shoot it straight on and they don't find it, it's not under there, they've shot themselves. [21]This side, they're going to pay four, they're going to pay them four. [22]They are going to try again. [23]When they finally find it as they're doing it, they might have shot it straight on, if they shoot straight on and find it, they will pay this side four. [24]If they didn't shoot straight on, when they uncover them and flip them over, and if it's in the fourth one, they will have uncovered (the other) three. [25]If it's under the fourth, this (side) is going to win. [26]So they're going to pay this (side) two. [27]So now they get to load (the moccasins), there. [28]They're going to take away the shoes. [29]This side is going to load now, and they're going to sing. [30]This drum (tapping on the table imitating the sound of the drum). [31]That's what they're going to do. [32]This (side) will hide it now, and this (side) is going to try and find that little ball. [33]Sometimes they'd play all day and even all night long. [34]In the process, what are these called now, I think they used to call them "counters." [35]What did they say? [36]There were two of them (the counters). [37]They used to connect those two together, some of them, as sort of markers; at first there is nothing to be seen. [38]If one has won, they would lean it up, and then push it into position. [39]There is only one going to be pointing this way (out of these two). [40]And when they're playing, if this side wins again, the second stick will be placed along side. [41]And after that if they win again that'll be the end. [42]Whatever they bet with each other, they did, even horses. [43]When they gambled with whatever, including money, maybe even women. [44]If this side wins, yes, all those things belongs to them. [45]"We'd like to challenge you," this (side) will say. [46]"Let's play again." [47]That's why they started to play again. [48]Whatever you're gambling with, they will gamble with it again. [49]These ones, whatever they won, they will gamble with something else, perhaps even a horse. [50]Most of them used to have four to six horses. [51]And then they would bet for horses again, and they would bet money again. [52]Thus they play and if this side wins this time, they take back all these

things, they win. [53]That's why it's called a gambling game, that's what they say. [54]That's all I am saying.

5 Child teaching (CD 1 track 4)

5.1 Text with analysis and translation

1. Nįįkjąk hookárakų́
nįįkjąk hoo<kara>kų
child <POSS.RFL>teach

Child teaching

2. 'Éegi ceekrégi wąąkšík, wąąkšíknąągre, jaasgé
'eegi ceek-regi wąąkšik wąąkšik=nąągre jaasge
and.then first/new-SIM/LOC Indian/person Indian/person=POS.NTL.PL:PROX how

wąąkšík'įįňegiži.
wąąkšik'įį-ire-giži
live-SBJ.3PL-TOP

In the beginning, this was the way the Indians, these Indians, lived.

3. Nįįkjąkra hižą́ gixetéregiží, hookárakų́įráanąga,
nįįkjąk-ra hižą gi-xete-ree-giži hoo<kara>kų-ire='anąga
child-DEF one APPL.BEN-be.big-go.there-TOP <POSS.RFL>teach-SBJ.3PL=and

'éejasgé coowéja wąąkšík'įįňekjąnégiži, wąąkšík ho'įra
'ee-jaasge coowe-'eeja wąąkšik'įį-ire-kjąne-giži wąąkšik_ho'į-ra
this-how in.the.future-there live-SBJ.3PL-FUT-TOP life-DEF

pį́į'ųųkje žéesge karagígųsirekjąnégi.
pįį-'ųų-kje] žeesge kara-gigųs-ire-kjąne-gi
be.good-do/make-FUT thus POSS.RFL-teach-SBJ.3PL-FUT-TOP

When a child was growing up, they taught him how to live in the future, so that he would live a good life.

4. Ceekjį́ra wa'ų́įňeže, cíihokisák honąžį́ňą,
ceek-xjį-ra wa'ų-ire-že cii-hokisak ho-nąąžį-ra
first/new-INTS-DEF do/be-SBJ.3PL-QUOT house-middle APPL.INESS-stand-DEF

himąrakíreže 'ųųxį́nįňą rúus, žéesge kiišíireže.
himąrak-ire-že 'ųųxįnį-ra ruus žeesge kii-šii-ire-že
point.at-SBJ.3PL-QUOT charcoal-DEF take thus RFL-tell.to.do-SBJ.3PL-QUOT

First they did this: They pointed to the fire (= stands in the center of the lodge), and ordered him to take the charcoal (to blacken his face).

5. Hąątáginąc hakikáražíreže.
hąątaginąc ha<kii>karaži-ire-že
fast.for.blessing(SBJ.3SG) <RFL>encourage(OBJ.3SG)-SBJ.3PL-QUOT

They encouraged him to fast for blessings.

6.

Ceekjį́ra,	xųnųnį́k	hąątáginącirégi,	wiirá	roocą́ąje
ceek-xjį-ra	xųųnų-nįk	hąątaginąc-ire-gi	wii-ra	roocą=jee
first/new-INTS-DEF	be.small-DIM	fast.for.blessing-SBJ.3PL-TOP	sun-DEF	be.straight=POS.VERT

hipá,	žéejąįxjį	hį́įpire,	žéejąįxjį	warúcireže.
hipa	žeejąįxjį	hįįp-ire	žeejąįxjį	waruc-ire-že
up.to.that.far	that.far	lie.down-SBJ.3PL	that.far	eat-SBJ.3PL-QUOT

The first time the little ones started to fast, they did it until noon (= sun stands straight) and then they ate.

7.

’Ųų	haráiregi,	hijáira	hiyaráireže,
’ųų	ha-ree-ire-gi	hijaira	hii<ha>re-ire-že
do/make	COLL-go.there-SBJ.3PL-TOP	more	<COLL>go.through-SBJ.3PL-QUOT

When they started out they did more along the way.

8.

Hahí	hąąpsérec	hąątáginącirégi,	hokipį́įregiži,	hahąhé
hahi	hąąp-serec	hąątaginąc-ire-gi	hokipį-ire-giži	hahąhe
finally	day-be.long	fast.for.blessing-SBJ.3PL-TOP	last/endure-SBJ.3PL-TOP	be.overtaken.by.night

híire	hąąhé	hokahí,	hahí	hagakírahąšge	ną́įňeže,
hii-ire	hąąhe	hokahi	hahi	hagakirahą-šge	nąą-ire-že
arrive.there-SBJ.3PL	night	every	finally	once-also	sleep-SBJ.3PL-QUOT

nųųbáhą	híi	nąįre,	’éejaxjį́	mą́ą	kerepąnąįžą,	’éeja
nųųp-ahą	hii	nąą-ire	’eeja-xjį	mąą	kerepąnąįžą	’eeja
two-times	arrive.there	sleep-SBJ.3PL	there-INTS	year	ten	there

nįgé	hereže,	joobáhą	hakewehášge	nąįňes’áže.
nįge	here-že	joop-ahą	hakewe-hą-šge	nąą-ire-s’a-že
somewhere	be-QUOT	four-times	six-times-also	sleep-SBJ.3PL-ITER-QUOT

All day long, when they fast, if they last that long, then they reached nightfall, and then they slept over one night, fasting, then they slept two, and at about ten years old they were accustomed to sleep four or even six nights while fasting.

Kere jų sep ska
07

9.

Žéežeegųgíži,	wąąknąągre	hižą́	hinįk	hiikį́,
žee-žeegų-giži	wąąk-nąągre	hižą	hinįk	hiikį
that-thus-TOP	man=POS.NTL.PL:PROX	one	son	wake.up(SBJ.3SG)

wookáragixétekjįgiži,	hą́įnįrégi,
woo<kara>gixete-xjį-giži	hąįnį-regi
<POSS.RFL>love(SBJ.3SG&OBJ.3SG)-INTS-TOP	morning-SIM/LOC

kiikáwa'ą́ągiži,	waasgéra	warúcra	hožú,	nąąpsánįkeja
kiikawa'a-'ąk-giži	waasge-ra	waruc-ra	hožu	nąąp-saanįk-'eeja
get.up.from.lying.position=POS.HOR-TOP	dish-DEF	food-DEF	put.into	hand-side-there

harukósanąga	žigé	nąąpsánįkejá	'ųųxį́nį,	hinįkrá	giwahá.
harukos='anąga	žige	nąąp-saanįk-'eeja	'ųųxįnį	hinįk-ra	gi-waha
hold(SBJ.3SG)=and	again	hand-side-there	charcoal	son-DEF	APPL.BEN-show

There was a man who loved his son very much, one morning when he got up he held a dish with food in one hand, and in the other charcoal, for his son to choose.

10.

Žéegųgają,	warucjáane	ruusgí,	ruusgí
žeegų-gają	waruc=jaane	ruus-gi	ruus-gi
thus-SEQ	food=POS.VERT:PROX	take(SBJ.3SG)-TOP	take(SBJ.3SG)-TOP

rúusgigiánąga,	rúuc	hikorohógają	raaxóc
ruus-gigi='anąga	ruuc	hikoroho-gają	raaxoc
take-let/cause(SBJ.3SG&OBJ.3PL)=and	eat	get.ready(SBJ.3SG)-SEQ	ashes

hogibéže.
ho<gi>be-že
<APPL.BEN>throw.into-QUOT

If he took the food, he let him take it, but when he got ready to eat, he threw ashes into it.

11.

Žéegųgiži	hi'ącrá	horğóc,	nąącgéra	téekjį
žeegų-giži	hi'ąc-ra	horogoc	nąącge-ra	teek-xjį
thus-TOP	father-DEF	look.at(SBJ.3SG)	heart-DEF	ache-INTS

horoğócše,	mąąňą	mąącgúra
horoğoc-še	mąą-ra	mąącgu-ra
look.at(SBJ.3SG&OBJ.3SG)-QUOT	arrow-DEF	bow-DEF

wagirúsanąga,	'áija	rukósanąga,	mąącguágre
wa-gi-ruus-'anąga	'aa-hija	rukos-'anąga	mąącgu-'agre
OBJ.3PL-APPL.BEN-take(SBJ.3SG)=and	arm-there	hold(SBJ.3SG)-and	bow-POS.HOR:PROX

mą́ąňą	hirasá	higipsį́canąga.
mąą-ra	hirasa	hi-gipsįc='anąga
arrow-DEF	in.addition	APPL.INST-whip=and

While he (the son) looked at him, sore at heart, his father took his bow and arrow, grasped him (the son) by the arm, and whipped him with the bow and arrow.

12.

’Ų̨ų̨xį́nį	wacópanąga	hišjára	séepgigiánąga	cąągrá
’ųųxįnį	wacop=’anąga	hišja-ra	seep-gigi=’anąga	cąąk-ra
charcoal	chop=and	face-DEF	be.black-let/cause(SBJ.3SG&OBJ.3SG)=and	outside-DEF

hut’ųňée(že).
hot’ųree-že
throw.out(SBJ.3SG&OBJ.3SG)-QUOT

Then he ground charcoal and blacked his (the son’s) face and threw him outside.

13.

Žéežeegų́giži,	nąącgéra	téekše,	nįįkją́knįkjaané.
žee-žeegų-giži	nąącge-ra	teek-še	nįįkjąk-nįk=jaane
that-thus-TOP	heart-DEF	ache-QUOT	child-DIM=POS.VERT:PROX

The child was sore at heart.

14.

Hocįcį́nįkjaané	nąącgéra	téekjįgiži,	hi’ącrá	hąąké	žéesge
hocįcį-nįk=jaane	nąącge-ra	teek-xjį-giži	hi’ąc-ra	hąąke	žeesge
boy-DIM=POS.VERT:PROX	heart-DEF	ache-INTS-TOP	father-DEF	NEG.IN	thus

giginį́nągają́,	’ųųgí	nąącgéra	téekjį	ğáakanągá,
gigi-nį-nąą-gają	’ųų-gi	nąącge-ra	teek-xjį	ğaak=’anąga
let/cause-NEG.FIN-POT-SEQ	do/make(SBJ.3SG)-TOP	heart-DEF	ache-INTS	cry=and

ciiróp	’eeja	hihinąpgi	gixará	hapahí	mąąnį
ciirop	’eeja	hihinąp-gi	gixa-ra	hapahi	mąąnį
door	there	go.outside(SBJ.3SG)-TOP	wilderness-DEF	go.toward	walk

réeže.
ree-že
go.there-QUOT

This boy had a real sore heart, his father should not have done it, (but) when he did, he cried broken hearted, when he went out the door, he went walking towards the wilderness.

15.

Ğáak	nąącgéra	téekjįže,	hąąké	haakjá	cii	’éeja
ğaak	nąącge-ra	teek-xjį-že	hąąke	haakja	cii	’eeja
cry	heart-DEF	ache-INTS-QUOT	NEG.IN	backwards	house	there

kirinį́ra.
kiri-nį-ra
arrive.back.here-NEG.FIN-DEF

He was crying with a broken heart, he did not return to the house.

16.

Žéesge,	žéesge	wiiwéwįňą	’ųųžé:
žeesge	žeesge	wiiwewį-ra	’ųų-že
thus	thus	thought/mind-DEF	be-QUOT

This is what he thought:

17.

“Žéegų	nįgé	hahí,	ceekjé,	jaajíga	nąącgéra
žeegų	nįge	ha-hii	cee-kje	jaaji-ga	nąącge-ra
thus	somewhere	1E.A-arrive.there	die\1E.U-FUT	father-PROP	heart-DEF

teek	wį́įňą.”
teek	hį-hii-ra
ache(OBJ.3SG)	1E.U-make/CAUS(SBJ.3SG)-DEF

“I will go somewhere and die, father made my heart ache.”

18.

Žéesge	hiiráanąga	gixára	howarégi	hahí
žeesge	hiire='anąga	gixa-ra	howare-gi	hahi
thus	think=and	wilderness-DEF	go.forward(SBJ.3SG)-TOP	finally

hahąhéanąga,	žigé	hinųbáhąra	hąąhé.
hahąhe='anąga	žige	hi-nųųp-ahą-ra	hąąhe
be.overtaken.by.night=and	again	ORD-two-times-DEF	night

Thinking that he went along towards the wilderness, and night came, and also the second night.

19.

Ğáak	goišíp	wa’ųákše,	t’éekjąne	žéesge,	jajáixjį
ğaak	goišip	wa’ų-’ąk-še	t’ee-kjąne	žeesge	jajaixjį
cry	always	do/be-POS.HOR-QUOT	die-FUT	thus	how.far

hokipį́giži,	žéejąįxjį	hį́įpanągá	t’éekje	žéesge	nąącgéra	téekše.
hokipį-giži	žeejąįxjį	hįįp='anąga	t’ee-kje	žeesge	nąącge-ra	teek-še
last/endure-TOP	that.far	lie.down=and	die-FUT	thus	heart-DEF	ache-QUOT

And still he went along crying, he would die, he would suffer to the end and then die, that is how sore-hearted he was.

20.

Žéegųgiži	nąą́c hokiją́xjįže,	jaasgé
žeegų-giži	nąąc_ho<kii>ją-xjį-že	jaasge
thus-TOP	<RFL>take.pity.on(SBJ.3SG)-INTS-QUOT	how

nąą́c hokiją́nągi,	žéesge	nąącgéra	téekše.
nąąc_ho<kii>ją-nąą-gi	žeesge	nąącge-ra	teek-še
<RFL>take.pity.on(SBJ.3SG)-POT-TOP	thus	heart-DEF	ache-QUOT

He felt very sorry for himself, he would pity himself; that is how sore-hearted he was.

21.

Hąąhéregi	mį́įki	ğáak,	jajáixjį	hiikį́gi	ğáak.
hąąhe-regi	mįįk-gi	ğaak	jajaixjį	hiikį-gi	ğaak
night-SIM/LOC	lie.down(SBJ.3SG)-TOP	cry	how.far	wake.up-TOP	cry(SBJ.3SG)

At night when he lay down he was crying, as long as he was awake he cried.

22.

Coowéxjį	nąą́	hiikį	jiikáranąga	žigé	hiikį́	ǧáak,	žée	žéesge
coowexjį	nąą	hiikį	jiikere='anąga	žige	hiikį	ǧaak	žee	žeesge
just.a.little	sleep	wake.up	be.started=and	again	wake.up	cry	that	thus

híireegí	hąąhé	hijoobáhą,	hąąhé	hisaacą́hą,	hirakéwehą
hii-regi	hąąhe	hi-joop-ahą	hąąhe	hi-saacą-hą	hi-hakewe-hą
make/CAUS-SIM/LOC	night	ORD-four-times	night	ORD-five-times	ORD-six-times

haiją́įšge	waxopį́nį	warácire	nąą́c hoją́įreže.
haiją-hišge	waxopįnį	wa-raac-ire	nąąc_hoją-ire-že
defeat(SBJ.3SG)-also	spirit	OBJ.3PL-name-SBJ.3PL	take.pity.on-SBJ.3PL-QUOT

He slept fitfully and waking, he was crying, he continued to do this, and on the fourth or fifth or perhaps the sixth night the spirits took pity on him.

23.

Wąąkšík ho'įrá,	jaasgé	hoxetéregi,	'ųįňékjąnégiži.
wąąkšik_ho'į-ra	jaasge	hoxete-regi	'ųų-ire-kjąne-giži
life-DEF	how	grow.up-SIM/LOC	do/make-SBJ.3PL-FUT-TOP

They blessed him with the life he would have when he grew up.

24.

Homąšją́	jaagú	žéesge	nąą́c hiroją́įrežé.
homąšją	jaagu	žeesge	nąąc_hiroją-ire-že
power	what	thus	take.pity.on(OBJ.3SG)-SBJ.3PL-QUOT

They blessed him with the power he would have.

Kere jų sep ska
07

25. Wąąktóšweešgekjaneáŋąga, wąąk wášošešge wooną́ğirešge cųųkjané
wąąktošewe-šge-kjąne='aŋąga wąąk wašoše-šge wooŋąğire-šge cųų-kjane
medicine.man-also-FUT=and man be.brave-also warrior-also have.much-FUT

'éegi hokicų́rašge jaasgé, pįįkjąnégi, coowéja
'eegi hokicų-ra-šge jaasge pįį-kjąne-gi coowe-'eeja
and.then descendants-DEF-also how be.good-FUT-TOP in.the.future-there

wąąkšík ho'įrá, haną́ąc gigų́siráanąga.
wąąkšik_ho'į-ra hanąąc gigųs-ire='anąga
life-DEF all teach-SBJ.3PL=and

Perhaps he would become a man of healing (a medicine man), or perhaps he would be a brave man if there was war; how good his family would be, all this they taught him.

26. 'Éegi wagáiranąže "Hąhó, haną́ąc téerenąą, jaagú hi'ąc
'eegi wage-ire-nąą-že hąho hanąąc tee-here-ną jaagu hi'ąc
and.then mean-SBJ.3PL-POT-QUOT INTJ all this-be-DECL what father

ráaga ronįgígųra.
raa-ga roo<nį-gi>gų-ra
have.kin\2.A-PROP <2.U-APPL.BEN>want-DEF

And they say to him, "Hąhóo! All this is what your father wanted for you.

27. Hi'ąc ráaga wooxéte nįįną́, 'éesge
hi'ąc raa-ga wooxete_hii-nįį-ną 'eesge
father have.kin\2.A-PROP love-1&2-DECL thus

wanįgí'ųną.
wa<nį-gi>'ų-ną
<2.U-APPL.BEN>do/be(SBJ.3SG)-DECL

"Because he loved you, he did this to you."

28. Tée žéegų nįgigígiži jaasgé nąą́cgéra nįtékjiire, žee
tee žeegų nį-gigi-giži jaasge nąącge-ra nį-teek-jiire žee
this thus 2.U-let/cause-TOP how heart-DEF 2.U-ache-begin that

nįgigígiži, 'éegi nąą́c horakíjągiži, waxopįnį warácire
nį-gigi-giži 'eegi nąąc_ho<ra-kii>ją-giži waxopįnį wa-raac-ire
2.U-let/cause-TOP and.then <2.A-RFL>take.pity.on-TOP spirit OBJ.3PL-name-SBJ.3PL

žéesge nąą́c honįją́įňekjąne 'éesge, nįgigíiną.
žeesge nąąc_ho<nį>ją-ire-kjąne 'eesge nį-gigi-ną
thus <2.U>take.pity.on-SBJ.3PL-FUT thus 2.U-let/cause-DECL

"Just as sore-hearted as you were, and as you pitied yourself, so the spirits would pity you, he did it to you."

29.

'Éegi	rakerékjąnąhéeną,	hi'ąc	ráaga	hąąké
'eegi	ra-kere-kjąnąhe-ną	hi'ąc	raa-ga	hąąke
and.then	2.A-go.back.there-FUT-DECL	father	have.kin\2.A-PROP	NEG.IN

honįš'íknį	wa'ų́ną.
ho<nį>š'ik-nį	wa'ų-ną
<2.U>dislike-NEG.FIN	do/be-DECL

"You should go home, your father did not hate you when he did this."

30.

Wonįgíxetéxjį	wa'ų́ną,	'éexjį	nąącgéra	téek,"	žée	žeesge,
woo<nį>gixete-xjį	wa'ų-ną	'ee-xjį	nąącge-ra	teek	žee	žeesge
<2.U>love-INTS	do/be-DECL	3EMPH-INTS	heart-DEF	ache	that	thus

higáiranąge.
hige-ire='anąga
say.to-SBJ.3PL=and

"He loved you very much, he was sore-hearted himself," they said to him.

31.

'Éegi,	haakjá,	cíira	howakéregi.
'eegi	haakja	cii-ra	howe-kere-gi
and.then	backwards	house-DEF	go.about-go.back.there(SBJ.3SG)-TOP

And so he went home.

Kere ju sep ska
07

32.

Hagoréižą,	ciéja	hagí	hoikéwegi,	hi'ącrá	t'ą́ąpjiiráanąga
hagoreižą	cii-'eeja	hagi	hoikewe-gi	hi'ąc-ra	t'ąąp-jiire='anąga
sometime	house-there	there	go.inside-TOP	father-DEF	get.down-begin=and

hinįkrá	nąąkárat'ųpanągá,	"Hinįk	háaxjį,
hinįk-ra	nąą<kara>t'ųp='anąga	hinįk	haa-xjį
son-DEF	<POSS.RFL>embrace(SBJ.3SG&OBJ.3SG)=and	son	have.kin\1E.A-INTS

rakirirá,	'éepįįną.
ra-kiri-ra	'ee-pįį-ną
2.A-arrive.back.here-DEF	this-be.good-DECL

When he entered the house, his father jumped up and threw his arms around him: "Dear son, it is good that you have come back.

33.

Hąąké	honįš'íknįną,	wonįgíxetéeną.
hąąke	ho<nįį>š'ik-nį-ną	woo<nįį>gixete-ną
NEG.IN	<1&2>dislike-NEG.FIN-DECL	<1&2>love-DECL

I did not hate you, I loved you.

34.

Žéegųgi	wąąkšík ho'į́,	gáagų	šerekjanąhé.
žeegų-gi	wąąkšik_ho'į	gaagų	še-ree-kjanąhe
thus-TOP	life	this.way	2.A-go.there-FUT

You're going to go this way with your living now.

35.

Hanąą́c	harakáraginąįce.
hanąąc	ha<ra-kara>giną(į)c=jee
all	<2.A-POSS.RFL>take.care.of=POS.VERT

You're going to be good to all that is yours.

36.

Žéesge	yaapéresge	žéesge	nįgigíiną.
žeesge	hi<ha>peres-ge	žeesge	nįį-gigi-ną
thus	<1E.A>know-CAUSAL	thus	1&2-let/cause-DECL

Because I knew this I did it to you.

37.

'Éegi	nąąğírak	hikarapéres	wąąkšíkra	'áireną.
'eegi	nąąğirak	hi<kara>peres	wąąkšik-ra	'ee-ire-ną
and.then	soul	<POSS.RFL>know	Indian/person-DEF	say-SBJ.3PL-DECL

The people said: know your soul.

38. Hižą́ žéesge wą̨ąkšík'į̨gížì, hagoréižą, róonągre, t'éešge,
hižą žeesge wą̨ąkšik'į̨-giži hagoreižą roo=nągre t'ee-šge
one thus live-TOP sometime body=POS.NTL:PROX die-also

nąąǧírak 'ée hanį̨ňą́ waxopį́nį warácire hagí
nąąǧirak 'ee hanį-ra waxopį̨nį wa-raac-ire hagi
soul 3EMPH have.NTL-DEF spirit OBJ.3PL-name-SBJ.3PL there

wą̨ąkšík'į̨į, mą̨ąnágre hikijá wą̨ąkšík'į́kjąnéeną.
wą̨ąkšik'į̨į mąą=nągre hikiją wą̨ąkšik'į̨į-kjąne-ną
live earth=POS.NTL:PROX reach live-FUT-DECL

One who lives this way might die in the body sometime, but his soul, reaching the spirits, will live as long as the earth.

39. Žée žéesge yaapéresnákšąną.
žee žeesge hi<ha>peres=nąk-šąną
that thus <1E.A>know=POS.NTL-DECL

That is what I know.

40. 'Éesge 'áajiirégi, žée hironį́gigųgé,
'eesge 'ee-jii-ire-gi žee hi-roo<nį̨-gi>gų-ge
thus say-arrive.here-SBJ.3PL-TOP that APPL.INST-<1&2-APPL.BEN>want-CAUSAL

wáa'ųųną.
wa<ha>'ų-ną
<1E.A>do/be(OBJ.3SG)-DECL

Because they said it traditionally (the ancestors said it) and because I wanted it for you, I did it.

41. 'Éegi žigé, mą̨ąxíwą̨gregi wą̨ąktóše hocíižą, jaanága,
'eegi žige mą̨ąxi-wą̨ąk-regi wą̨ąktosewe hoci-ižą jaanąga
and.then again sky/cloud-upper.region-SIM/LOC medicine.man house-one how.many

wanį́k, wapakánąkra, nááną́ągre, 'éeja hapahí wakirí
wanįk wapakąnąk-ra nąą=nąągre 'eeja hapahi wakiri
bird be.wise-DEF wood=POS.NTL.PL:PROX there go.toward insect

hikišérenáąki.
hikišere-nąą-gi
deal.with-POT-TOP

Up in the sky there is a medicine lodge, the lodge of woodpecker spirits (those that can see worms in the trees).

42. Jaagúra, hižą́ heregí, hąąké ruš'ákiranį.
jaagu-ra hižą here-gi hąąke ruš'ak-ire-nį
what-DEF one be-TOP NEG.IN fail.at-SBJ.3PL-NEG.FIN

They don't fail at anything.

43. Hišjasúra wapakąnąkire.
hišjasu-ra wapakąnąk-ire
eye-DEF be.wise-SBJ.3PL

Their eyes see everything.

44. Žée žéesge, jaanąga, wanįrák rakįį wąąktóšewe hocíižą
žee žeesge jaanąga wanįk-ra ra-kįį wąąktošewe hoci-ižą
that thus how.many bird-DEF 2.A-make.self medicine.man house-one

wąąkrégiák, že'é nąąc honįjąįñegiži,
wąąk-regi-'ąk že'e nąąc_ho<nį>ją-ire-giži
upper.region-SIM/LOC-POS.HOR that <2.U>take.pity.on-SBJ.3PL-TOP

mąąxíwąkrégi howáji, homąšją nįcųąnąga.
mąąxi-wąąk-regi howe-jii homąšją nį-cųų='anąga
sky/cloud-upper.region-SIM/LOC go.about-arrive.here power 2.U-have.much=and

How many of you turn into birds, there's a medicine man's lodge in the sky, if they bless you with that, from up in the sky you'll have strength.

45. Wąąkšíknąągre hižą hotek šíišik jaagúižą hanįąnąga,
wąąkšik=nąągre hižą hotek šiišik jaagu-ižą hanį='anąga
Indian/person=POS.NTL.PL:PROX one sore.spot be.bad what-one have.NTL=and

hanįkárahásiregíži, hoték žée, rušją raanąą.
hanįkarahas-ire-giži hotek žee rušją raa-nąą
help-SBJ.3PL-TOP sore.spot that quit make/CAUS\2.A-POT

If of these Indians one has a bad sore, whatever he has, when they rely on you, that sore you can cure it.

46. Žee žeesgé homąšjąižą že'é haraginąc žéesge, wáa'ųną,
žee žeesge homąšją-ižą že'e ha<ra>ginąc žeesge wa<ha>'ų-ną
that thus power-one that <2.A>take.care.of thus <1E.A>do/be-DECL

jáagu nįįgi'ųñą.
jaagu nįį-gi-'ųų-ra
what 1&2-APPL.BEN-do/make-DEF

So that you would suffer for this kind of power, I did what I did to you.

47. 'Éegi žigé xeexétera hižą nįgenąki, waxopįnį
'eegi žige xee-xete-ra hižą nįge=nąk-gi waxopįnį
and.then again hill-be.big-DEF one somewhere=POS.NTL-TOP spirit

warácire hocí wa'ųnąkšąną.
wa-raac-ire hoci wa'ų=nąk-šąną
OBJ.3PL-name-SBJ.3PL house do/be=POS.NTL-DECL

And if there is a big mountain somewhere, it is a spirits' house.

48. Žéesge horakáwanąga, waxopį́nį warácire ceewą́ąk
žeesge ho<ra>kewe=’anąga waxopįnį wa-raac-ire cee-wąąk
thus <2.A>go.inside=and spirit OBJ.3PL-name-SBJ.3PL cow-man

céexi, hųųcížą céexi, jaagúra hížą, žéesge
ceexi hųųc-ižą ceexi jaagu-ra hižą žeesge
holy/expensive bear-one holy/expensive what-DEF one thus

wa’ųą́ki nąąc honįją́giži wáinį hąkága wanąjonįją́įsganį.
wa’ų-’ąk-gi nąąc_ho<nį>ją-giži wainį hąkaga wanąjo<nį>jąįsge-nį
do/be-POS.HOR-TOP <2.U>take.pity.on-TOP clothing NEG.IN.never <2.U>be.poor-NEG.FIN

If you go there, and some spirit, a holy buffalo or a holy bear, whatever it is, takes pity on you, you will never lack clothes.

49. Wąąkšík jáagu hanį́įňera hiną́ wąąkšíkš’į́į haní̧
wąąkšik jaagu hanį-ire-ra hiną wąąkšik<š>’įį hanį
Indian/person what have.NTL-SBJ.3PL-DEF enough <2.A>live have.NTL

wąąkšíkš’į́įkjąneną.
wąąkšik<š>’įį-kjąne-ną
<2.A>live-FUT-DECL

You will have enough of the things that people have.

50. Žée róogų nįgigí wáa’ų́ųną.
žee roogų nįį-gigi wa<ha>’ų-ną
that want 1&2-let/cause <1E.A>do/be-DECL

Wishing this for you, I did it.

Kere jy sep ska
07

51.

“Xeenąą́gre	hižą́	’éeja	rahigí,	ciiróp	hižą́	’éeja
xee=nąągre	hižą	’eeja	ra-hii-gi	ciirop	hižą	’eeja
hill=POS.NTL.PL:PROX	one	there	2.A-arrive.there-TOP	door	one	there

jéeną,	‘gígįgįgįgįgíš’	’áajire,	ciirópra	gihásgi,
jee-ną	gįgįgįgį-gįgįš	’ee-jiire	ciirop-ra	gihas-gi
POS.VERT-DECL	RDP:INTS-make.squeaking.noise	say-begin	door-DEF	open-TOP

horakéwegi,	rookrá	jáagu	hiratáža híirešgé,	žéesge
ho<ra>kewe-gi	rook-ra	jaagu	hi-hataža_hii-ire-šge	žeesge
<2.A>go.inside-TOP	inside-DEF	what	APPL.INST-light-SBJ.3PL-also	thus

wąąkšík	’éeja	nąą́kikjąnąhéeną.
wąąkšik	’eeja	nąąk-i-kjąnąhe-ną
Indian/person	there	POS.NTL.PL-0-FUT-DECL

“When you get to one of these hills, there is a door, it starts saying “gįgįgįgįgįgįš” (= it squeaks) when it opens, and when you go inside, it’ll be lit with whatever (= something) and there will be Indians sitting there.

52.

Žee	nąą́c honįją́įñegiží,	hąkagá	wažąñą́	hižą́
žee	nąąc_ho<nį>ją-ire-giži	hąkaga	wažą-ra	hižą
that	<2.U>take.pity.on-SBJ.3PL-TOP	NEG.IN.never	something-DEF	one

roorágųnį.
roo<ra>gų-nį
<2.A>want-NEG.FIN

If they take pity on you, you will never want (lack) anything.

53.

Wąąkšíkš’įį́kjąne	žée	žéesge	ronįgígų,	wáa’ųųną.
wąąkšik<š>’įį-kjąne	žee	žeesge	roo<nįį-gi>gų	wa<ha>’ų-ną
<2.A>live FUT	that	thus	<1&2-APPL.BEN>want	<1E.A>do/be-DECL

Because I wanted you to live that way, I did it to you.

54.

’Éegi	nįį́kų́hąregi,	nįį́nąą́gre	kųųhą́
’eegi	nįį-kųųhą-regi	nįį=nąągre	kųųhą
and.then	water-underneath-SIM/LOC	water=POS.NTL.PL:PROX	underneath

híirera	cíi	nąągú	wa’ųnąą́kšąną.
hii-ire-ra	cii	nąągu	wa’ų=nąąk-šąną
make/CAUS-SBJ.3PL-DEF	house	road	do/be=POS.NTL.PL-DECL

Under the water, under these rivers, are their home-made roads.

55.

Žée	žéesge,	žéesgeeja	žigé	wažą́	hižą́	hirahą́tegi,
žee	žeesge	žeesge-'eeja	žige	wažą	hižą	hi<ra>hąte-gi
that	thus	thus-there	again	something	one	<2.A>dream.of-TOP

mąąnągre	hąąké	wažą́	hižą́	šuruš'áknįkjąné.
mąą=nągre	hąąke	wažą	hižą	šu-ruš'ak-nį-kjąne
earth=POS.NTL:PROX	NEG.IN	something	one	2.A-fail.at-NEG.FIN-FUT

If you dream of those, nothing on this earth will be impossible for you.

56.

Nįéja,	jáagu,	wanóicge	horajánąąki	jáagu	gipį́
nįį-'eeja	jaagu	wanoicge	horaje=nąąk-gi	jaagu	gipį
water-there	what	animal	travel=POS.NTL.PL-TOP	what	like

wawaš'ų́kjąne,	žéegųgi	jáagu,	wanóicge	jáagu
wa-wa<š>'ų-kjąne	žeegų-gi	jaagu	wanoicge	jaagu
OBJ.3PL-<2.A>do/be-FUT	thus-TOP	what	animal	what

wiirorákųkjąnegiži,	hirakáraperés,	wapaką́nąkra	waš'ų́,
wa-hiro<ra>kų-kjąne-giži	hi<ra-kara>peres	wapakąnąk-ra	wa<š>'ų
OBJ.3PL-<2.A>utilize-FUT-TOP	<2.A-POSS.RFL>know	be.wise-DEF	<2.A>do/be

wąąkšíkš'į́įkjąnąhe.
wąąkšik<š>'įį-kjąnąhe
<2.A>live-FUT

You will do as you please with the live things in the water, with the animals, you will live by your power.

57.

Žée	žéegųgíži	hįkága	waašaragésnį́.	hiną́
žee	žeegų-giži	hįkaga	wa-ha<ša>rages-nį	hiną
that	thus-TOP	NEG.IN.never	OBJ.3PL-<2.A>have.not.enough.to.eat-NEG.FIN	enough

woorúcra	š'ų́ųkjąne.
wooruc-ra	š-'ųų-kjąne
food.serving-DEF	2.A-do/make-FUT

You will never not have enough to eat, you will always have enough food.

58.

Nįéja,	jáagu	wanóicgeną́ągre	nįįkų́hąregi,	žée	žéesge,
nįį-'eeja	jaagu	wanoicge=nąągre	nįį-kųųhą-regi	žee	žeesge
water-there	what	animal=POS.NTL.PL:PROX	water-underneath-SIM/LOC	that	thus

mąąnągre	kųųhą́regi,	tiiránąąkšąną.
mąą=nągre	kųųhą-regi	tiire=nąąk-šąną
earth=POS.NTL:PROX	underneath-SIM/LOC	move=POS.NTL.PL-DECL

Whatever animals are under the water, there beneath the earth, this is going on.

59. Waxopį́nį warácire, kųųhą́ ho'ųnąąkšąną.
waxopįnį wa-raac-ire kųųhą ho-'ųų=nąąk-šąną
spirit OBJ.3PL-name-SBJ.3PL underneath APPL.INESS-do/make=POS.NTL.PL-DECL

The spirits, they roam underground.

60. Nįįkų́hąra mą́ąra hociéja goojáxjį, hacį́įja
nįį-kųųhą-ra mąą-ra ho-cii-'eeja gooja-xjį hacįįja
water-underneath-DEF earth-DEF APPL.INESS-live-there over.there-INTS where

kųųhą́ra žéejąįxjipá, horajánąąkšąną žéesgexjį wapakánąk
kųųhą-ra žeejąįxjį-hipa horaje=nąąk-šąną žeesge-xjį wapakąnąk
underneath-DEF that.far-up.to.that.far travel=POS.NTL.PL-DECL thus-INTS be.wise

wa'ųnąąkšąną.
wa'ų=nąąk-šąną
do/be=POS.NTL.PL-DECL

Under the water, far away at the very bottom of the earth, they move about, this is how powerful they are.

61. Žée wiiráperés tee žéesge ronįgígų, 'eesge
žee wa-hi<ra>peres tee žeesge roo<nįį-gi>gų 'eesge
that OBJ.3PL-<2.A>know this thus <1&2-APPL.BEN>want thus

wanįgí'ųųną jaagu nįįgí'ųųra.
wa<nįį-gi>'ų-ną jaagu nįį-gi-'ųų-re
<1&2-APPL.BEN>do/be-DECL what 1&2-APPL.BEN-do/make-DEF

Wanting you to learn this, I did what I did to you.

62. 'Éegi žigé, mąąxíwąąkrégi, wíi hašjašą́nągre,
'eegi zige mąąxi-wąąk-regi wii ha<š>ja-ša=nąk-re
and.then again sky/cloud-upper.region-SIM/LOC sun <2.A>see-2.A=POS.NTL-DEM.PROX

hąąhéwi, hašjašą́nągre, wiirágųšge,
hąąhe-wii ha<š>ja-ša=nąk-re wiiragųšge
night-sun <2.A>see-2.A=POS.NTL-DEM.PROX star

waašjášąnągre, hą́ąp kirijé
wa-ha<š>ja-ša=nąk-re hąąp kiri-jee
OBJ.3PL-<2.A>see-2.A=POS.NTL-DEM.PROX day arrive.back.here-POS.VERT

híijaané, nįįžú gúujaane,
hii=jaane nįįžu guu=jaane
arrive.there=POS.VERT:PROX rain come.back.here=POS.VERT:PROX

k'óonąągre hokawás kirijé híijaané,
k'oo=nąągre hokawas kiri=jee hii=jaane
thunder=POS.NTL.PL:PROX be.dark arrive.back.here-POS.VERT arrive.there=POS.VERT:PROX

jąąjáp,	tee	hanąącį	waxopįnį	warácire	wa'ųnąąkšąną.
jąąjąp	tee	hanąącį	waxopįnį	wa-raac-ire	wa'ų=nąąk-šąną
lightning	this	all	spirit	OBJ.3PL-name-SBJ.3PL	do/be=POS.NTL.PL-DECL

And also up in the sky, up there, the sun that you see, the moon that you see, the stars that you see, when it becomes daylight, when the rain is coming, when it's thundering, when it becomes dark, the lightning, these all are spirits.

63.

Hąąprá	pįįxjį	kirijéhiánąga,	žigé	mąąxíwi
hąąp-ra	pįį-xjį	kiri-jee-hii='anąga	žige	mąąxi-wi
day-DEF	be.good-INTS	arrive.back.here-POS.VERT-make/CAUS=and	again	sky/cloud-PL

šiišíkjį	kirijéhiánąga,	mąą'é,	jáasge
šiišik-xjį	kiri-jee-hii='anąga	mąą'e	jaasge
be.bad-INTS	arrive.back.here-POS.VERT-make/CAUS=and	tornado	how

kirijéhiánąga	sįnįhíxjį	kirijéhiánąga
kiri-jee-hii='anąga	sįnįhi-xjį	kiri-jee-hii='anąga
arrive.back.here-POS.VERT-make/CAUS=and	be.cold-INTS	arrive.back.here-POS.VERT-make/CAUS=and

jáasgexjį	hąąprá	hokiráracjaane,	taanąącį	waxopįnį
jaasge-xjį	hąąp-ra	hoki<ra>rac=jaane	tee-hanąącį	waxopįnį
how-INTS	day-DEF	<RDP:INTS>various=POS.VERT:PROX	this-all	spirit

warácire	wa'ųnąąkšąną.
wa-raac-ire	wa'ų=nąąk-šąną
OBJ.3PL-name-SBJ.3PL	do/be=POS.NTL.PL-DECL

The fall of darkness and bad clouds and wind and cold, all different kinds of weather, they are spirits.

64.

'Éegi	mąąnągre	jáasgexjį,	woogų́sranągre,
'eegi	mąą=nągre	jaasge-xjį	woogųs-ra=nągre
and.then	earth=POS.NTL:PROX	how-INTS	creation-DEF=POS.NTL:PROX

nįįkų́hąregi	mąąkų́hąregi	mąįhákregi	mąąxí
nįį-kųųhą-regi	mąą-kųųhą-regi	mąą-hihak-regi	mąąxi
water-underneath-SIM/LOC	earth-underneath-SIM/LOC	earth-on.top-SIM/LOC	sky/cloud

hožuágre,	hanąącįxjįra,	waxopįnį	warácire,	hokirácra
hožu-'agre	hanąącį-xjį-ra	waxopįnį	wa-raac-ire	hokirac-ra
put.into-POS.HOR:PROX	all-INTS-DEF	spirit	OBJ.3PL-name-SBJ.3PL	various-DEF

hanąącį	tíire	wa'ųnąągre,	hąąké,	hakíkijawiánąga
hanąącį	tiire	wa'ų=nąągre	hąąke	ha<kiki>ja-wi='anąga
all	move	do/be=POS.NTL.PL:PROX	NEG.IN	<RCP>see-PL=and

hokikít'anągre,	žéesge	hikisgéeną.
ho<kii>kit'e=nąągre	žeesge	hikisge-ną
<RCP>talk.to=POS.NTL.PL:PROX	thus	resemble-DECL

And this land, how it was created, under the water, under the earth, on top of the earth, where it's full of clouds, all of that, this spirit (responsible for all that), all kinds of things that are moving, they don't see each other, the ones that are speaking, that is what it is like.

65.

Mą̨ąsánįk	móožejąsánįgeja	waxopį́nį	warácireną́ąkišge,
mąą-saanįk	mąą-hožeją-saanįk-'eeja	waxopįnį	wa-raac-ire-nąąk-išge
earth-side	earth-end-side-there	spirit	OBJ.3PL-name-SBJ.3PL-POS.NTL.PL-also

jáagu	hiiranąąkiži,	wiiwéwį	'éeja	howáaji,	wiiwéwįra
jaagu	hiire-nąąk-giži	wiiwewį	'eeja	howe-jii	wiiwewį-ra
what	think-POS.NTL.PL-TOP	thought/mind	there	go.about-arrive.here	thought/mind-DEF

hirahígiži	hiperesšą́ną.
hirahi-giži	hiperes-šąną
go.to.find-TOP	know(SBJ.3SG)-DECL

The other side of the earth, on the side where the earth ends, this spirit, whatever he is thinking, where the thoughts come from, when his thoughts reach him, he knows.

66.

Hokikít'aire,	žéesge	hikisgéeną.
ho<kii>kit'e-ire	žeesge	hikisge-ną
<RCP>talk.to-SBJ.3PL	thus	resemble-DECL

It is just like speaking to one another.

67.

Hąąké	homąkíkinįranį́	woorák	cų́įñe,	wiiwéwįrašąną
hąąke	homą<kii>kįnį-ire-nį	woorak	cųų-ire	wiiwewį-ra-šąną
NEG.IN	<RCP>visit-SBJ.3PL-NEG.FIN	story	have.much-SBJ.3PL	thought/mind-DEF-only

hi'ų́įñeánąga,	hokikít'aireną,	žéesge
hi-'ųų-ire=nąga	ho<kii>kit'e-ire-ną	žeesge
APPL.INST-do/make-SBJ.3PL=and	<RCP>talk.to-SBJ.3PL-DECL	thus

wa'ųnáąkšąną.
wa'ų=nąąk-šąną
do/be=POS.NTL.PL-DECL

They don't visit each other, they have many stories, all they use to talk is their mind, that's the way they are.

68.

'Éegi	žigé,	xeerókeja,	nįįkų́hąįja,	jáagu	hiratážairéšge
'eegi	žige	xee-rook-'eeja	nįį-kųųhą-hija	jaagu	hirataža-ire-šge
and.then	again	hill-inside-there	water-underneath-there	what	light.with-SBJ.3PL-also

wíinągre	hiratážairanį́,	hąąké	péec	hiratážairanąąšge
wii=nągre	hirataža-ire-nį	hąąke	peec	hirataža-ire-nąą-šge
sun=POS.NTL:PROX	light.with-SBJ.3PL-NEG.FIN	NEG.IN	fire	light.with-SBJ.3PL-POT-also

wapaką́nąknąąągre	wooką́cąk	že'é,	hihą́p,	hohą́p	mįįnákirešge.
wapakąnąk=nąągre	wakącąk	že'e	hi-hąąp	hohąp	mįįnąk-ire-šge
be.wise=POS.NTL.PL:PROX	be.holy	that	APPL.INST-day	daylight	sit-SBJ.3PL-also

Inside the hill, under the water, whatever they light it with, they don't light it by the sun, and they don't light it by the fire, the wise ones are lit by the sacred, and they are sitting there lit.

69.

'Éesge,	homąšją́ňą	hanį́įňege	žéesge	ciirá
'eesge	homąšją-ra	hanį-ire-ge	žeesge	cii-ra
thus	power-DEF	have.NTL-SBJ.3PL-CAUSAL	thus	house-DEF

giháąpnáąkšąną.
gi-hąąp=nąąk-šąną
APPL.BEN-light=POS.NTL.PL-DECL

Because they have this power, their home is lit.

70.

Hacį́įjaregí,	kųųháregi	mą́įhakrégi	wąąkrégi
hacįįja-regi	kųųhą-regi	mąą-hihak-regi	wąąk-regi
where-SIM/LOC	underneath-SIM/LOC	earth-on.top-SIM/LOC	upper.region-SIM/LOC

mąąxíwąąkeja	hanáąacįxjįra	mąąnágre	hoixjį́xjįra
mąąxi-wąąk-'eeja	hanąącį-xjį-ra	mąą=nągre	hoixjį-xjį-ra
sky/cloud-upper.region-there	all-INTS-DEF	earth=POS.NTL:PROX	be.full-INTS-DEF

waxopį́nį	warácire,	tíire	wa'ųnáąagre.
waxopįnį	wa-raac-ire	tiire	wa'ų=nąągre
spirit	OBJ.3PL-name-SBJ.3PL	move	do/be=POS.NTL.PL:PROX

Everywhere, underneath, on the earth and up above in the sky, all this creation is full of spirits moving.

71.

Wiiwéwįrašąną	hitiráire	žéesge	hokikít'e
wiiwewį-ra-šąną	hi-tiire-ire	žeesge	ho<kii>kit'e
thought/mind-DEF-only	APPL.INST-move-SBJ.3PL	thus	<RCP>talk.to

wa'ųnáąakšąną.
wa'ų=nąąk-šąną
do/be=POS.NTL.PL-DECL

They are moving in thought alone, speaking to one another that way.

72.

'Éesge	žée	žéesge	homąšją́	cų́ų,	wa'ųnáąakšąną
'eesge	žee	žeesge	homąšją	cųų	wa'ų=nąąk-šąną
thus	that	thus	power	have.much	do/be=POS.NTL.PL-DECL

mąąnágre.
mąą=nągre
earth=POS.NTL:PROX

They are having much power, on earth.

73.

'Éesge	tée	hirapéresgíži	hanąąc	tee	hirapéresgíži,	wąąkšík ho'į
'eesge	tee	hi<ra>peres-giži	hanąąc	tee	hi<ra>peres-giži	wąąkšik_ho'į
thus	this	<2.A>know-TOP	all	this	<2.A>know-TOP	life

hašįnįňą́,	hąkagá	roorá	kšiikší	wąąkšíkš'į́įnį́kjąnéeną.
ha<šį>nį-ra	hąkaga	roo-ra	kšiikši	wąąkšik<š>'įį-nį-kjąne-ną
<2.A>have.NTL-DEF	NEG.IN.never	body-DEF	be.weak	<2.A>live-NEG.FIN-FUT-DECL

If you know this, if you know all this, the life that you have, you will never live with a weak body.

74.

'Éegi	žigé	hąkagá	warucnįánąga,	hąąpsánįki
'eegi	žige	hąkaga	waruc-nį='anąga	hąąp-saanįk-gi
and.then	again	NEG.IN.never	eat-NEG.FIN=and	day-side-TOP

hąątáginącjaane.
hąątaginąc=jaane
fast.for.blessing=POS.VERT:PROX

He never ate and he was fasting half the day, if you accomplish two, three, four, or ten times (days).

75.

Žigé	hą́ąpnųųbáhą	taanį́hą	joobą́hą	kerepąną́įžą	šuruxúrukíisge,
žige	hąąp-nųųp-ahą	taanį-hą	joop-ahą	kerepąnąįžą	šu-ruxuruk-'isge
again	day-two-times	three-times	four-times	ten	2.A-accomplish-perhaps

žéegų	higé	roorá	mąąnį́šją́nąga,	hąkága	hotekšíišik,
žeegų	hige	roo-ra	mąą<nį>šją='anąga	hąkaga	hotek-šiišik
thus	again	body-DEF	<2.U>be.strong=and	NEG.IN.never	sore.spot-be.bad

hąkága	hošawažánįánąga	žéesge	wąąkšíkš'įįną́ną.
hąkaga	ho<ša>waža-nį='anąga	žeesge	wąąkšik<š>'įį-nąą-ną
NEG.IN.never	<2.A>be.sick-NEG.FIN=and	thus	<2.A>live-POT-DECL

Again, your body gets stronger and you will never get sick that's the way you will live.

Kere jų sep ska
07

76.

“’Éegi	waxopį́nį	warácire	mée	wąąkšík
’eegi	waxopįnį	wa-raac-ire	mee	wąąkšik
and.then	spirit	OBJ.3PL-name-SBJ.3PL	this	Indian/person

wiiš’į́įnąąną.
wa-hi-š-’įį-nąą-ną
OBJ.3PL-APPL.INST-2.A-live-POT-DECL

“With the spirits you (people) can live.

77.

Taaní	woorágižu;	jaagúgi	homąšją́ra	wąąkšíkš’į́kje	žéesge
taanį	wa-ho<ra>gižu	jaagu-gi	homąšją-ra	wąąkšik<š>’įį-kje	žeesge
tobacco	OBJ.3PL-<2.A>offer.to	what-TOP	power-DEF	<2.A>live-FUT	thus

ratá,	wąąkšík ho’į́	hirukąnąnągre	žéesge	waragíta;
ra-taa	wąąkšik_ho’į	hirukąną=nągre	žeesge	wa-ra-gi-taa
2.A-ask.for	life	control=POS.NTL:PROX	thus	OBJ.3PL-2.A-APPL.BEN-ask.for

žéesge	wąąkšíkš’į́gíži,	hąąké	roorá	nįkšikšínįkjąnéną.
žeesge	wąąkšik<š>’įį-giži	hąąke	roo-ra	nį-kšikši-nį-kjąne-ną
thus	<2.A>live-TOP	NEG.IN	body-DEF	2.U-be.weak-NEG.FIN-FUT-DECL

If you offer them tobacco and ask for power, asking for it from the masters of life, if you live this way, your body will never be weak.

78.

Sįnįhíjaane,	hosįnį́jaane	žeesgé	hirukąnąňą,	hosįnįňą́
sįnįhi=jaane	hosįnį=jaane	žeesge	hirukąną-ra	hosįnį-ra
be.cold=POS.VERT:PROX	be.cold=POS.VERT:PROX	thus	control-DEF	be.cold-DEF

waažírekúhira	hižą́	wa’ųnąkra,	himąnį́šją́ną.
waažirekuhi-ra	hižą	wa’ų=nąk-ra	himą<nį>šją-ną
northwind-DEF	one	do/be=POS.NTL-DEF	<2.U>be.strengthened-DECL

By the cold weather, the master of cold, the northwind, you will be strengthened.

79.

Hąąké	hironį́cooxnį́ną.
hąąke	hiro<nį>cox-nį-ną
NEG.IN	<2.U>affect.negatively-NEG.FIN-DECL

This does not harm you.

80.

Žigé	mąįtajéwehi	šiišíkra	žigé	nįįžújaane	žigé,	waxopį́nį
žige	mąįtajewehi	šiišik-ra	žige	nįįžu=jaane	žige	waxopįnį
again	wind	be.bad-DEF	again	rain=POS.VERT:PROX	again	spirit

warácire	wa’ųnąąkra,	wakąjá	wa’ųnąkra,
wa-raac-ire	wa’ų=nąąk-ra	wakąja	wa’ų=nąk-ra
OBJ.3PL-name-SBJ.3PL	do/be=POS.NTL.PL-DEF	thunder	do/be=POS.NTL-DEF

hanįnį́žuišge	žigé	himąnį́šjąną́ną.
ha-nį-nįįžu-išge	žige	himą<nį>šją-nąą-ną
APPL.SUPESS-2.U-rain-also	again	<2.U>be.strengthened-POT-DECL

And the bad wind and this rain they are spirits, they are the thunder spirit, if it rains on you, you will be strengthened.

81.

Wiiną́gre	hatanį́kącgíišge	žigé,	wiirá	hicóoke
wii=nągre	hata<nį>kac-gi-šge	žige	wii-ra	hicoke
sun=POS.NTL:PROX	<2.U>be.hot-TOP-also	again	sun-DEF	grandfather

hííranąga	taanį́karaną,	hatakácra	himąnį́šjąną́ną,
hii-ire='anąga	taa<nį>kara-ną	hatakac-ra	himą<nį>šją-nąą-ną
make/CAUS-SBJ.3PL=and	<2.U>limber-DECL	be.hot-DEF	<2.U>be.strengthened-POT-DECL

jaasgé	taakácregiži.
jaasge	taakac-ree-giži
how	be.hot-go.there-TOP

Even if the sun is hot on you again, they made the sun their grandfather, (the sun) limbering you, its heat will strengthen you, however hot it gets.

82.

Tee	haną́ącįxjį,	hohuhíną́gre,	jaasgé,	woogų́sra
tee	hanąącį-xjį	hohuhi=nągre	jaasge	woogųs-ra
this	all-INTS	direction=POS.NTL:PROX	how	creation-DEF

mąąną́gre	gųųsrá	jaasgánąk	haną́ąc	homąšją́	te'é	née
mąą=nągre	gųųs-ra	jaasge=nąk	hanąąc	homąšją	te'e	nee
earth=POS.NTL:PROX	create-DEF	how=POS.NTL	all	power	this	2EMPH

hirapéresgi,	wiiwéwį	hirapéresgiži,	róo	hašįnįñą́
hi<ra>peres-gi	wiiwewį	hi<ra>peres-giži	roo	ha<šį>nį-ra
<2.A>know-TOP	thought/mind	<2.A>know-TOP	body	<2.A>have.NTL-DEF

himąnį́šją	wąąkšíkš'į́įnąną.
hi-mąą<nį>šją	wąąkšik<š>'įį-nąą-ną
APPL.INST-<2.U>be.strong	<2.A>live-POT-DECL

All these directions, however the Creator created this earth how it is, if you know the strength, if you know these thoughts your body will be strengthened from it as you live.

83.

Wąąkšík ho'įrá	hožeją́įjipá,	rahiną́ąną.
wąąkšik_ho'į-ra	hožeją-hija-hipa	ra-hii-nąą-ną
life-DEF	end-there-up.to.that.far	2.A-arrive.there-POT-DECL

You can reach the end of life.

84.

Žée	žeegų́gi	nąąğírak	hikaráperes	wąąkšíkš'į́inągiži,	roorá
žee	žeegų-gi	nąąğirak	hi<kara>peres	wąąkšik<š>'įį-nąk-giži	roo-ra
that	thus-TOP	soul	<POSS.RFL>know	<2.A>live-POS.NTL-TOP	body-DEF

nįgižéjągi	bookéwe	hirakísganą́ąną	hąąké	šjeerá
nį-gižeją-gi	bookewe	hi<ra>kisge-nąą-ną	hąąke	šjee-ra
2.U-end-TOP	stumble	2.A-resemble-POT-DECL	NEG.IN	die\2.U-DEF

hirapéresnįną́ąną
hi<ra>peres-nį-nąą-ną
<2.A>know-NEG.FIN-POT-DECL

And if you live knowing the spirits, when the end of the body comes for you, it will be as if you stumble, you will not know that you are dying.

85.

Žéegųgi	mąąną́gre	hikiją́	wąąkšíkš'į́iną́ąną,	waxopį́nį
žeegų-gi	mąą=nągre	hikiją	wąąkšik<š>'įį-nąą-ną	waxopįnį
thus-TOP	earth=POS.NTL:PROX	reach	<2.A>live-POT-DECL	spirit

warácire	hagí	wąąkšíkš'į́iną́ąną.
wa-raac-ire	hagi	wąąkšik<š>'įį-nąą-ną
OBJ.3PL-name-SBJ.3PL	there	<2.A>live-POT-DECL

You will live as long as the earth, with the spirits you will live.

86.

Žée	woo'éhi	te'é,	hirapéresną́ąną	waxopį́nį	warácire
žee	woo'ehi	te'e	hi<ra>peres-nąą-ną	waxopįnį	wa-raac-ire
that	law	this	<2.A>know-POT-DECL	spirit	OBJ.3PL-name-SBJ.3PL

hąątáginącanąga,	hąątáraginą́cra	mąą	haną́ąc	hinįk
hąątaginąc='anąga	hąąta<ra>ginąc-ra	mąą	hanąąc	hinįk
fast.for.blessing=and	<2.A>fast.for.blessing-DEF	earth	all	son

háaxjį	hirapéresgiži,	wąąkšík ho'į́	te'é	pį́ixjį
haa-xjį	hi<ra>peres-giži	wąąkšik_ho'į	te'e	pįį-xjį
have.kin\1E.A-INTS	<2.A>know-TOP	life	this	be.good-INTS

wąąkšíkš'į́kjąnéeną.
wąąkšik<š>'įį-kjąne-ną
<2.A>live-FUT-DECL

If you know the law, if you fast for blessings from the spirits, if you fast for blessings from the earth, my son, you will have a good life.

87.

Tée	haaní̜	nąnįgí'įge	wáa'ų́ųną.
tee	hanį	nąą<nįį-gi>'į-ge	wa<ha>'ų-ną
this	have.NTL	<1&2-APPL.BEN>try-CAUSAL	<1E.A>do/be-DECL

Because I wished this for you, I did it.

©
Keve jy sep ska
07

88.

“Hinįk	háaxjį	nįįpsįcanąga	cąąkrá	honįt’ųteera
hinįk	haa-xjį	nįį-gipsįc=’anąga	cąąk-ra	ho<nįį>t’ųtee-ra
son	have.kin\1E.A-INTS	1&2-whip=and	outside-DEF	<1&2>throw.out\1E.A-DEF

nąącgéra	nįtékšąną.
nąącge-ra	nį-teek-šąną
heart-DEF	2.U-ache-DECL

“My son, I whipped you and threw you out and your heart ached.

89.

Jáasge	nįték	nąącgéra	nįtéká,	hijáira	nąącgéra
jaasge	nį-teek	nąącge-ra	nį-teek-ga	hijaira	nąącge-ra
how	2.U-ache	heart-DEF	2.U-ache-CONT	more	heart-DEF

hįtéknųnįgé,	woocéxi	wáa’ųųną.
hį-teek-nųnįge	woocexi	wa<ha>’ų-ną
1E.U-ache-nevertheless	be.difficult	<1E.A>do/be-DECL

Your heart ached, but my heart ached even more, it was difficult to do it.

90.

Žéesge	nįįgígigi	nee	hirapéresikjąnégi,	héesge	méežeesge
žeesge	nįį-gigi-gi	nee	hi<ra>peres-i-kjąne-gi	heesge	mee-žeesge
thus	1&2-let/cause-TOP	2EMPH	<2.A>know-0-FUT-TOP	that’s.why	this-thus

nįgigíiną.
nįį-gigi-ną
1&2-let/cause-DECL

That you could know this yourself I did it to you, therefore I did it to you.

91.

Mée	woorák	te’é,	hirapéresgi	harakížu	wąąkšíkš’įįkjąnégiži.
mee	woorak	te’e	hi<ra>peres-gi	ha<ra>kižu	wąąkšik<š>’įį-kjąne-giži
this	story	this	<2.A>know-TOP	<2.A>be.together	<2.A>live-FUT-TOP

If you know this story you will live by means of it.

92.

Mąąnągre	’éegi	hąąké	wažąną́	hižą́	roorágųnįkjąne,
mąą=nągre	’eegi	hąąke	wažą-ra	hižą	roo<ra>gų-nį-kjąne
earth=POS.NTL:PROX	and.then	NEG.IN	something-DEF	one	<2.A>want-NEG.FIN-FUT

hąkága	roorá	nįkšikšínį.
hąkaga	roo-ra	nį-kšikši-nį
NEG.IN.never	body-DEF	2.U-be.weak-NEG.FIN

You will need nothing on earth, your body will never be weak.

93.

Roonągre	kąąňéšge	nąąǧírak	hašįnįňą	wąąkšíkš'įįkjąne	mąąnągre	hikiją́
roo=nągre	kąąre-šge	nąąǧirak	ha<ši>nį-ra	wąąkšik<š>'įį-kjąne	mąą=nągre	hikiją
body=POS.NTL:PROX	fall.over-also	soul	<2.A>have.NTL-DEF	<2.A>live-FUT	earth=POS.NTL:PROX	reach

Your body will drop, but your soul will live as long as the earth.

94.

Woorák	te'é,	hiperés	nąnįgí'įgé,	'éesge	wáa'ųųną.
woorak	te'e	hiperes	nąą<nįį-gi>'į-ge	'eesge	wa<ha>'ų-ną
story	this	know	<1&2-APPL.BEN>try-CAUSAL	thus	<1E.A>do/be-DECL

Because I wanted you to know this story I did this.

95.

Mąąnągre	jáasgenągre	žéegų	'ée	hanąąc	hirapéresgíži	pį́į	wąąkšíkš'įįkjąne	wanįgí'ųnąąną.
mąą=nągre	jaasge=nągre	žeegų	'ee	hanąąc	hi<ra>peres-giži	pįį	wąąkšik<š>'įį-kjąne	wa<nįį-gi>'ų-nąą-ną
earth=POS.NTL:PROX	how=POS.NTL:PROX	thus	this	all	<2.A>know-TOP	be.good	<2.A>live-FUT	<1&2-APPL.BEN>do/be-POT-DECL

If you know how this earth is, if you know all this, you will live well, therefore I did this.

96.

Hąhą́,	hinįk	háaxjį	méežeegų́ną,	'ée	pį́įną
hąhą	hinįk	haa-xjį	mee-žeegų-ną	'ee	pįį-ną
yes	son	have.kin\1E.A-INTS	this-thus-DECL	this	be.good-DECL

My son, this is the way, it is good.

97.

Jaagu	ronįgų́ra	žéesge	hirapéresrá
jaagu	roo<nįį>gų-ra	žeesge	hi<ra>peres-ra
what	<1&2>want-DEF	thus	<2.A>know-DEF

What it is that I wanted for you (is that) you know.

98.

'Ée	pį́įną."
'ee	pįį-ną
this	be.good(OBJ.3SG)-DECL

It is good."

99.

Žéejáiįxjįňą.
žeejąįxjį-ra
that.far-DEF

This is the end.

100. Hąhó!
hąho
INTJ

Hąho!

5.2 The complete Hocąk text without analysis

[1]Nįįkjąk hookárakų́ [2]'Éegi ceekrégi wąąkšík, wąąkšíknąągre, jaasgé wąąkšík'į́įňegiži. [3]Nįįkjąkra hižą́ gixetéregiží, hookárakų́įráanąga, 'éejasgé coowéja wąąkšík'į́įňekjąnégiži, wąąkšík ho'įra pį́i'ųųkje žéesge karagígųsirekjąnégi. [4]Ceekjį́ra wa'ų́įňeže, cíihokisák honąžį́ňą, himąrakíreže 'ųųxį́nįňą rúus, žéesge kiišíireže. [5]Hąątáginąc hakikáražíreže. [6]Ceekjį́ra, xųnųník hąątáginącirégi, wiirá roocą́ąje hipá, žéejąįxjį hį́ipire, žéejąįxjį warúcireže. [7]'Ųų haráiregi, hijáira hiyaráireže, [8]Hahí hąąpsérec hąątáginącirégi, hokipį́įregiži, hahąhé híire hąąhé hokahí, hahí hagakírahąšge nąį́ňeže, nųųbáhą hii nąįre, 'éejaxjį́ mą́ą kerepąnąį́žą, 'éeja nįgé hereže, joobáhą hakewehášge nąį́ňes'áže.

[9]Žéežeegųgíži, wąąknąągre hižą́ hinį́k hiikį́, wookáragixétekjįgiži, hą́įnįrégi, kiikáwa'ą́ągiži, waasgéra warúcra hožú, nąąpsánįkeja harukósanąga žigé nąąpsánįkejá 'ųųxį́nį, hinįkrá giwahá. [10]Žéegųgają, warucjáane ruusgí, ruusgí rúusgigiánąga, rúuc hikorohógają raaxóc hogibéže. [11]Žéegųgiži hi'ącrá horğóc, nąącgéra téekjį horoğócše, mąąňą mąącgúra wagirúsanąga, 'áija rukósanąga, mąącguágre mą́ąňą hirasá higipsį́canąga. [12]'Ųųxį́nį wacópanąga hišjára séepgigiánąga cąągrá hut'ųňée(že). [13]Žéežeegų́giži, nąącgéra téekše, nįįkjąknįkjaané. [14]Hocįcį́nįkjaané nąącgéra téekjįgiži, hi'ącrá hąąké žéesge giginį́nągają́, 'ųųgí nąącgéra téekjį ğáakanągá, ciiróp 'eeja hihinąpgi gixará hapahí mąąnį réeže. [15]Ğáak nąącgéra téekjįže, hąąké haakjá cii 'éeja kirinį́įra. [16]Žéesge, žéesge wiiwéwįňą 'ųųžé: [17]"Žéegų nįgé hahí, ceekjé, jaajíga nąącgéra teek wį́įňą." [18]Žéesge hiiráanąga gixára howarégi hahí hahąhéanąga, žigé hinųbáhąra hąąhé. [19]Ğáak goišíp wa'ų́ákše, t'éekjąne žéesge, jajáixjį hokipį́giži, žéejąįxjį hį́ipanąga t'éekje žéesge nąącgéra téekše. [20]Žéegųgiži nąą́c hokiją́xjįžé, jaasgé nąą́c hokiją́nągi, žéesge nąącgéra téekše. [21]Hąąhéregi mį́įki ğáak, jajáixjį hiikį́gi ğáak. [22]Coowéxjį nąą́ hiikį jiikáranąga žigé hiikį́ ğáak, žée žéesge híireegí hąąhé hijoobáhą, hąąhé hisaacą́hą, hirakéwehą haiją́įšge waxopį́nį warácire nąą́c hoją́įreže. [23]Wąąkšík ho'įrá, jaasgé hoxetéregi, 'ųįňékjąnégiži. [24]Homąšją́ jaagú žéesge nąą́c hirojąį́režé.

[25]Wąąktóšweešgekjaneánąga, wąąk wášošešge woonąğiresge cųųkjané 'éegi hokicų́rašge jaasgé, pįįkjąnégi, coowéja wąąkšík ho'įrá, hanąąc gigų́siráanąga. [26]'Éegi wagáiranąže "Hąhó, hanąąc téerenąą, jaagú hi'ąc ráaga ronįgígųra. [27]Hi'ąc ráaga wooxéte nįįną́, 'éesge wanįgí'ųną. [28]Tée žéegų nįgigígiži jaasgé nąącgéra nįtékjiire, žee nįgigígiži, 'éegi nąą́c horakį́jągiži, waxopį́nį warácire žéesge nąą́c honįją́įňekjąne 'éesge, nįgigíiną. [29]'Éegi rakerékjąnąhéeną, hi'ąc ráaga hąąké honįš'íknį wa'ų́ną. [30]Wonįgíxetéxjį wa'ų́ną, 'éexjį nąącgéra téek," žée žeesge, higáiranąge. [31]'Éegi, haakjá, cíira howakéregi.

[32]Hagoréižą, ciéja hagí hoikéwegi, hi'ącrá t'ą́ąpjiiráanąga hinįkrá nąąkárat'ųpanągá, "Hinįk háaxjį, rakirirá, 'éepįįną. [33]Hąąké honįš'íknįną, wonįgíxeteéną. [34]Žéegųgi wąąkšík ho'į́, gáagų šerekjanąhé. [35]Hanąąc harakáraginąį́ce. [36]Žéesge yaapéresge žéesge nįgigíiną. [37]'Éegi nąąğírak hikarapéres wąąkšíkra 'áireną. [38]Hižą́ žéesge wąąkšík'įįgíži, hagoréižą, róonągre, t'éešge, nąąğírak 'ée hanįňą́ waxopį́nį warácire hagí wąąkšík'įį,

mąąnągre hikiją wąąkšík'įkjąnéeną. [39]Žée žéesge yaapéresnąąkšąną. [40]'Éesge 'áajiirégi, žée hironįgigųgé, wáa'ųųną. [41]'Égi žigé, mąąxíwągregi wąąktóše hocíižą, jaanąga, wanįk, wapakąnąkra, nąąnąągre, 'éeja hapahí wakirí hikišérenąąki. [42]Jaagúra, hižą heregí, hąąké ruš'ákiranį. [43]Hišjasúra wapakąnąkire. [44]Žée žéesge, jaanąga, wanįrák rakįį wąąktóšewe hocíižą wąąkrégiák, že'é nąąc honįjąįňegiži, mąąxíwąkrégi howáji, homąšją nįcųąnąga. [45]Wąąkšíknąągre hižą hotek šíišik jaagúižą hanįąnąga, hanįkárahásiregíži, hoték žée, rušją raanąą. [46]Žee žeesgé homąšjąįžą že'é haraginąc žéesge, wáa'ųną, jáagu nįįgi'ų́ňą. [47]'Égi žigé xeexétera hižą nįgenąki, waxopį́nį warácire hocí wa'ųnąkšąną. [48]Žéesge horakáwanąga, waxopį́nį warácire ceewąąk céexi, hųųcížą céexi, jaagúra hížą, žéesge wa'ųąki nąąc honįjągiži wáinį hąkága wanąjonįjąįsganį. [49]Wąąkšík jáagu hanįįňera hiną wąąkšíkš'įį hanį wąąkšíkš'įįkjąnéną. [50]Žée róogų nįgigí wáa'ųųną.

[51]"Xeenąągre hižą 'éeja rahigí, ciiróp hižą 'éeja jéeną, 'gįgįgįgįgįgįš' 'áajire, ciirópra gihásgi, horakéwegi, rookrá jáagu hiratáža híirešgé, žéesge wąąkšík 'éeja nąąkikjąnąhéeną. [52]Žee nąąc honįjąįňegiží, hąkagá wažąňą hižą roorágųnį. [53]Wąąkšíkš'įįkjąne žée žéesge ronįgígų, wáa'ųųną. [54]'Égi nįįkųhąregi, nįįnąągre kųųhą híirera cíi nąągú wa'ųnąąkšąną. [55]Žée žéesge, žéesgeeja žigé wažą hižą hirahątegi, mąąnągre hąąké wažą hižą šuruš'áknįkjąné. [56]Nįéja, jáagu, wanóicge horajánąąki jáagu gipį wawaš'ųkjąne, žéegųgi jáagu, wanóicge jáagu wiirorákųkjąnegiži, hirakáraperés, wapakąnąkra waš'ų, wąąkšíkš'įįkjąnąhe. [57]Žée žéegųgíži hįkága waašaragésnį. hiną woorúcra š'ų́ųkjąne. [58]Nįéja, jáagu wanóicgenąągre nįįkų́hąregi, žée žéesge, mąąnągre kųųhąregi, tiiránąąkšąną. [59]Waxopį́nį warácire, kųųhą ho'ųnąąkšąną. [60]Nįįkų́hąra mąąra hociéja goojáxjį, hacį́ja kųųhąra žéejąįxjipá, horajánąąkšąną žéesgexjį wapakąnąk wa'ųnąąkšąną. [61]Žée wiiráperés tee žéesge ronįgígų, 'eesge wanįgí'ųųną jaagu nįįgí'ųųra. [62]'Égi žigé, mąąxíwąąkrégi, wíi hašjašąnągre, hąąhéwi, hašjašąnągre, wiirágųsge, waašjášąnągre, hąąp kirijé híijaané, nįįžú gúujaane, k'óonąągre hokawás kirijé híijaané, jąąjąp, tee hanąącį waxopį́nį warácire wa'ųnąąkšąną. [63]Hąąprá pį́įxjį kirijéhiánąga, žigé mąąxíwi šiišíkjį kirijéhiánąga, mąą'é, jáasge kirijéhiánąga sįnįhíxjį kirijéhiánąga jáasgexjį hąąprá hokiráracjaane, taanąącį waxopį́nį warácire wa'ųnąąkšąną. [64]'Égi mąąnągre jáasgexjį, woogų́sranągre, nįįkų́hąregi mąąkų́hąregi mąįhákregi mąąxí hožuágre, hanąącįxjįra, waxopį́nį warácire, hokirácra hanąącį tíire wa'ųnąągre, hąąké, hakíkijawiánąga hokikít'anągre, žéesge hikisgéeną. [65]Mąąsánįk móožejąsánįgeja waxopį́nį warácirenąąkišge, jáagu hiiranąąkiži, wiiwéwį 'éeja howáaji, wiiwéwįra hirahígiži hiperesšąną. [66]Hokikít'aire, žéesge hikisgéeną. [67]Hąąké homąkíkinįranį woorák cų́įňe, wiiwéwįrašąną hi'ų́įňeánąga, hokikít'aireną, žéesge wa'ųnąąkšąną. [68]'Égi žigé, xeerókeja, nįįkų́hąjja, jáagu hiratážairéšge wíinągre hiratážairanį, hąąké péec hiratážairanąąšge wapakąnąknąągre wookącąk že'é, hihąp, hohąp mįįnąkirešge. [69]'Éesge, homąšjąňą hanįįňege žéesge ciirá gihąąpnąąkšąną. [70]Hacįįjaregí, kųųhąregi mąįhakrégi wąąkrégi mąąxíwąąkeja hanąącįxjįra mąąnągre hoixjįxjįra waxopį́nį warácire, tíire wa'ųnąągre. [71]Wiiwéwįrašąną hitiráire žéesge hokikít'e wa'ųnąąkšąną. [72]'Éesge žée žéesge homąšją cų́ų, wa'ųnąąkšąną mąąnągre. [73]'Éesge tée hirapéresgíži hanąąc tee hirapéresgíži, wąąkšík ho'į hašįnįňą, hąkagá roorá kšiikší

wąąkšíkš'į́įnį́kjąnéeną. [74]'Éegi žigé hąkagá warucnįánąga, hąąpsánįki hąątáginącjaane. [75]Žigé hą́ąpnųųbáhą taanį́hą joobą́hą kerepąnąį́žą šuruxúrukíisge, žéegų higé roorá mąąnį́šją́nąga, hąkága hotekšíišik, hąkága hošawažánįánąga žéesge wąąkšíkš'įįnąną.

[76]"'Éegi waxopį́nį warácire mée wąąkšík wiiš'į́įnąną. [77]Taanį woorágižu; jaagúgi homąšją́ra wąąkšíkš'į́kje žéesge ratá, wąąkšík ho'į́ hirukąnąnągre žéesge waragíta; žéesge wąąkšíkš'į́įgíži, hąąké roorá nįkšikšínįkjąnéną. [78]Sįnįhíjaane, hosįnį́jaane žeesgé hirukąnąňą, hosįnįňą́ waažírekúhira hižą́ wa'ųnąkra, himąnį́šją́ną. [79]Hąąké hironį́cooxnį́ną. [80]Žigé mą́įtajéwehi šiišíkra žigé nįįžújaane žigé, waxopį́nį warácire wa'ųnąąkra, wakąjá wa'ųnąkra, hanįnį́žuišge žigé himąnį́šjąnąną. [81]Wiinągre hatanį́kącgíišge žigé, wiirá hicóoke híiranąga taanį́karaną, hatakácra himąnį́šjąnąną, jaasgé taakácregiži. [82]Tee hanąącįxjį, hohuhínągre, jaasgé, woogų́sra mąąnągre gųųsrá jaasgánąk hanąąc homąšją́ te'é née hirapéresgi, wiiwéwį hirapéresgiži, róo hašįnįňą́ himąnį́šją wąąkšíkš'į́įnąną. [83]Wąąkšík ho'įrá hožejąįjipá, rahinąąną. [84]Žée žeegų́gi nąąǧírak hikaráperes wąąkšíkš'į́įnągiži, roorá nįgižéjągi bookéwe hirakísganąąną hąąké šjeerá hirapéresnįnąąną [85]Žéegųgi mąąnągre hikiją́ wąąkšíkš'įįnąąną, waxopį́nį warácire hagí wąąkšíkš'įįnąąną. [86]Žée woo'éhi te'é, hirapéresnąąną waxopįnį warácire hąątáginącanąga, hąątáraginącra mąą hanąąc hinįk háaxjį hirapéresgiži, wąąkšík ho'į́ te'é pį́įxjį wąąkšíkš'į́kjąnéeną. [87]Tée haanį́ nąnįgí'įge wáa'ų́ųną.

[88]"Hinįk háaxjį nįįpsį́canąga cąąkrá honįt'ų́teera nąącgéra nįtékšąną. [89]Jáasge nįték nąącgéra nįtéká, hijáira nąącgéra hįtéknųnįgé, woocéxi wáa'ųųną. [90]Žéesge nįįgígigi nee hirapéresikjąnégi, héesge méežeesge nįgigíiną. [91]Mée woorák te'é, hirapéresgi harakížu wąąkšíkš'į́įkjąnégiži. [92]Mąąnągre 'éegi hąąké wažąňą́ hižą́ roorágųnįkjąne, hąkága roorá nįkšikšínį. [93]Roonągre kąąňéšge nąąǧírak hašįnįňą wąąkšíkš'į́įkjąne mąąnągre hikiją́ [94]Woorák te'é, hiperés nąnįgí'įgé, 'éesge wáa'ųųną. [95]Mąąnągre jáasgenągre žéegų 'ée hanąąc hirapéresgíži pį́į wąąkšíkš'į́įkjąne wanįgí'ųnąąną. [96]Hąhą́, hinįk háaxjį méežeegų́ną, 'ée pį́įną [97]Jaagu ronįgų́ra žéesge hirapéresrá [98]'Ée pį́įną." [99]Žéejáiįxjįňą. [100]Hąhó!

5.3 The complete English translation

[1]Child teaching [2]In the beginning, this was the way the Indians, these Indians, lived. [3]When a child was growing up, they taught him how to live in the future, so that he would live a good life. [4]First they did this: They pointed to the fire (= stands in the center of the lodge), and ordered him to take the charcoal (to blacken his face). [5]They encouraged him to fast for blessings. [6]The first time the little ones started to fast, they did it until noon (= sun stands straight) and then they ate. [7]When they started out they did more along the way. [8]All day long, when they fast, if they last that long, then they reached nightfall, and then they slept over one night, fasting, then they slept two, and at about ten years old they were accustomed to sleep four or even six nights while fasting.

[9]There was a man who loved his son very much, one morning when he got up he held a dish with food in one hand, and in the other charcoal, for his son to choose. [10]If he took the food, he let him take it, but when he got ready to eat, he threw ashes into it. [11]While he (the son) looked at him, sore at heart, his father took his bow and arrow, grasped him (the son) by the arm, and whipped him with the bow and arrow. [12]Then he ground charcoal and blacked his (the son's) face and threw him outside. [13]The child was sore at heart. [14]This boy had a real sore heart, his father should not have done it, (but) when he did, he cried broken hearted, when he went out the door, he went walking towards the wilderness. [15]He was crying with a broken heart, he did not return to the house. [16]This is what he thought: [17]"I will go somewhere and die, father made my heart ache." [18]Thinking that he went along towards the wilderness, and night came, and also the second night. [19]And still he went along crying, he would die, he would suffer to the end and then die, that is how sore-hearted he was. [20]He felt very sorry for himself, he would pity himself; that is how sore-hearted he was. [21]At night when he lay down he was crying, as long as he was awake he cried. [22]He slept fitfully and waking, he was crying, he continued to do this, and on the fourth or fifth or perhaps the sixth night the spirits took pity on him. [23]They blessed him with the life he would have when he grew up. [24]They blessed him with the power he would have.

[25]Perhaps he would become a man of healing (a medicine man), or perhaps he would be a brave man if there was war; how good his family would be, all this they taught him. [26]And they say to him, "Hąhóo! All this is what your father wanted for you. [27]Because he loved you, he did this to you. [28]Just as sore-hearted as you were, and as you pitied yourself, so the spirits would pity you, he did it to you. [29]You should go home, your father did not hate you when he did this. [30]He loved you very much, he was sore-hearted himself," they said to him. [31]And so he went home.

[32]When he entered the house, his father jumped up and threw his arms around him: "Dear son, it is good that you have come back. [33]I did not hate you, I loved you. [34]You're

going to go this way with your living now. [35]You're going to be good to all that is yours. [36]Because I knew this I did it to you. [37]The people said: know your soul. [38]One who lives this way might die in the body sometime, but his soul, reaching the spirits, will live as long as the earth. [39]That is what I know. [40]Because they said it traditionally (the ancestors said it) and because I wanted it for you, I did it. [41]Up in the sky there is a medicine lodge, the lodge of woodpecker spirits (those that can see worms in the trees). [42]They don't fail at anything. [43]Their eyes see everything. [44]How many of you turn into birds, there's a medicine man's lodge in the sky, if they bless you with that, from up in the sky you'll have strength. [45]If of these Indians one has a bad sore, whatever he has, when they rely on you, that sore you can cure it. [46]So that you would suffer for this kind of power, I did what I did to you. [47]And if there is a big mountain somewhere, it is a spirits' house. [48]If you go there, and some spirit, a holy buffalo or a holy bear, whatever it is, takes pity on you, you will never lack clothes. [49]You will have enough of the things that people have. [50]Wishing this for you, I did it.

[51]"When you get to one of these hills, there is a door, it starts saying 'gįgįgįgįgįgįš' (= it squeaks) when it opens, and when you go inside, it'll be lit with whatever (= something) and there will be Indians sitting there. [52]If they take pity on you, you will never want (lack) anything. [53]Because I wanted you to live that way, I did it to you. [54]Under the water, under these rivers, are their home-made roads. [55]If you dream of those, nothing on this earth will be impossible for you. [56]You will do as you please with the live things in the water, with the animals, you will live by your power. [57]You will never not have enough to eat, you will always have enough food. [58]Whatever animals are under the water, there beneath the earth, this is going on. [59]The spirits, they roam underground. [60]Under the water, far away at the very bottom of the earth, they move about, this is how powerful they are. [61]Wanting you to learn this, I did what I did to you. [62]And also up in the sky, up there, the sun that you see, the moon that you see, the stars that you see, when it becomes daylight, when the rain is coming, when it's thundering, when it becomes dark, the lightning, these all are spirits. [63]The fall of darkness and bad clouds and wind and cold, all different kinds of weather, they are spirits. [64]And this land, how it was created, under the water, under the earth, on top of the earth, where it's full of clouds, all of that, this spirit (responsible for all that), all kinds of things that are moving, they don't see each other, the ones that are speaking, that is what it is like. [65]The other side of the earth, on the side where the earth ends, this spirit, whatever he is thinking, where the thoughts come from, when his thoughts reach him, he knows. [66]It is just like speaking to one another. [67]They don't visit each other, they have many stories, all they use to talk is their mind, that's the way they are. [68]Inside the hill, under the water, whatever they light it with, they don't light it by the sun, and they don't light it by the fire, the wise ones are lit by the sacred, and they are sitting there lit. [69]Because they have this power, their home is lit. [70]Everywhere, underneath, on the earth and up above in the sky, all this creation is full of spirits moving.

[71]They are moving in thought alone, speaking to one another that way. [72]They are having much power, on earth. [73]If you know this, if you know all this, the life that you have, you will never live with a weak body. [74]He never ate and he was fasting half the day, if you accomplish two, three, four, or ten times (days). [75]Again, your body gets stronger and you will never get sick that's the way you will live.

[76]"With the spirits you (people) can live. [77]If you offer them tobacco and ask for power, asking for it from the masters of life, if you live this way, your body will never be weak. [78]By the cold weather, the master of cold, the northwind, you will be strengthened. [79]This does not harm you. [80]And the bad wind and this rain they are spirits, they are the thunder spirit, if it rains on you, you will be strengthened. [81]Even if the sun is hot on you again, they made the sun their grandfather, (the sun) limbering you, its heat will strengthen you, however hot it gets. [82]All these directions, however the Creator created this earth how it is, if you know the strength, if you know these thoughts your body will be strengthened from it as you live. [83]You can reach the end of life. [84]And if you live knowing the spirits, when the end of the body comes for you, it will be as if you stumble, you will not know that you are dying. [85]You will live as long as the earth, with the spirits you will live. [86]If you know the law, if you fast for blessings from the spirits, if you fast for blessings from the earth, my son, you will have a good life. [87]Because I wished this for you, I did it.

[88]"My son, I whipped you and threw you out and your heart ached. [89]Your heart ached, but my heart ached even more, it was difficult to do it. [90]That you could know this yourself I did it to you, therefore I did it to you. [91]If you know this story you will live by means of it. [92]You will need nothing on earth, your body will never be weak. [93]Your body will drop, but your soul will live as long as the earth. [94]Because I wanted you to know this story I did this. [95]If you know how this earth is, if you know all this, you will live well, therefore I did this. [96]My son, this is the way, it is good. [97]What it is that I wanted for you (is that) you know. [98]It is good." [99]This is the end. [100]Hąho!

6 Horses (Bill O'Brien & Chloris Lowe Sr.) (CD 2 track 1)

6.1 Text with analysis and translation

1. CL: Germannąągre hit'et'e wąąkšik hit'et'e roįgųnąąk
CL: German-nąągre hit'et'e wąąkšik hit'et'e roo<hį>gų-nąąk
CL: German-POS.NTL.PL:PROX talk Indian/person talk <1DI.A>want-POS.NTL

nųnįge, 'eesge... BO: Tağiriįkra. CL: Tağiriįkra, 'eesge
nųnįge 'eesge BO: Tağiri-įk-ra CL: Tağiri-įk-ra 'eesge
nevertheless that's.why BO: German-DIM-DEF CL: German-DIM-DEF that's.why

Bill O'Brien and nee Chloris Lowega wahanąkšąną,
Bill O'Brien and nee Chloris Lowe-ga wahe-nąk-šąną
Bill O'Brien and 1EMPH Chloris Lowe-PROP talk\1E.A-POS.NTL-DECL

'eegi wąąkšik yaat'et'ekjene, hiyaicgakjanawi.
'eegi wąąkšik hi<ha>t'et'e-kjene hi<ha>gicga-kjane-wi
and.then Indian/person <1E.A>talk-FUT <1E.A>attempt-FUT-PL

CL: These Germans want me to talk Indian, that's why, BO: Germans, CL: Germans, that's why Bill O'Brien and me Chloris Lowe, I'm going to talk Indian, we're going to try.

2. BO: Yaa'ųcakjanawi.
BO: hi<ha>'ųja-kjane-wi
BO: <1E.A>try-FUT-PL

BO: We're going to try.

3. CL: Hihą, jaagu hįį'e hiikjene?
CL: hihą jaagu hį-ha'e_hii-kjene
CL: INTJ what 1DI.A-talk.about-FUT

CL: Yes, what are we going to talk about?

4. BO: Hąąke yaaperesnį jaagu hįį'e hiikjene.
BO: hąąke hi<ha>peres-nį jaagu hį-ha'e_hii-kjene
BO: NEG.IN <1E.A>know-NEG.FIN what 1DI.A-talk.about-FUT

BO: I don't know what we're going to talk about.

5. CL: Tee 'eegi wažą waxja nįįsge hijašge ha'e hiiną.
CL: tee 'eegi wažą waxja nįįsge hija-šge ha'e_hii-ną
CL: this and.then something be.funny VAGUE there-also talk.about-POT

CL: We could talk about something sort of funny.

6.

Hįxųnųįkregi...	BO:	Hižą	hokarakre.	CL:	Hąhą'o,
hį-xųnų-įk-regi	BO:	hižą	ho<ka>rak-re	CL:	hąhą'o
1E.U-be.small-DIM-SIM/LOC	BO:	one	<POSS.RFL>tell-IMP	CL:	yes

heesge	haakje.
heesge	haa-kje
that's.why	make/CAUS\1E.A-FUT

When I was little... BO: Tell one of your stories. CL: Yes I'll do that.

7.

Hąą,	hįxųnųįkregi,	'ųųsge,	cooka	'eeraanąga
hąą	hį-xųnų-įk-regi	'ųųsge	cooka	'ee-ra-'anąga
yes	1E.U-be.small-DIM-SIM/LOC	something:HESIT	grandfather	have.kin\1E.A-DEF-and

nąąnį	'eerašge	hegų	ciinąkra	'eeja	howare	hikorohoire.
nąąnį	'ee-ra-šge	hegų	ciinąk-ra	'eeja	howare	hikoroho-ire
mother	have.kin\1E.A-DEF-also	that.way	village-DEF	there	go.forward	get.ready-SBJ.3PL

Yes, when I was little, my grandpa and mother were getting ready to go to town.

8.

BO:	Hąą.	CL:	'Eesge	hegų	šųųkxetera	hahi
BO:	hąą	CL:	'eesge	hegų	šųųkxete-ra	hahi
BO:	yes	CL:	that's.why	that.way	horse-DEF	over.there

wootoğoc	nįįsge	'anąga	hegų,	hegų,	hižą	hamįąnąkikje
wa-hotoğoc	nįįsge	'anąga	hegų	hegų	hižą	hamį<ha>nąk-i-kje
OBJ.3PL-look.at\1E.A	VAGUE	and	that.way	that.way	one	<1E.A>sit.on-0-FUT

yaare	nįįsge.	BO:	Hąą.
hii<ha>re	nįįsge	BO:	hąą
<1E.A>think	VAGUE	BO:	yes

BO: Yes. CL: So I went to look at the horses, I thought I'd sort of sit on one. BO: Yes.

9.

CL:	'Eesge	hegų	waagipe,	hegų	ciinąkra	hegų
CL:	'eesge	hegų	wa-ha<ha>gipe	hegų	ciinąk-ra	hegų
CL:	that's.why	that.way	OBJ.3PL-<1E.A>wait.for	that.way	village-DEF	that.way

xapge	howarairegi	pįįnągųnį	yaare.
xapge	howare-ire-gi	pįį-ną-gųnį	hii<ha>re
shortly	go.forward-SBJ.3PL-TOP	be.good-POT-DUB	<1E.A>think

CL: I waited for them, I wish they'd hurry up and go to town, I thought.

10.

Hegų	hegų	'ųųnąk'ų	hicągeere	jiikaraire.	BO:	Hąą.
hegų	hegų	'ųų-nąk-'ų	hicągeere	jiikere-ire	BO:	hąą
that.way	that.way	be-POS.NTL-SIM	with.difficuty/finally	be.started-SBJ.3PL	BO:	yes

CL:	Hegų	hahi	xawanį.
CL:	hegų	hahi	xawanį
CL:	that.way	finally	be.lost

They finally got going. BO: Yes. CL: They finally went out of sight.

11.

'Eesge	hegų	'eeja	šųųkxete	hocira	'eeja	haapahi.
'eesge	hegų	'eeja	šųųkxete	hoci-ra	'eeja	ha<ha>pahi
that's.why	that.way	there	horse	house-DEF	there	1E.A>go.toward

So then I went towards the horse shed.

12.

Hegų	hija	hahi	'anąga	hegų...	wažąsu	xųnųįk	nįįsge	jaagušge	wiigairera?
hegų	hija	hahi	'anąga	hegų	wažąsu	xųnų-įk	nįįsge	jaagu-šge	wa-hige-ire-ra
that.way	there	finally	and	that.way	seeds	be.small-DIM	VAGUE	what-also	OBJ.3PL-say.to-SBJ.3PL-DEF

I got there and I proceeded... what did you call them... the little seeds?

13.

Šųųkxete	wook'ųiňešųnų,	waruc	wook'ųiňešųnų.
šųųkxete	wa-hok'ų-ire-šųnų	waruc	wa-hok'ų-ire-šųnų
horse	OBJ.3PL-give-SBJ.3PL-HAB	food	OBJ.3PL-give-SBJ.3PL-HAB

The ones they used to feed to the horses.

14.

BO:	Žee	'eeja	jagu	wiicąwąsruucopšge	'aire.
BO:	žee	'eeja	jagu	wiicąwąsruucop-šge	'ee-ire
BO:	that	there	and.so	corn.meal-also	say-SBJ.3PL

BO: Well, they said ground corn.

15.

CL:	Heesgešge	'airegųnį.
CL:	heesge-šge	'ee-ire-gųnį
CL:	that's.why-also	say-SBJ.3PL-DUB

CL: Yeah, I guess that is what they said.

16.

BO:	'Eegi	(wažą	wažą,)	wažąrustakšge	'airešųnų.	CL:	Hąhą'ą.
BO:	'eegi	(wažą	wažą)	wažą-rustak-šge	'ee-ire-šųnų	CL:	hąhą'ą
BO:	and.then	(something	something)	something-flatten-also	say-SBJ.3PL-HAB	CL:	yes

BO: Or they used to call them oatmeal (something flat). CL: Yes.

17.

Žeešge	jagu	'ee	hopase	nįįsge	'eeja	kook	xete	hižą
žee-šge	jagu	'ee	hopase	nįįsge	'eeja	kook	xete	hižą
that-also	and.so	3EMPH	corner	VAGUE	there	box	be.big(OBJ.3SG)	one

'eeja	nąąžįjeera	pąąňą	nųųp	hige	'eeja	hajawi...
'eeja	nąąžį-jee-ra	pąą-ra	nųųp	hige	'eeja	ha-jee-wi
there	stand-POS.VERT-DEF	bag-DEF	two	again	there	COLL-POS.VERT-PL

BO:	Hąą.	CL:	'Eesge	hegų	hahi.
BO:	hąą	CL:	'eesge	hegų	ha-hii
BO:	yes	CL:	that's.why	that.way	1E.A-arrive.there

Kind of in the corner there was a big box and two bags... BO: Yes. CL: That's where I went.

18.

BO:	Hąhą'o.
BO:	hąhą'o
BO:	yes

BO: Yes.

19.

CL:	Mąąs	kookra	nųųp	hegų	haiğe	nįįsgeanąga	hegų
CL:	mąąs	kook-ra	nųųp	hegų	ha-giğe	nįįsge-'anąga	hegų
CL:	metal	box-DEF	two	that.way	1E.A-bring.out	VAGUE-and	that.way

šųųkxetera	'eeja	nųųp	hajawi.
šųųkxete	'eeja	nųųp	ha-jee-wi
horse	there	two	COLL-POS.VERT-PL

CL: I scooped up two cans full and there were two horses.

20.

'Eesgeegų,	wooruceja	hacįįja	warucnąka	'eeja	hahi,
'eesge-hegų	wooruc-'eeja	hacįįja	waruc-nąka	'eeja	ha-hii
thus-that.way	eating.place-there	where	food-POS.NTL:DIST	there	1E.A-arrive.there

wažąňą	waak'ų	hegų,	hegų	waruc
wažą-ra	wa-ho<ha>k'ų	hegų	hegų	waruc
something-DEF	OBJ.3PL-<1E.A>give	that.way	that.way	eat

hajiharaire.
ha-jii-ha-ree-ire
COLL-arrive.here-COLL-go.there-SBJ.3PL

I went to where they eat, I gave them the stuff, they started to eat.

21.

Hižą	woowąknįįsgešųnų,	šųųkxete	wąąk	hižą	hija	nąąžį,
hižą	woowąk-nįįsge-šųnų	šųųkxete	wąąk	hižą	hija	nąąžį
one	be.naughty-VAGUE-HAB	horse	man	one	there	stand(SBJ.3SG)

že'e	waxja	nįįsge	hiranąą'įšųnų.
že'e	waxja	nįįsge	hiraną<ha>'į-šųnų
that.way	be.pretty	VAGUE	<1E.A>think.of-HAB

One of the horses was bad/wild, a male horse, and he was standing there, I used to think he was kind of cute.

22.

Žee	'eesge,	hamįąnąkšųnų	warucjaa'ų	hegų	hamįąnąkšųnų.
žee	'eesge	hamį<ha>nąk-šųnų	waruc-jee-'ų	hegų	hamį<ha>nąk-šųnų
that	that's.why	<1E.A>sit.on-HAB	eat-POS.VERT-SIM	that.way	<1E.A>sit.on-HAB

That's why I used to ride him, when he was eating I got on him.

23.

Hegų,	hegų,	hegų	jaagunįįsge	hamįąnąknąga	hegų
hegų	hegų	hegų	jaagu-nįįsge	hamį<ha>nąk-šąną	hegų
that.way	that.way	that.way	what-VAGUE	<1E.A>sit.on-DECL	that.way

hotoǧocnaga	hegų	šįįcrašge	hegų	nąąsura...	hoipįnįnįįsge
hotoǧoc-nąga	hegų	šįįc-ra-šge	hegų	nąąsu-ra	hoipįnį-nįįsge
look.at\1E.A-and	that.way	rear-DEF-also	that.way	head-DEF	spin-VAGUE

haakirinąk	hegų	hakjoopahišge	hamįąnąknągašge,	hegų
ha<ha>kirinąk	hegų	hakja-ho-hapahi-šge	hamį<ha>nąk-nąga-šge	hegų
<1E.A>land.on	that.way	back-APPL.INESS-go.toward-also	<1E.A>sit.on-and-also	that.way

'eeja	cąąkejašge	hegųągaira	horoǧoc	reehanįįsgešųnų.
'eeja	cąąk-'eeja-šge	hegų-hagaira	horoǧoc	ree-haa-nįįsge-šųnų
there	outside-there-also	that.way-sometimes	look.at	go.there-make/CAUS\1E.A-VAGUE-HAB

I got on him and spun around on him glancing outside once in a while, while I was looking over the back end.

24.

BO:	Hąą.	CL:	'Eeja	hegų	ha'ųnąk'ų	šųųkxetejka
BO:	hąą	CL:	'eeja	hegų	ha-'ųų-nąk-'ų	šųųkxete-įk-ga
BO:	yes	CL:	there	that.way	1E.A-do/make-POS.NTL-SIM	horse-DIM-PROP

warucra	rušjąšgųnį.	BO:	Hąą.
waruc-ra	rušją-šgųnį	BO:	hąą
eat-DEF	quit(SBJ.3SG)-DUB	BO:	yes

BO: Yes. CL: While I was doing that, the horse must have got done eating. BO: Yes.

25.

CL:	Hegų	'eeja	hegų	t'ąąt'ąpjiire.
CL:	hegų	'eeja	hegų	t'ąąt'ąp-jiire
CL:	that.way	there	that.way	jump-begin

CL: The horse started jumping up and down.

26. Ciira ciira jaagu kuužiįknįįsge wa'ųnąke. BO: Hey...
cii-ra cii-ra jaagu kuuži-įk-nįįsge wa'ų-nąk-ge BO hey
house-DEF house-DEF what low-DIM-VAGUE do/be-POS.NTL-CAUSAL BO hey

The barn was kind of low. BO: Hey...

27. CL: Nąąsura hegų hegų 'aara hegų giwawa nįįsge
CL: nąąsu-ra hegų hegų 'aa-ra hegų giwawa nįįsge
CL: head-DEF that.way that.way arm-DEF that.way flopping VAGUE

mįąnąk wa'ųnąk hegų, (he)gųągaira nąąpra hakara...
mįį<ha>nąk wa'ų-nąk hegų hegų-hagaira nąąp-ra hakara
<1E.A>sit do/be-POS.NTL that.way that.way-sometimes hand-DEF (incomplete)

CL: My arms, hands, were flopping around while I sat on it, once in a while my hands...

28. Hegų hija ha'ųxjįnąk'ų hegų hicągeere ciiropra
hegų hija ha-'ųų-xjį-nąk-'ų hegų hicągeere ciirop-ra
that.way there 1E.A-do/make-INTS-POS.NTL-SIM that.way with.difficulty/finally door-DEF

hapahaare, hegų 'ųųnąk'ų jaagu mąąšjąxjį
ha<ha>pahi-hare hegų 'ųų-nąk-'ų jaagu mąąšją-xjį
<1E.A>go.toward-go.there that.way do/make-POS.NTL-SIM what be.strong-INTS

t'ąąpjikeregają hegų nąąsura 'eeja hegų (hipa)
t'ąąp-jiikere-gają hegų nąąsu-ra 'eeja hegų (hipa)
get.down(SBJ.3SG)-be.started-SEQ that.way head-DEF there that.way (SLIP)

yaakipa, ciira.
hi<ha>kipa cii-ra
<1E.A>meet house-DEF

I was really working hard, and finally he headed towards the door, and as we were going he jumped very hard, so my head met the building.

29. 'Eeja hegų... BO: Hąą, nąąsura 'eeja hirojiną. CL: Hąą,
'eeja hegų BO: hąą nąąsu-ra 'eeja hirojį-ną CL: hąą
there that.way BO: yes head-DEF there strike.with-DECL CL: yes

hegų šųųkxeteįka jagu hegų hahi xawanįgi hegų
hegų šųųkxete-įk-ga jagu hegų hahi xawanį-gi hegų
that.way horse-DIM-PROP and.so that.way finally be.lost(SBJ.3SG)-TOP that.way

waną'įňą 'įįxawanį jiikere, hegų tee 'eeja jagu, yaaperes
waną'į-ra 'įį-xawanį ha-jiikere hegų tee 'eeja jagu hi<ha>peres
mind-DEF live-be.lost 1E.A-be.started that.way this there and.so <1E.A>know

nįįsge hakirinąkgają, tee 'eeja huu joop mįąnąknąk mąija.
nįįsge ha<ha>kirinąk-gają tee 'eeja huu joop mįį<ha>nąk mąą-ija
VAGUE <1E.A>land.on-SEQ this there leg four <1E.A>sit earth-there

There... BO: Hitting the head there. CL: Yes, and of course that horse just disappeared, I was unconscious, and then when I finally came to, here I was on all four on the ground.

30. Šųųkxeteįka 'eeja nųųgiwąkjį hegų t'ąąt'ąp nįįsge rahe.
šųųkxete-ik-ga 'eeja nųųgiwąk-jį hegų t'ąąt'ąp nįįsge rahe
horse-DIM-PORP there run-INTS that.way jump VAGUE be.going.there

BO: Hąą.
BO: hąą
BO: yes

There goes the horse running and bucking over there. BO: Yes.

31. CL: Že'e woorak waxja niisge hiranąą'įšųnų.
CL: že'e woorak waxja nįįsge hiraną<ha>'į-šųnų
CL: that story be.funny VAGUE <1E.A>think.of-HAB

CL: I used to think that was a funny story.

32. Hegų hegų hąąkešge nąąnį 'eerašge jaaji
hegų hegų hąąke-šge nąąnį 'ee-ra-šge jaaji
that.way that.way NEG.IN-also mother have.kin\1E.A-DEF-also father

'eerašge hegų waagitaknį, s'iixjį.
'ee-ra-šge hegų ho<ha-gi>tak-nį s'ii-xjį
have.kin\1E.A-DEF-also that.way <1E.A-APPL.BEN>tell\1E.A-NEG.FIN long.time-INTS

Well, I didn't even tell mom and dad for a long time.

33. Hegų 'eeja hicągeerexjį nįįsge howe mąąnį hąąp
hegų 'eegi hicągeere-xjį nįįsge howe mąą<ha>nį hąąp-ra
that.way and.then with.difficulty-INTS VAGUE go.about <1E.A>walk day-DEF

nųųpahą hegų.
nųųp-ahą hegų
two-times that.way

There I was, barely able to walk for two days.

34. Hegų wažą 'ųų hįgigi nąą'įirešge ğerexjįįk nįįsge
hegų wažą 'ųų hį-gigi nąą'i-ire-šge ğere-xjį-įk nįįsge
that.way something do/make 1E.U-let/cause try-SBJ.3PL-also be.slow-INTS-DIM VAGUE

howe yaaxgąxgą.
howe hi<ha>xgąxgą
go.about <1E.A>move.around

When they tried to make me do something, I was moving around real slow.

35. BO: Hegų žee šųųkxete wanąą'į šiišik hirakipa? CL: Hąhą'o.
BO: hegų žee šųųkxete wanąą'į šiišik hi<ra>kipa CL: hąhą'o
BO: that.way that horse mind be.bad <2.A>meet CL: yes

BO: You met with an ill tempered horse? CL: Yes.

36.

Hąhą'o,	jagu	šųųk	šųųkjeega	jagu,	woowąk	nįįsgera
hąhą'o	jagu	šųųk	šųųk-jeega	jagu	woowąk	nįįsge-ra
yes	and.so	dog	dog-POS.VERT:DIST	and.so	be.naughty(OBJ.3SG)	VAGUE-DEF

šųųkxetejeega	jagu	woowąk	nįįsge	hiranąą'įšųnų.
šųųkxete-jeega	jagu	woowąk	nįįsge	hiraną<ha>'į-šųnų
horse-POS.VERT:DIST	and.so	be.naughty(OBJ.3SG)	VAGUE	<1E.A>think.of-HAB

Yes, that dog (= horse), he was kind of naughty, I used to think he was wild.

37.

BO:	Že'e	waną'į	šiišik	wawigairešųnų.	CL:	Hąhą.
BO:	žee	waną'į	šiišik	wa-hige-ire-šųnų	CL:	hąhą
BO:	that	mind	be.bad	OBJ.3PL-say.to-SBJ.3PL-HAB	CL:	yes

BO: They used to call those ill tempered. CL: Yes.

38.

Hąąke	hamįnąk	pįnį.	BO:	Hey...	CL:	Žee	heesge...
hąąke	hamįnąk	pįį-nį	BO:	hey	CL:	žee	heesge
NEG.IN	sit.on	be.good-NEG.FIN	BO:	hey	CL:	that	that's.why

BO:	Nųnįge	waš'ųšąnąk?	CL:	Hąhą.
BO:	nųnįge	wa<š>'ų-šą-nąk	CL:	hąhą
BO:	nevertheless	<2.A>do/be-2.A-POS.NTL	CL:	yes

It wasn't good for riding. BO: Hey... CL: That's why... BO: But there you were? CL: Yes.

39.

Žee	hagoreižąxjį	žige	Wakąja	Hagipeirega...	BO:	Hąą.	CL:
žee	hagoreižą-xjį	žige	Wakąja	hagipe-ire-ga	BO:	hąą	CL:
that	sometime-INTS	again	Thunderbird	wait.for-SBJ.3PL-PROP	BO:	yes	CL:

'Eesge	haawįňą,	šųųkxetera	hakuhawi	'anąga
'eesge	haa-wį-ra	šųųkxete-ra	ha-kuhe-wi	'anąga
that's.why	make/CAUS\1E.A-PL-DEF	horse-DEF	1E.A-be.coming.back.here\1E.A-PL	and

hegų	xee	kųųhąija	hahi	wooğe	haakjanawi.
hegų	xee	kųųhą-hija	ha-hii	wooğe	haa-kjene-wi
that.way	hill	underneath-there	1E.A-arrive.there	noise	make/CAUS\1E.A-FUT-PL

Then one time Wakąja Hagipeire... BO: Yes CL: And I went and got the horse and went down the hill and we were going to have a big time.

40.

'Eesge	hegų	Wakąja	Hagipeirega	hamįnąk	'anąga
'eesge	hegų	Wakąja	hagipe-ire-ga	hamįnąk	'anąga
that's.why	that.way	Thunderbird	wait.for-SBJ.3PL-PROP	sit.on(SBJ.3SG)	and

hegų	hazohinįįsge	hegų	hakikaranį,	šųųkxetera.
hegų	hazohi-nįįsge	hegų	ha<kii-kara>nį	šųųkxete-ra
that.way	calmly-VAGUE	that.way	<RFL-POSS.RFL>have.NTL(SBJ.3SG)	horse-DEF

BO: Hąą.
BO: hąą
BO: yes

And then Wakąja Hagipeire got on the horse and it acted real gentle. BO: Yes.

41. CL: 'Eeja hegų cieja hagiwigają hegų "Hey"
CL: 'eeja hegų cii-'eeja ha-gii-wi-gają hegų hey
CL: there that.way house-there 1E.A-arrive.back.there-PL-SEQ that.way hey

hegų, Wakąja Hagipeirega 'een, "hegų nąąk'as
hegų Wakąja hagipe-ire-ga 'ee-ną hegų nąąk'as
that.way Thunderbird wait.for-SBJ.3PL-PROP say(SBJ.3SG)-DECL that.way take.off.suddenly

hagigikjene."
ha-gigi-kjene
1E.A-let/cause(OBJ.3SG)-FUT

CL: And when we got home Wakąja Hagipeire said, "Hey, I'm going to make him go fast.

42. Hegų jaasgegi, 'eesge hegų "gooja hahi 'anąga hegų
hegų jaasgegi heesge hegų gooja ha-hii 'anąga hegų
that.way however that's.why that.way over.there 1E.A-arrive.there and that.way

hikaraiwįx hagigi 'anąga hakirikjene" hige 'ee.
hikaraiwįx ha-gigi 'anąga ha-kiri-kjene hige 'ee
turn.around 1E.A-let/cause and 1E.A-arrive.back.here-FUT again say(SBJ.3SG)

I'm going to go over there and make him turn around and come back," he said.

43. BO: Hąą. CL: "Yaa, hegų raare!" hegų hihe.
BO: hąą CL: yaa hegų ree-re hegų hihe
BO: yes CL: AFFRM that.way go.there-IMP that.way say\1E.A

BO: Yes. CL: "Go ahead and go!" that's what I said.

44. Hegų gipsapsak nįįsge 'anąga hegų 'eeja
hegų gi<psa>psak nįįsge 'anąga hegų 'eeja
that.way <RDP:ITER>slap(SBJ.3SG&OBJ.3SG) VAGUE and that.way there

šųųkxetera nųųgiwąkxjį jiire.
šųųkxete-ra nųųgiwąk-xjį jiire
horse-DEF run-INTS begin(SBJ.3SG)

He kind of slapped the horse and it started running.

45. Hegų giš'įš'į nįįsge ('anąga) hegų hahi xawanį.
hegų giš'įš'į nįįsge ('anąga) hegų hahi xawanį
that.way bounce(SBJ.3SG) VAGUE (and) that.way finally be.lost(SBJ.3SG)

And he was kind of bouncing and disappeared.

46.

Hegų	'eeja	nąąžį	'anąga	hegų	haagipe
hegų	'eeja	nąą<ha>žį	'anąga	hegų	ha<ha-gi>pe
that.way	there	<1E.A>stand	and	that.way	<1E.A-APPL.BEN>wait(OBJ.3SG)

nįįsge	'eeja,	tee	'eeja	jagu	ruuk'asjį	hiraicera	saagrexjį	hegų
nįįsge	'eeja	tee	'eeja	jagu	ruuk'as-jį	hiraicera	saagre-xjį	hegų
VAGUE	there	this	there	and.so	fast-INTS	more	be.fast-INTS	that.way

haji	hağep	jinąkšąną.
haji	hağep	jiinąk-šąną
come.about	appear	become-DECL

While I was standing there waiting, he came into sight real fast.

47.

BO:	Hąą.	CL:	Hegų	nųųgiwąkjį.
BO:	Hąą	CL:	hegų	nųųgiwąk-jį
BO:	yes	CL:	that.way	run(SBJ.3SG)-INTS

BO: Yes. CL: Galloping real fast.

48.

Hegų	ruporoporok	nįįsge	hegų	ruuk'asjį	wa'ųnąk.
hegų	ruporo<poro>k	nįįsge	hegų	ruuk'as-jį	wa'ų-nąk
that.way	<RDP>be.balled.up	VAGUE	that.way	be.fast-INTS	do/be(SBJ.3SG)-POS.NTL

He was kind of balled up and hunched over, he was fast.

49.

Hegų	šųųkra	hotoğocga	'eeja	hegų,	"Hey"	yaage,
hegų	šųųk-ra	hotoğoc-ga	'eeja	hegų	hey	hi<ha>ge
that.way	dog-DEF	look.at\1E.A-CONT	there	that.way	hey	<1E.A>say.to

"Rexga,	ruxare,"	hegų	yaage.
Rex-ga	ruxe-re	hegų	hi<ha>ge
Rex-PROP	chase-IMP	that.way	<1E.A>say.to

So then I glanced at the dog and I said, "Hey, Rex, chase him," I said it that way.

50.

"Hagurare,"	hegų	yaage,	hegų	nąąk'asjį	hegų
hagure-re	hegų	hi<ha>ge	hegų	nąąk'as-xjį	hegų
go.after-IMP	that.way	<1E.A>say.to	that.way	take.off.suddenly(SBJ.3SG)-INTS	that.way

šųųkra	'eeja	šųųkxetera,	Wakąja	Hagipeirega
šųųk-ra	'eeja	šųųkxete-ra	Wakąja	hagipe-ire-ga
dog-DEF	there	horse-DEF	Thunderbird	wait.for-SBJ.3PL-PROP

wiikipa	jinąkanąga	hegų,	šųųkįka
wa-hikipa	jii-nąk-ire	hegų	šųųk-įk-ga
OBJ.3PL-meet(SBJ.3SG)	arrive.here-POS.NTL-SBJ.3PL	that.way	dog-DIM-PROP

šųųkxetejeega	haracap	nąą'į.
šųųkxete-jeega	haracap	nąą'į
horse-POS.VERT:DIST	taste/bite	try(SBJ.3SG)

"Go after him," I said and the dog took off real fast after the horse, he met Wakąja Hagipeire there and the dog tried to bite the horse.

51.

Hegų	hegų	sįįcrašge	hegų	ragąšjį	hegų
hegų	hegų	sįįc-ra-šge	hegų	ragąš-jį	hegų
that.way	that.way	tail-DEF-also	that.way	miss(SBJ.3SG)-INTS	that.way

wąąkjį	'eeja	t'ąąp	jiikere	nįįsge,	hegų	heesge
wąąk-jį	'eeja	t'ąąp	jiikere	nįįsge	hegų	heesge
upper.region-INTS	there	get.down	be.started(SBJ.3SG)	VAGUE	that.way	that's.why

hiigają,	jaasge	wažą	'ųųgi,	hąąke	yaaperesnį,
hii-gają	jaasge	wažą	'ųų-gi	hąąke	hi<ha>peres-nį
make/CAUS(SBJ.3SG)-SEQ	how	something	do/make-TOP	NEG.IN	<1E.A>know-NEG.FIN

hegų	šųųkxetejeega	hegų	hiwušaxjį	jinąkšąną
hegų	šųųkxete-jeega	hegų	hiwuša-xjį	jii-nąk-šąną
that.way	horse-POS.VERT:DIST	that.way	stop-INTS	arrive.here(SBJ.3SG)-POS.NTL-DECL

hegų,	'eeja	hegų	Wakąja	Hagipeirega	hegų	jagu,
hegų	'eeja	hegų	Wakąja	hagipe-ire-ga	hegų	jagu
that.way	there	that.way	Thunderbird	wait.for-SBJ.3PL-PROP	that.way	and.so

wąąkra howaregają,	hegų	mąįja	gišgįkjį	kįnįpšąną.
wąąkra_howare-gają	hegų	mąą-hija	gišgįk-jį	kįnįp-šąną
go.up\1E.A-SEQ	that.way	earth-there	thud-INTS	fall.down(SBJ.3SG)-DECL

Even the tail he just barely missed it, and the horse jumped way up in the air, and as he did that, I don't know what he did, that horse stopped suddenly, and there Wakąja Hagipeire went up in the air he landed with a thud on the ground.

52.

BO:	Hąą.	CL:	Hegų	'įįxjį	nįįsge,	hegų	ruuhira
BO:	hąą	CL:	hegų	'įįx-jį	nįįsge	hegų	ruuhi-ra
BO:	yes	CL:	that.way	grunt(SBJ.3SG)-INTS	VAGUE	that.way	rib-DEF

hakurukos	mįąnąkga	hegų	'eeja	įįx	nįįsge	jiire.
ha<ku>rukos	mįį<ha>nąk-ga	hegų	'eeja	'įįx	nįįsge	jiire
<POSS.RFL>hold(SBJ.3SG)	<1E.A(slip)>sit-CONT	that.way	there	grunt	VAGUE	begin

BO: Yes. CL: He was groaning, and he held his ribs and sat up, he started to groan.

53.

Hegų	hegų	woogitekji	hųųroğoc	wa'ųąkšąną.
hegų	hegų	woogitek-xjį	ho<hį>roğoc	wa'ų-'ąk-šąną
that.way	that.way	be.angry-INTS	<1E.U>look.at	do/be(SBJ.3SG)-POS.HOR-DECL

He was looking at me real mad.

54.

Hegų	'eeja	nųųgiwąkjį	kirikere	haa.
hegų	'eeja	nųųgiwąk-jį	kiri-kere	haa
that.way	there	run-INTS	arrive.back.here-go.back.there	make/CAUS\1E.A

So I quickly ran away.

55.

Hegų	jaasge	hiiregi	hąąke	yaaperesnį.
hegų	jaasge	hii-ire-gi	hąąke	hi<ha>peres-nį
that.way	how	make/CAUS-SBJ.3PL-TOP	NEG.IN	<1E.A>know-NEG.FIN

I don't know what happened after that.

56.

Žee	('ųų)	waxja	hiranąą'įšųnų.
žee	('ųų)	waxja	hiraną<ha>'į-šųnų
that	(do/make)	be.funny	<1E.A>think.of-HAB

I used to think that story was funny.

57.

Že'e	woorak	waxja	nįįsge	here	hiranąą'įgųnį
že'e	woorak	waxja	nįįsge	here	hiraną<ha>'į-gųnį
that	story	be.funny	VAGUE	be	<1E.A>think.of-POT-DUB

yaarege	'eesge	wahakšąną.
hi<ha>re-ge	'eesge	wahe-nąk-šąną
<1E.A>think-CAUSAL	that's.why	talk\1E.A-POS.NTL-DECL

I used to think that story was funny, that's why I'm saying it.

58.

Jagu	wažą	hišege	rooragųgają	(ke	yaa)?
jagu	wažą	hiše-ge	roo<ra>gų-gają	(hąąke	yaa)
and.so	something	say\2.A-CAUSAL	<2.A>want-SEQ	(NEG.IN(HESIT)	yaa)

Maybe you want to say something?

59.

BO:	'Eegi	jagu	jagu	hegų	hišagįnįgają...	CL:	Hąą.	BO:
BO:	'eegi	jagu	jagu	hegų	hiše-gįnį-gają	CL:	hąą	BO:
BO:	and.then	and.so	and.so	that.way	say\2.A-already-SEQ	CL:	yes	BO:

Hąą,	waxjagųnį	hegų	žee	jagu...	CL:	Yaa.	BO:	Šųųkxete
hąą	waxja-gųnį	hegų	žee	jagu	CL:	yaa	BO:	šųųkxete
yes	be.funny-DUB	that.way	that	and.so	CL:	ARRFM	BO:	horse

waną'į	šiišiknąągre	hegų	hąąke	hiperes
waną'į	šiišik-nągre	hegų	hąąke	hiperes
mind	be.bad(OBJ.3SG)-POS.NTL:PROX	that.way	NEG.IN	know

pįįňąnį	jaagu	'ųirekjenegi,	hegų...	CL:	Hąąhą
pįį-ire-nį	jaagu	'ųų-ire-kjene-gi	hegų	CL:	hąąhą
be.good-SBJ.3PL-NEG.FIN	what	do/make-SBJ.3PL-FUT-TOP	that.way	CL:	yes

nįįšge hagoreižą jagu heesge haagają.
nįį-šge hagoreižą jagu heesge haa-gają
1EMPH-also sometime and.so that's.why make/CAUS\1E.A-SEQ

BO: Well, you've already said it... CL: Yes. BO: Yes, that must have been funny... CL: Yes. BO: They're unpredictable, these ill tempered horses, when they're going to do something... CL: Yeah, I did that too.

60. Mąąxi Sgaaga... hegų šųųkxete seep hižą ruwįire. CL:
mąąxi sgaa-ga hegų šųųkxete seep hižą ruwį-ire CL:
sky/cloud be.white-PROP that.way horse be.black one buy-SBJ.3PL CL:

Mhmm... BO: Wacekįk šųųkxete hinųk hižą.
mhmm BO: wacek-įk šųųkxete hinųk hižą
mhmm BO: be.young-DIM horse woman one

Mąąxi Sgaa... they bought a black horse. CL: Mhmm... BO: A young female.

61. Hegų jagu hiraati rutikje wagi'ųįñera... CL: Yaa.
hegų jagu hiraati ruti-kje wa<gi>'ų-ire-ra CL: yaa
that.way and.so wagon pull-FUT <APPL.BEN>do/be-SBJ.3PL-DEF CL: AFFRM

BO: Hegų hąąke 'ųųsge waišgera ke
BO: hegų hąąke 'ųųsge waišge-ra hąąke
BO: that.way NEG.IN something:HESIT harness-DEF NEG.IN

'ųmąknį.
'ųmąk-nį
get.used.to(SBJ.3SG)-NEG.FIN

They bought two for the wagon... CL: Yaa. BO: But she wasn't used to a harness.

62. Hegų hegų 'eeja hikijąįja hijąnejeega hikiją
hegų hegų 'eeja hikiją-hija hijąne-jeega hikiją
that.way that.way there on.side-there the.other.one-POS.VERT:DIST on.side

kereire nąąžį kereiregają, hegų, hegų hirajakį,
kere-ire nąąžį kere-gają hegų hegų hirajakį
set.upright-SBJ.3PL stand go.back.there-SEQ that.way that.way hold.one's.position

hegų, 'ųųja'ų, hegų hišera heesge hegų t'ąąp
hegų 'ųų-jee-'ų hegų hiše-ra heesge hegų t'ąąp
that.way do/make-POS.VERT-SIM that.way say\2.A-DEF that's.why that.way get.down

jiikerekere nįįsge hegų hegų waišgerašge hegų
jikere-kere nįįsge hegų hegų waišge-ra-šge hegų
be.started(SBJ.3SG)-RDP:ITER VAGUE that.way that.way harness-DEF-also that.way

hanąąc waruwawaxšąną.
hanąąc wa-ra-wawax-šąną
all OBJ.3PL-by.mouth-break-DECL

They put her alongside the other horse, they stood her there, she resisted, and like you said, she was getting jumpy, and she even broke the harness.

63.

CL:	Wiyahį̨cį!	BO:	Hąąhą.
CL:	wiyahį̨cį	BO:	hąąhą
CL:	too.much	BO:	yes

CL: That's too much! BO: Yes.

64.

Hegų	'eeja	hegų	waišgera	hegų	giruxguire.
hegų	'eeja	hegų	waišge-ra	hegų	giruxgu-ire
that.way	there	that.way	harness-DEF	that.way	take.off-SBJ.3PL

Then they took her harness off.

65.

CL:	Hegų	t'ąąt'ąpjee?
CL:	hegų	t'ąąt'ąp-jee
CL:	that.way	jump-POS.VERT

CL: Was she still jumping?

66.

BO:	Hąą,	ka.
BO:	hąą	ka
BO:	yes	no

BO: Yes, no.

67.

Hegų	žee	'eeja	giseweną.
hegų	tee	'eeja	gisewe-ną
that.way	this	there	be.quiet(SBJ.3SG)-DECL

And then she settled down.

68.

CL:	Hąą.	BO:	Hegų	'eeja	Mąąxi	Sgaaga
CL:	hąą	BO:	hegų	'eeja	mąąxi	sgaa-ga
CL:	yes	BO:	that.way	there	sky/cloud	be.white(OBJ.3SG)-PROP

wąįgeną,	"Te'e	hamįšąnąknągi	hiš'ųnąą,"
wa-hį-hige	te'e	hamį<šą>nąk-nąą-gi	hi-š-'ųų-nąą
OBJ.3PL-1E.U-say.to(SBJ.3SG)	this	<2.A>sit.on-POT-TOP	APPL.INST-2.A-do/make-POT

hį̨ige.
hi<hį>ge
<1E.U>say.to(SBJ.3SG)

CL: Yes. BO: Mąąxi Sgaa turned to me and said, "If you can ride her you can use her."

69. CL: Hąą. BO: Hąą, heesge hegų nįį 'eeja (waną)
CL: hąą BO: hąą heesge hegų nįį 'eeja (waną)
CL: yes BO: yes that's.why that.way water there SLIP

hanį teegają... CL: Hąą. BO: Nįį 'eeja
hanį tee-gają CL: hąą BO: nįį 'eeja
have.NTL(SJB.3SG) go.there\1E.A-SEQ CL: yes BO: water there

waanį tee.
wa-hanį tee
OBJ.3PL-have.NTL go.there(SBJ.3SG)\1E.A

CL: yes, BO: Yes, and so I took her down to the river, CL: yes, BO: I took her to the water.

70. Hegų 'eeja, jagu halter kiira nįįsgešge hegų
hegų 'eeja jagu halter kiira nįįsgešge hegų
that.way there and.so halter only or that.way

haanąk, 'iirusgicrašąnąšge kiira hi'ų 'anąga...
haa-nąk 'ii-hirusgic-ra-šąną kiira hi-'ųų 'anąga
make/CAUS\1E.A-POS.NTL mouth-tie.with-DEF-only only APPL.INST-do/make and

CL: Hąą. BO: Hegų nįį 'eeja nįįxa nįįxara hikijaixjį
CL: hąą BO: hegų nįį 'eeja nįįxa nįįxa-ra hikijaixjį
CL: yes BO: that.way water there belly(HESIT) belly-DEF same.height

nįįsge nįį hošewera. CL: Hašįnį rahi?
nįįsge nįį hošewe-ra CL: ha<šį>nį ra-hii
VAGUE water deep.place-DEF CL: <2.A>have.NTL(OBJ.3SG) 2.A-arrive.there

And there using just a halter... CL: Yes. BO: I took her belly deep into the water. CL: You took her there?

71. BO: Hąą, 'eeja hanį hahi.
BO: hąą 'eeja ha<ha>nį ha-hii
BO: yes there <1E.A>have.NTL 1E.A-arrive.there

BO: Yes, I took her there.

72. Hegų žeejąną hamįnąkšąną.
hegų žeejąną hamį<ha>nąk-šąną
that.way finally <1E.A>sit.on(OBJ.3SG)-only

Then, just like that, I sat on her.

73. CL: Hąą. BO: Jagu hegų hįgixgu ną'įkje
CL: hąą BO: jagu hegų hį-gixgu nąą'į-kje
CL: yes BO: and.so that.way 1E.U-buck.off try(SBJ.3SG)-FUT

wagi'ųňą žee jaagu, (paa) paara hegų nąąsura
wa<gi>'ų-ra žee jaagu (paa) paa-ra hegų nąąsu-ra
<APPL.BEN>do/be(SBJ.3SG)-DEF what that (nose) nose-DEF that.way head-DEF

hąąke nįį howacip (ro) rokigųnįge,
hąąke nįį ho-wacip (ro) roo<kii>gų-nį-ge
NEG.IN water APPL.INESS-dump (HESIT) <RFL>want(SBJ.3SG)-NEG.FIN-CAUSAL

hegų hegų hazohixjį hegų hegų 'eeja howe ha'ų
hegų hegų hazohi-xjį hegų hegų 'eeja howe ha-'ųų
that.way that.way carefully-INTS that.way that.way there go.about 1E.A-do/make

hajawi.
ha-jee-wi
1E.A-POS.VERT-PL

CL: Yes. BO: I meant for her to try and buck me off, but she didn't want her face in the water, so we were moving around real easily.

74. Hegų nįįnąka 'eeja hegų hegų mąąnį hagigi.
hegų nįį-nąka 'eeja hegų hegų mąąnį ha-gigi
that.way water-POS.NTL:DIST there that.way that.way walk 1E.A-let/cause

CL: Ya. BO: Hegų hamįąnąknąga waa'ųnąkšąną.
CL: ya BO: hegų hamį<ha>nąk-nąga wa<ha>'ų-nąk-šąną
CL: AFFRM BO: that.way <1E.A>sit.on-and <1E.A>do/be-POS.NTL-DECL

I just let her walk in that water. CL: Yes. BO: I was sitting on her.

75. CL: Hąąke waxjanį?
CL: hąąke waxja-nį
CL: NEG.IN be.funny-NEG.FIN

CL: It wasn't fun?

76. BO: Hąą, hegų, hegų wažą 'ųųxjį hiregųnį,
BO: hąą hegų hegų wažą 'ųų-xjį hire-gųnį
BO: yes that.way that.way something be-INTS think(SBJ.3SG)-DUB

nąįxgukje hirege wa'ųjeešgųnį.
ną<hį>xgu-kje hire-ge wa'ų-jee-šgųnį
<1E.U>buck.off(SBJ.3SG)-FUT think(SBJ.3SG)-CAUSAL do/be-POS.VERT-DUB

BO: Yes, she must've really thought she was doing something.

77. Hegų... CL: Yaa. BO: Hegų 'ųųjaa'ų gisewe.
hegų CL: yaa BO: hegų 'ųų-jee-'ų gisewe
that.way CL: AFFRM BO: that.way be-POS.VERT-SIM be.quiet(SBJ.3SG)

Then... CL: Yes. BO: Eventually she settled down.

78. Heesge hąą hegų, nąįži hiną hagigigųnį yaaregają.
heesge hąą hegų nąįži hiną ha-gigi-gųnį hii<ha>re
that's.why yes that.way about.now enough 1E.A-let/cause(OBJ.3SG)-DUB <1E.A>think

That's why I thought I had done enough to her now.

79.

CL:	Jaagušge...	BO:	Hegų	hamįąnąk	hegų	hakarawi
CL:	jaagu-šge	BO:	hegų	hamį<ha>nąk	hegų	ha-kere-wi
CL:	what-also	BO:	that.way	<1E.A>sit.on	that.way	1E.A-go.back.there-PL

hegų	hazohixjį	ha'ų	hanąkwi'ų	hija	hagiwi.
hegų	hazohi-xjį	ha-'ųų	ha-nąk-wi-'ų	hija	ha-gii-wi
that.way	carefully-INTS	1E.A-do/make	1E.A-POS.NTL-PL-SIM	there	1E.A-arrive.there-PL

CL: What else... BO: And then I sat on her back real calmly and we eventually got home.

80.

CL:	Jaagųšge	'airešųnųňą	že'e?
CL:	jaagu-šge	'ee-ire-šųnų-ra	že'e
CL:	what-also	say-SBJ.3PL-HAB-DEF	that

CL: What did they use to say to that?

81.

Nįį	'eeja	kirikere,	nįį	'ąąc	nįį	'ąąc	kere
nįį	'eeja	kiri-kere	nįį	'ąąc	nįį	'ąąc	kere
water	there	arrive.back.here-go.back.there	water	off.shore	water	off.shore	go.back.there

(or	or)	jaagušge	'airešųnųną?
(or	or)	jaagu-šge	'ee-ire-šųnų-ra
(or	or)	what-also	say-SBJ.3PL-HAB-DEF

To come by through the water, out of the water, what did they say?

82.

Jaagu	nįį	'eeja	rahįp	nąga	kirikere
jaagu	nįį	'eeja	ra-hįįp	nąga	kiri-kere
what	water	there	2.A-reach	and	arrive.back.here-go.back.there

raagišge	wooracrašge	hegų	te'e	waakįkųnųnį.
ra-gii-šge	woorac-ra-šge	hegų	te'e	wa<ha>kikųnųnį
2.A-arrive.back.there-also	word-DEF-also	that.way	this	<1E.A>forget

You got to the river, I forgot the word.

83.

Jagu	hegų	kaga	wąąkšik	yaat'et'enį	wa'ųhaje.
jagu	hegų	kaga	wąąkšik	hi<ha>t'et'e	wa'ų-ha-jee
and.so	that.way	NEG.IN.never	Indian/person	<1E.A>talk	do/be-1E.A-POS.VERT

BO:	Hąą,	CL:	Hegų	hagairaxjišąną.
BO:	hąą	CL:	hegų	hagaira-xjį-šąną
BO:	yes	CL:	that.way	sometimes-INTS-only

I hardly ever speak Indian. BO: Yes. CL: Just once in a while.

84.

BO:	Hąą,	hegų	'ąącra	howakuuwi.
BO:	hąą	hegų	'ąąc-ra	howe-kuu-wi
BO:	yes	that.way	off.shore-DEF	go.about-come.back.here-PL

BO: Yes, so we came back to shore.

85.	CL:	Hąą	hąą,	žeesge	hihe	nąą'į.
	CL:	hąą	hąą	žeesge	hihe	nąą<ha>'į
	CL:	yes	yes	thus	say\1E.A	<1E.A>try

CL: Yes, yes, I was trying to say that.

86.	BO:	Hąą,	'ąącra	howakuuwi	nįį	'ąącra.	CL:
	BO:	hąą	'ąąc-ra	howe-kuu-wi	nįį	'ąąc-ra	CL:
	BO:	yes	off.shore-DEF	go.about-come.back.here-PL	water	off.shore-DEF	CL:

Hąąhą.
hąąhą
yes

BO: Yes, we came out of the water and back to shore. CL: Yes.

87.	CL:	Heesgegają...	BO:	Žige	hagoreižą,	šųųkxetera	nųųp	(ru),
	CL:	heesge-gają	BO:	žige	hagoreižą	šųųkxete-ra	nųųp	(ru)
	CL:	that's.why-SEQ	BO:	again	sometime	horse-DEF	two	(SLIP)

šųųkxete	hižą	žige	ruwįįňe,	hagoreižą.	CL:	Yaa.
šųųkxete	hižą	žige	ruwį-ire	hagoreižą	CL:	yaa
horse	one	again	buy(OBJ.3SG)-SBJ.3PL	sometime	CL:	AFFRM

CL: That's it... BO: Then one day they bought two horses, bought one horse one day. CL: Yes.

88.	BO:	Hąą,	'Ųųsgega	jaagušge	higairerašge,	Shankey
	BO:	hąą	'ųųsge-ga	jaagu-šge	hige-ire-ra	Shankey
	BO:	yes	something:HESIT-PROP	what-also	say.to-SBJ.3PL-DEF	Shankey

hišge	wawigaire.
hisge	wa-hige-ire
also	OBJ.3PL-say.to-SBJ.3PL

BO: What did they call him, they called him Shankey.

89.	CL:	Warejkra...	BO:	Merrillan	heepregi,	'eeja	ciirašųnų.
	CL:	wareįk-ra	BO:	Merrillan	heep-regi	'eeja	cii-ire-šųnų
	CL:	white.man-DEF	BO:	Merrillan	side-SIM/LOC	there	live-SBJ.3PL-HAB

CL: The white man... BO: He used to live on this side of Merrillan.

90.	CL:	Hm.	BO:	Heesge	hegų,	nįįja	nįįsgejee.
	CL:	hm	BO:	heesge	hegų	nįįja	nįįsge-jee
	CL:	hm	BO:	that's.why	that.way	be.flooded	VAGUE-POS.VERT

CL: Hm. BO: They told me to take it back and because it was flooding.

91.

CL:	Hąą.	BO:	"Hihą,	tee	hanį	karare,"	hįįgaire.
CL:	hąą	BO:	hihą	tee	hanį	kere-re	hi<hį>ge-ire
CL:	yes	BO:	INTJ	this	have.NTL	go.back.there-IMP	<1E.U>say.to-SBJ.3PL

CL: Yes. BO: "Okay, take this back with you," they told me.

92.

Heesge	hegų	jagu	nįįja	nįįsge	jeegi	hegų
heesge	hegų	jagu	nįį-hija	nįįsge	jee-gi	hegų
that's.why	that.way	and.so	water-there	POS.VERT-TOP	VAGUE	that.way

ciinąkra	waaginąkšąną.	CL:	Yaa.
ciinąk-ra	wa-ha-gii-nąk-šąną	CL:	yaa
village-DEF	OBJ.3PL-1E.A-arrive.back.there-POS.NTL-DECL	CL:	AFFRM

Because it was flooding I went through town. CL: Yaa.

93.

BO:	Nąąxąąmąnįnąkšge	'eeja	hagiwigająšge	hegų
BO:	nąąxąąmąnį-nąk-šge	'eeja	ha-gii-wi-gają-sge	hegų
BO:	bridge-there-POS.NTL-also	there	1E.A-arrive.back.there-PL-SEQ-also	that.way

hat'ąp	nąga	hegų	tuuti	hegų	nąąxąąmąnįňą
ha-t'ąąp	nąga	hegų	tuuti	hegų	nąąxąąmąnį-ra
1E.A-get.down	and	that.way	pull(OBJ.3SG)\1E.A	that.way	bridge-DEF

hatucawiną.	CL:	Hąą.	BO:	Hegų	'aakeja
hatuce-wi-ną	CL:	hąą	BO:	hegų	'ageja
cross\1E.A-PL-DECL	CL:	yes	BO:	that.way	across

hagiwiigają	žige	hamįąnąkšąną.
ha-gii-wi-gają	žige	hamį<ha>nąk-šąną
1E.A-arrive.back.there-PL-SEQ	again	<1E.A>sit.on-DECL

BO: We got to the bridge and I got off and led him across the bridge. CL: Yes. BO: When we got across I got back on again.

94.

Hegų	hakarawį	hegų	box	factorynąka	'eeja	hagi
hegų	ha-kere-wį	hegų	box	factory-nąka	'eeja	hagi
that.way	1E.A-go.back.there-PL	that.way	box	factory-POS.NTL:DIST	there	over.there

waaginąkwi.
ho<ha>ginąk-wi
<1E.A>go.via-PL

On the way back we went by that box factory.

95. 'Eegi hirocąnągrešge hige 'eeja waaginąk
`eegi hirocą-nągre-šge hige 'eeja ho<ha>ginąk-wi
and.then take.shortcut-POS.NTL:PROX-also again there <1E.A>go.via-PL

hakarawįną.
ha-kere-wį-ną
1E.A-go.back.there-PL-DECL

We took the shortcut going home.

96. Hegų hakarahawį, hegų hakocąk nąąk
hegų ha-karahe-wį hegų hakocąk nąąk
that.way 1E.A-be.going.back.there-PL that.way for.a.little.while run

haigikje. CL: Hąą.
ha-gigi-kje CL: hąą
1E.A-let/cause(OBJ.3SG)-FUT CL: yes

On the way back I let him run for a little while. CL: Yes.

97. BO: Heesge hegų nąąmąąmą reeha nąga hegų hazohixjį
BO: heesge hegų nąąmą<mą>_reeha nąga hegų hazohi-xjį
BO: that's.why that.way <RDP:ITER>spur.horse\1E.A and that.way carefully-INTS

hegų 'eeja hakarahawį, nųųwąk.
hegų 'eeja ha-karahe-wį nųųwąk
that.way there 1E.A-be.going.back.there-PL run

BO: I kicked him (the horse) with my heels in and we headed back at a real easy pace, running.

98. Hegų hegų gaagų taawigają, hegų 'eeja
hegų hegų gaagų tee-wi-gają hegų 'eeja
that.way that.way this.way go.there\1E.A-PL-SEQ that.way there

taahawių wakąįžą wakaižą nąągura haruce(ire).
taahe-wi-'ų waką-ižą waką-ižą nąągu-ra haruce
be.going.there\1E.A-PL-SIM snake-one snake-one road-DEF cross(SBJ.3SG)

As we were going, headed that way, a snake crossed the road.

99. Šųųkxetejka hegų 'eeja nąąğire, gaaja hoginąkšąną. CL:
šųųkxete-įk-ga hegų 'eeja nąąğire gaaja hoginąk-šąną CL:
horse-DIM-PROP that.way there be.scared over.there go.via(SBJ.3SG)-DECL CL:

Hąą.
hąą
yes

The horse got scared and went that way through there. CL: Yes.

100.	BO:	Hegų	gaaja	hoginąk	nąga	jagu	nįįšge	roocą
	BO:	hegų	gaaja	hoginąk	nąga	jagu	nįį-šge	roocą
	BO:	that.way	over.there	go.via(SBJ.3SG)	and	and.so	1EMPH-also	be.straight

t'ąąp	[...]	CL:	Roocącą,	hąą.
t'ąąp	[...]	CL:	roocą-cą	hąą
jump	[...]	CL:	be.straight-RDP	yes

BO: And when he went that way I went straight [...] he jumped straight ahead. CL: Really straight, yes.

101.	BO:	Yaa,	hija	taahegają	hegų.	CL:	Ya,	"cia!"
	BO:	yaa	hija	taahe-gają	hegų	CL:	ya,	"cia!"
	BO:	AFFRM	there	be.going.there\1E.A-SEQ	that.way	CL:	AFFRM	INTJ

hiše?	BO:	'Eeja	hįrušąnąire.
hiše?	BO:	'eeja	hį-rušąną-ire
say\2.A	BO:	there	1E.U-drop-SBJ.3PL

BO: Yes, I kept on going. CL: Did you say "shucks"? BO: There they (it) dropped me.

102.	Xee	š'ooknąka	hegų	'eeja	hagi	waa'ų.
	xee	š'ook-nąka	hegų	'eeja	ha-gii	wa<ha>'ų
	hill	be.lumpy-POS.NTL_DIST	that.way	there	1E.A-arrive.back.there	<1E.A>do/be

CL:	Mhmm.
CL:	mhmm
CL:	mhmm

I got back to the little round hill. CL: Mhmm.

103.	BO:	Hegų	cieja	hagi	gajeere.	CL:	wakąįka
	BO:	hegų	cii-'eeja	ha-gii	gajeere	CL:	waką-įk-ga
	BO:	that.way	house-there	1E.A-arrive.back.there	HYP	CL:	snake-DIM-PROP

nąąğire?
nąąğire
be.scared(SBJ.3SG)

BO: I got home finally. CL: That little snake, did it get scared?

104.	BO:	'Eesge,	hąą,	waką	nąąkewe.
	BO:	'eesge	hąą	waką	nąąkewe
	BO:	that's.why	yes	snake	be.afraid(SBJ.3SG)

BO: That way, yes, he was afraid of the snake.

105. Waką nąąğire hiiregi hegų.
waką nąąğire hii-regi hegų
snake be.scared make/CAUS(SBJ.3SG)-SIM/LOC that.way

The snake scared him.

106. Hegų xatapra howakere, šųųkxetejeega
hegų hoxatap-ra howe-kere šųųkxete-jeega
that.way woods-DEF go.about-go.back.there(SBJ.3SG) horse-POS.VERT:DIST

hiroanąkšąną. CL: Hąą.
hiro<ha>nąk-šąną CL: hąą
<1E.A>follow-DECL CL: yes

The horse headed back into the woods, I followed that horse. CL: Yes.

107. 'Eeja hagi nįįňą haruce.
'eeja hagi nįį-ra haruce
there there water-DEF cross

He crossed that water there.

108. CL: Kere? BO: Hąhą hegų kere wa'ų.
CL: kere BO: hąhą hegų kere wa'ų
CL: go.back.there(SBJ.3SG) BO: yes that.way go.back.there do/be(SBJ.3SG)

CL: Was he headed home? BO: Yes, he was heading back home.

109. Hegų 'eeja (hąįnįgają) hąįnįgają žige hija hahiwįgają, tee
hegų 'eeja hąįnį-gają hąįnį-gają žige hija ha-hii-wį tee
that.way there morning-SEQ morning-SEQ again there 1E.A-arrive.there-PL this

'eeja jee.
'eeja jee
there POS.VERT

Then the next day we went over there again, and there he was.

110. CL: Hą, hacįįja ciira hiperes?
CL: hą hacįįja cii-ra hiperes
CL: yes where live-DEF know(SBJ.3SG)

CL: Yes, he knew where he lived?

111. BO: Hąą hacįįja 'eeja howajii wa'ųjera
BO: hą hacįįja 'eeja howajii wa'ų-jee-ra
BO: yes where there come.from do/be(SBJ.3SG)-POS.VERT-DEF

hiperesgają. CL: Mhmm.
hiperes-gają CL: mhmm
know(SBJ.3SG)-SEQ CL: mhmm

BO: Yes, he knew where he came from. CL: Mhmm.

112. Šųųkxete hamįnąkra waxja hiranąą'įšųnų,
šųųkxete hamįnąk-ra waxja hiraną<ha>'į-šųnų
horse sit.on-DEF be.funny(OBJ.3SG) <1E.A>think.of-HAB

hįxųnųįkregi, hegų goišip.
hį-xųųnų-įk-regi hegų goišip
1E.U-be.small-DIM-SIM/LOC that.way always

When I was little I used to think it was fun to ride on horseback all the time.

113. Hegų wažąňą hižą ha'ųgi hegų goišip hegų
hegų wažą-ra hižą ha-'ųų-gi hegų goišip hegų
that.way something-DEF one 1E.A-do/make-TOP that.way always that.way

šųųkxete hamįąnąk tee tuuxuruks'aže 'eegi, cooka
šųųkxete hamį<ha>nąk tee tuuxuruk-s'a'že 'eegi cooka
horse <1E.A>sit.on this accomplish\1E.A-ITER-QUOT and.then grandfather

'eera hegų 'ee "Jaasge raakjegi," yaa
'ee-ra hegų 'ee jaasge raa-kje-gi yaa
have.kin\1E.A-DEF that.way say(SBJ.3SG) how make/CAUS\2.A-FUT-TOP AFFRM

hegų 'eešųnų.
hegų 'ee-šųnų
that.way say(SBJ.3SG)-HAB

Whenever I did anything, I would ride a horse, grandpa told me "whatever you want to do," yes that's what he used to tell me.

6.2 The complete Hocąk text without analysis

[1]CL: Germannąągre hit'et'e wąąkšik hit'et'e roįgųnąąk nųnįge, 'eesge... BO: Tağiriįkra. CL: Tağiriįkra, 'eesge Bill O'Brien and nee Chloris Lowega wahanąkšąną, 'eegi wąąkšik yaat'et'ekjene, hiyaicgakjanawi. [2]BO: Yaa'ųcakjanawi. [3]CL: Hihą, jaagu hįį'e hiikjene? [4]BO: Hąąke yaaperesnį jaagu hįį'e hiikjene. [5]CL: Tee 'eegi wažą waxja nįįsge hijašge ha'e hiiną. [6]Hįxųnųįkregi... BO: Hižą hokarakre. CL: Hąhą'o, heesge haakje. [7]Hąą, hįxųnųįkregi, 'ųųsge, cooka 'eeraanąga nąąnį 'eerašge hegų ciinąkra 'eeja howare hikorohoire. [8]BO: Hąą. CL: 'Eesge hegų šųųkxetera hahi wootoğoc nįįsge 'anąga hegų, hegų, hižą hamįąnąkikje yaare nįįsge. BO: Hąą. [9]CL: 'Eesge hegų waagipe, hegų ciinąkra hegų xapge howarairegi pįįnągųnį yaare. [10]Hegų hegų 'ųųnąk'ų hicągeere jiikaraire. BO: Hąą. CL: Hegų hahi xawanį. [11]'Eesge hegų 'eeja šųųkxete hocira 'eeja haapahi. [12]Hegų hija hahi 'anąga hegų... wažąsu xųnųįk nįįsge jaagušge wiigairera? [13]Šųųkxete wook'ųiňešųnų, waruc wook'ųiňešųnų. [14]BO: Žee 'eeja jagu wiicąwąsruucopšge 'aire. [15]CL: Heesgešge 'airegųnį. [16]BO: 'Eegi (wažą wažą,) wažąrustakšge 'airešųnų. CL: Hąhą'ą. [17]Žeešge jagu 'ee hopase nįįsge 'eeja kook xete hižą 'eeja nąąžįjeera pąąňą nųųp hige 'eeja hajawi... BO: Hąą. CL: 'Eesge hegų hahi. [18]BO: Hąhą'o. [19]CL: Mąąs kookra nųųp hegų haiğe nįįsgeanąga hegų šųųkxetera 'eeja nųųp hajawi. [20]'Eesgeegų, wooruceja hacįįja warucnąka 'eeja hahi, wažąňą waak'ų hegų, hegų waruc hajiharaire. [21]Hižą woowąknįįsgešųnų, šųųkxete wąąk hižą hija nąąžį, že'e waxja nįįsge hiranąą'įšųnų. [22]Žee 'eesge, hamįąnąkšųnų warucjaa'ų hegų hamįąnąkšųnų. [23]Hegų, hegų, hegų jaagunįįsge hamįąnąknąga hegų hotoğocnaga hegų šįįcrašge hegų nąąsura... hoipįnįnįįsge haakirinąk hegų hakjoopahišge hamįąnąknągašge, hegų 'eeja cąąkejašge hegųągaira horoğoc reehanįįsgešųnų. [24]BO: Hąą. CL: 'Eeja hegų ha'ųnąk'ų šųųkxeteįka warucra rušjąšgųnį. BO: Hąą. [25]CL: Hegų 'eeja hegų t'ąąt'ąpjiire. [26]Ciira ciira jaagu kuužiįknįįsge wa'ųnąke. BO: hey [27]CL: Nąąsura hegų hegų 'aara hegų giwawa nįįsge mįąnąk wa'ųnąk hegų, (he)gųągaira nąąpra hakara... [28]Hegų hija ha'ųxjįnąk'ų hegų hicągeere ciiropra hapahaare, hegų 'ųųnąk'ų jaagu mąąšjąxjį t'ąąpjikeregają hegų nąąsura 'eeja hegų (hipa) yaakipa, ciira. [29]'Eeja hegų BO: hąą, nąąsura 'eeja hirojiną. CL: hąą, hegų šųųkxeteįka jagu hegų hahi xawanįgi hegų waną'įňą 'įįxawanį jiikere, hegų tee 'eeja jagu, yaaperes nįįsge hakirinąkgają, tee 'eeja huu joop mįąnąknąk mąija. [30]Šųųkxeteįka 'eeja nųųgiwąkjį hegų t'ąąt'ąp nįįsge rahe. BO: Hąą. [31]CL: Že'e woorak waxja niisge hiranąą'įšųnų. [32]Hegų hegų hąąkešge nąąnį 'eerašge jaaji 'eerašge hegų waagitaknį, s'iixjį. [33]Hegų 'eeja hicągeerexjį nįįsge howe mąąnį hąąp nųųpahą hegų. [34]Hegų wažą 'ųų hįgigi nąą'įirešge ğerexjįįk nįįsge howe yaaxgąxgą. [35]BO: Hegų žee šųųkxete waną'į šiišik hirakipa? CL: Hąhą'o. [36]Hąhą'o, jagu šųųk šųųkjeega jagu, woowąk nįįsgera šųųkxetejeega jagu woowąk nįįsge hiranąą'įšųnų. [37]BO: Že'e waną'į šiišik wawigairešųnų. CL: Hąhą. [38]Hąąke hamįnąk pįnį. BO: Hey... CL: Žee heesge... BO: Nųnįge waš'ųšąnąk? CL: Hąhą. [39]Žee hagoreižąxjį žige Wakąja Hagipeirega... BO: Hąą. CL: 'Eesge haawįňą, šųųkxetera hakuhawi 'anąga hegų xee kųųhąija hahi wooğe haakjanawi. [40]'Eesge hegų Wakąja Hagipeirega hamįnąk 'anąga hegų hazohinįįsge hegų hakikaranį, šųųkxetera. BO: Hąą. [41]CL: 'Eeja hegų

cieja hagiwigają hegų "Hey" hegų, Wakąja Hagipeirega 'een, "hegų nąąk'as hagigikjene." [42]Hegų jaasgegi, 'eesge hegų "gooja hahi 'anąga hegų hikaraiwįx hagigi 'anąga hakirikjene" hige 'ee. [43]BO: Hąą. CL: "Yaa, hegų raare!" hegų hihe. [44]Hegų gipsapsak nįįsge 'anąga hegų 'eeja šųųkxetera nųųgiwąkxjį jiire. [45]Hegų giš'įš'į nįįsge ('anąga) hegų hahi xawanį. [46]Hegų 'eeja nąąžį 'anąga hegų haagipe nįįsge 'eeja, tee 'eeja jagu ruuk'asjį hiraicera saagrexjį hegų haji hağep jinąkšąną. [47]BO: Hąą. CL: Hegų nųųgiwąkjį. [48]Hegų ruporoporok nįįsge hegų ruuk'asjį wa'ųnąk. [49]Hegų šųųkra hotoğocga 'eeja hegų, "Hey" yaage, "Rexga, ruxare," hegų yaage. [50]"Hagurare," hegų yaage, hegų nąąk'asjį hegų šųųkra 'eeja šųųkxetera, Wakąja Hagipeirega wiikipa jinąkanąga hegų, šųųkįka šųųkxetejeega haracap nąą'į. [51]Hegų hegų sįįcrašge hegų ragąšjį hegų wąąkjį 'eeja t'ąąp jiikere nįįsge, hegų heesge hiigają, jaasge wažą 'ųųgi, hąąke yaaperesnį, hegų šųųkxetejeega hegų hiwušaxjį jinąkšąną hegų, 'eeja hegų Wakąja Hagipeirega hegų jagu, wąąkra howaregają, hegų mąįja gišgįkjį kįnįpšąną. [52]BO: Hąą. CL: Hegų 'įįxjį nįįsge, hegų ruuhira hakurukos mįąnąkga hegų 'eeja įįx nįįsge jiire. [53]Hegų hegų woogitekji hųųroğoc wa'ųąkšąną. [54]Hegų 'eeja nųųgiwąkjį kirikere haa. [55]Hegų jaasge hiiregi hąąke yaaperesnį. [56]Žee ('ųų) waxja hiranąą'įšųnų. [57]Že'e woorak waxja nįįsge here hiranąą'įgųnį yaarege 'eesge wahakšąną. [58]Jagu wažą hišege rooragųgają (ke yaa)? [59]BO: 'Eegi jagu jagu hegų hišagįnįgają... CL: Hąą. BO: Hąą, waxjagųnį hegų žee jagu... CL: Yaa. BO: Šųųkxete wanąʼį šiišiknąągre hegų hąąke hiperes pįįñąnį jaagu 'ųirekjenegi, hegų... CL: Hąąhą nįįšge hagoreižą jagu heesge haagają. [60]Mąąxi Sgaaga... hegų šųųkxete seep hižą ruwįire. CL: Mhmm... BO: Wacekįk šųųkxete hinųk hižą. [61]Hegų jagu hiraati rutikje wagi'ųįñera... CL: Yaa. BO: Hegų hąąke 'ųųsge waišgera ke 'ųmąknį. [62]Hegų hegų 'eeja hikijąįja hijąnejeega hikiją kereire nąąžį kereiregają, hegų, hegų hirajakį, hegų, 'ųųja'ų, hegų hišera heesge hegų t'ąąp jiikerekere nįįsge hegų hegų waišgerašge hegų hanąąc waruwawaxšąną. [63]CL: Wiyahįcį! BO: Hąąhą. [64]Hegų 'eeja hegų waišgera hegų giruxguire. [65]CL: Hegų t'ąąt'ąpjee? [66]BO: Hąą, ka. [67]Hegų žee 'eeja giseweną. [68]CL: Hąą. BO: Hegų 'eeja Mąąxi Sgaaga wajgeną, "Te'e hamįšąnąknągi hiš'ųnąą," hįįge. [69]CL: Hąą. BO: Hąą, heesge hegų nįį 'eeja (waną) hanį teegają... CL: Hąą. BO: Nįį 'eeja waanį tee. [70]Hegų 'eeja, jagu halter kiira nįįsgešge hegų haanąk, 'iirusgicrašąnąšge kiira hi'ų 'ąnąga... CL: Hąą. BO: Hegų nįį 'eeja nįįxa nįįxara hikijaixjį nįįsge nįį hošewera. CL: Hašįnį rahi? [71]BO: Hąą, 'eeja hanį hahi. [72]Hegų žeejąną hamįąnąkšąną. [73]CL: Hąą. BO: Jagu hegų hįgixgu ną'įkje wagi'ųñą žee jaagu, (paa) paara hegų nąąsura hąąke nįį howacip (ro) rokigųnįge, hegų hegų hazohixjį hegų hegų 'eeja howe ha'ų hajawi. [74]Hegų nįįnąka 'eeja hegų hegų mąąnį hagigi. CL: Ya. BO: Hegų hamįąnąknąga waa'ųnąkšąną. [75]CL: Hąąke waxjanį? [76]BO: Hąą, hegų, hegų wažą 'ųųxjį hiregųnį, nąįxgukje hirege wa'ųjeešgųnį. [77]Hegų... CL: Yaa. BO: Hegų 'ųųjaa'ų gisewe. [78]Heesge hąą hegų, nąįži hiną hagigigųnį yaaregają. [79]CL: Jaagušge... BO: Hegų hamįąnąk hegų hakarawi hegų hazohixjį ha'ų hanąkwi'ų hija hagiwi. [80]CL: Jaagųšge 'airešųnųñą že'e? [81]Nįį 'eeja kirikere, nįį 'ąąc nįį 'ąąc kere (or or) jaagušge 'airešųnųną? [82]Jaagu nįį 'eeja rahįp nąga kirikere raagišge wooracrašge hegų te'e waakįkųnųnį. [83]Jagu hegų kaga wąąkšik yaat'et'enį wa'ųhaje. BO: Hąą. CL: Hegų hagairaxjišąną. [84]BO: Hąą, hegų 'ąącra howakuuwi. [85]CL: Hąą hąą, žeesge hihe nąą'į. [86]BO: Hąą, 'ąącra howakuuwi nįį 'ąącra. CL: Hąąhą. [87]CL: Heesgegają... BO: Žige hagoreižą, šųųkxetera nųųp (ru), šųųkxete hižą žige ruwįįňe, hagoreižą. CL: Yaa. [88]BO: Hąą, 'Ųųsgega jaagušge higairerašge, Shankey hišge wawigaire. [89]CL: Wareįkra... BO: Merrillan heepregi, 'eeja ciirašųnų. [90]CL: Hm. BO: Heesge hegų, nįįja nįisgejee. [91]CL: Hąą. BO: "Hihą, tee hanį karare," hįįgaire. [92]Heesge hegų jagu nįįja nįisge jeegi hegų ciinąkra waaginąkšąną. CL: Yaa. [93]BO: Nąąxąąmąnįnąkšge 'eeja hagiwigająšge hegų hat'ąp nąga hegų tuuti hegų nąąxąąmąnįňą hatucawiną. CL: Hąą. BO: Hegų 'aakeja hagiwiigają žige hamįąnąkšąną. [94]Hegų hakarawį hegų box factorynąka 'eeja hagi waaginąkwi. [95]'Eegi hirocąnąągrešge hige 'eeja waaginąk hakarawįną. [96]Hegų hakarahawį, hegų hakocąk nąąk haigikje. CL: Hąą. [97]BO: Heesge hegų nąąmąąmą reeha nąga hegų hazohixjį hegų 'eeja hakarahawį, nųųwąk. [98]Hegų hegų gaagų taawigają, hegų 'eeja taahawių wakaįžą wakaižą nąągura haruce(ire). [99]Šųųkxeteįka hegų 'eeja nąąğire, gaaja hoginąkšąną. CL: Hąą. [100]BO: Hegų gaaja hoginąk nąga jagu nįįšge roocą t'ąąp [...] CL: Roocącą, hąą. [101]BO: Yaa, hija taahegają hegų. CL: Ya, "cia!" hiše? BO: 'Eeja hįrušąnąire. [102]Xee š'ooknąka hegų 'eeja hagi waa'ų. CL: Mhmm. [103]BO: Hegų cieja hagi gajeere. CL: wakąįka nąąğire? [104]BO: 'Eesge, hąą, waką nąąkewe. [105]Waką nąąğire hiiregi hegų. [106]Hegų xatapra howakere, šųųkxetejeega hiroanąkšąną. CL: Hąą. [107]'Eeja hagi nįįňą haruce. [108]CL: Kere? BO: Hąhą hegų kere wa'ų. [109]Hegų 'eeja (hąįnįgają) hąįnįgają žige hija hahiwįgają, tee 'eeja jee. [110]CL: Hą, hacįįja ciira hiperes? [111]BO: Hąą hacįįja 'eeja howajii wa'ųjera hiperesgają. CL: Mhmm. [112]Šųųkxete hamįnąkra waxja hiranąą'įšųnų, hįxųnųįkregi, hegų goišip. [113]Hegų wažąňą hižą ha'ųgi hegų goišip hegų šųųkxete hamįąnąk tee tuuxuruks'aže 'eegi, cooka 'eera hegų 'ee "Jaasge raakjegi," yaa hegų 'eešųnų.

6.3 The complete English translation

[1]CL: These Germans want me to talk Indian, that's why... BO: Germans. CL: Germans, that's why Bill O'Brien and me Chloris Lowe, I'm going to talk Indian, we're going to try. [2]BO: We're going to try. [3]CL: Yes, what are we going to talk about? [4]BO: I don't know what we're going to talk about. [5]CL: We could talk about something sort of funny. [6]When I was little... BO: Tell one of your stories. CL: Yes I'll do that. [7]Yes, when I was little, my grandpa and mother were getting ready to go to town. [8]BO: Yes. CL: So I went to look at the horses, I thought I'd sort of sit on one. BO: Yes. [9]CL: I waited for them, I wish they'd hurry up and go to town, I thought. [10]They finally got going. BO: Yes. CL: They finally went out of sight. [11]So then I went towards the horse shed. [12]I got there and I proceeded... what did you call them... the little seeds? [13]The ones they used to feed to the horses. [14]BO: Well, they said ground corn. [15]CL: Yeah, I guess that is what they said. [16]BO: Or they used to call them oatmeal (something flat). CL: Yes. [17]Kind of in the corner there was a big box and two bags... BO: Yes. CL: That's where I went. [18]BO: Yes. [19]CL: I scooped up two cans full and there were two horses. [20]I went to where they eat, I gave them the stuff, they started to eat. [21]One of the horses was bad/wild, a male horse, and he was standing there, I used to think he was kind of cute. [22]That's why I used to ride him, when he was eating I got on him. [23]I got on him and spun around on him glancing outside once in a while, while I was looking over the back end. [24]BO: Yes. CL: While I was doing that, the horse must have got done eating. BO: Yes. [25]CL: The horse started jumping up and down. [26]The barn was kind of low. BO: Hey... [27]CL: My arms, hands, were flopping around while I sat on it, once in a while my hands... [28]I was really working hard, and finally he headed towards the door, and as we were going he jumped very hard, so my head met the building. [29]There... BO: Hitting the head there. CL: Yes, and of course that horse just disappeared, I was unconscious, and then when I finally came to, here I was on all four on the ground. [30]There goes the horse running and bucking over there. BO: Yes. [31]CL: I used to think that was a funny story. [32]Well, I didn't even tell mom and dad for a long time. [33]There I was, barely able to walk for two days. [34]When they tried to make me do something, I was moving around real slow. [35]BO: You met with an ill tempered horse? CL: Yes. [36]Yes, that dog (= horse), he was kind of naughty, I used to think he was wild. [37]BO: They used to call those ill tempered. CL: Yes. [38]It wasn't good for riding. BO: Hey... CL: That's why... BO: But there you were? CL: Yes. [39]Then one time Wakąja Hagipeire... BO: Yes CL: And I went and got the horse and went down the hill and we were going to have a big time. [40]And then Wakąja Hagipeire got on the horse and it acted real gentle. BO: Yes. [41]CL: And when we got home Wakąja Hagipeire said, "Hey, I'm going to make him go fast. [42]I'm going to go over there and make him turn around and come back," he said. [43]BO: Yes. CL: "Go ahead and go!" that's what I said. [44]He kind of slapped the horse and it started running. [45]And he was kind of bouncing and disappeared. [46]While I was standing there waiting, he came into sight real fast. [47]BO: Yes. CL: Galloping real fast. [48]He was kind of balled up and hunched

over, he was fast. [49]So then I glanced at the dog and I said, "Hey, Rex, chase him," I said it that way. [50]"Go after him," I said and the dog took off real fast after the horse, he met Wak̨ąja Hagipeire there and the dog tried to bite the horse. [51]Even the tail he just barely missed it, and the horse jumped way up in the air, and as he did that, I don't know what he did, that horse stopped suddenly, and there Wak̨ąja Hagipeire went up in the air he landed with a thud on the ground. [52]BO: Yes. CL: He was groaning, and he held his ribs and sat up, he started to groan. [53]He was looking at me real mad. [54]So I quickly ran away. [55]I don't know what happened after that. [56]I used to think that story was funny. [57]I used to think that story was funny, that's why I'm saying it. [58]Maybe you want to say something? [59]BO: Well, you've already said it... CL: Yes. BO: Yes, that must have been funny... CL: Yes. BO: They're unpredictable, these ill tempered horses, when they're going to do something... CL: Yeah, I did that too. [60]Mąąxi Sgaa... they bought a black horse. CL: Mhmm... BO: A young female. [61]They bought two for the wagon... CL: Yaa. BO: But she wasn't used to a harness. [62]They put her alongside the other horse, they stood her there, she resisted, and like you said, she was getting jumpy, and she even broke the harness. [63]CL: That's too much! BO: Yes. [64]Then they took her harness off. [65]CL: Was she still jumping? [66]BO: Yes, no. [67]And then she settled down. [68]CL: Yes. BO: Mąąxi Sgaa turned to me and said, "If you can ride her you can use her." [69]CL: Yes. BO: Yes, and so I took her down to the river... CL: Yes. BO: I took her to the water. [70]And there using just a halter... CL: Yes. BO: I took her belly deep into the water. CL: You took her there? [71]BO: Yes, I took her there. [72]Then, just like that, I sat on her. [73]CL: Yes. BO: I meant for her to try and buck me off, but she didn't want her face in the water, so we were moving around real easily. [74]I just let her walk in that water. CL: Yes. BO: I was sitting on her. [75]CL: It wasn't fun? [76]BO: Yes, she must've really thought she was doing something. [77]Then... CL: Yes. BO: Eventually she settled down. [78]That's why I thought I had done enough to her now. [79]CL: What else... BO: And then I sat on her back real calmly and we eventually got home. [80]CL: What did they use to say to that? [81]To come by through the water, out of the water, what did they say? [82]You got to the river, I forgot the word. [83]I hardly ever speak Indian. BO: Yes. CL: Just once in a while. [84]BO: Yes, so we came back to shore. [85]CL: Yes, yes, I was trying to say that. [86]BO: Yes, we came out of the water and back to shore. CL: Yes. [87]CL: That's it... BO: Then one day they bought two horses, bought one horse one day. CL: Yes. [88]BO: What did they call him, they called him Shankey. [89]CL: The white man... BO: He used to live on this side of Merrillan. [90]CL: Hm. BO: They told me to take it back and because it was flooding. [91]CL: Yes. BO: "Okay, take this back with you," they told me. [92]Because it was flooding I went through town. CL: Yaa. [93]BO: We got to the bridge and I got off and led him across the bridge. CL: Yes. BO: When we got across I got back on again. [94]On the way back we went by that box factory. [95]We took the shortcut going home. [96]On the way back I let him run for a little while. CL: Yes. [97]BO: I kicked him (the horse) with my heels in and we headed back at a real easy pace, running. [98]As we were going, headed that way, a snake crossed the road. [99]The horse got scared and went that way through there. CL: Yes. [100]BO: And when he went that way I went straight [...] he jumped straight ahead. CL: Really straight, yes. [101]BO: Yes, I kept on going. CL: Did you say "shucks"? BO: There they (it) dropped me. [102]I got back to the little round hill. CL: Mhmm. [103]BO: I got home finally. CL: That little snake, did it get scared? [104]BO: That way, yes, he was afraid of the snake. [105]The snake scared him. [106]The horse headed back into the woods, I followed that horse. CL: Yes. [107]He crossed that water there. [108]CL: Was he headed home? BO: Yes, he was heading back home. [109]Then the next day we went over there again, and there he was. [110]CL: Yes, he knew where he lived? [111]BO: Yes, he knew where he came from. CL: Mhmm. [112]When I was little I used to think it was fun to ride on horseback all the time. [113]Whenever I did anything, I would ride a horse, grandpa told me "whatever you want to do," yes that's what he used to tell me.

7 Connection (Cecil Garvin) (CD 2 track 2)

7.1 Text with analysis and translation

1. CG: Mąąnąąpe hakį hahiregi... BO: Hąą. CG: Mąą (mąą) šaagowįnįįsge ha'ųanįhera, hagaira higi hakiri waawešųnų.
   CG: mąąnąąpe ha-kįį ha-hii-regi BO: hąą CG: mąą (mąą) šaagowį-nįįsge ha-'ųų-ha-nįhe-ra hagaira higi ha-kiri ho<ha>we-šųnų
   CG: soldier 1E.A-act/become 1E.A-arrive.there-SIM/LOC BO: yes CG: year (year) seven-VAGUE 1E.A-be-1E.A-be/PROG-DEF sometimes here 1E.A-arrive.back.here <1E.A>go.about-HAB

   CG: When I was in the military... BO: Yes. CG: I was in (there) for around seven years, I used to come back through here every once in a while.

2. CG: Virgilga, Virgil Pettibonega Minneapolis 'eeja ciišųnų.
   CG: Virgil-ga Virgil Pettibone-ga Minneapolis 'eeja cii-šųnų
   CG: Virgil-PROP Virgil Pettibone-PROP Minneapolis there live(SBJ.3SG)-HAB

   Virgil Pettibone used to live in Minneapolis.

3. BO: Hąą. CG: Hagoreižą 'eejašge hakirira 'eeja hipuša.
   BO: hąą CG: hagoreižą 'eeja-šge ha-kiri-ra 'eeja hipuša
   BO: yes CG: sometime there-also 1E.A-arrive.back.here-DEF there stop\1E.A

   BO: Yes. CG: At one time when I came back there, I stopped in there.

4. CG: Hija (hija) 'ųųnąkšąną. BO: Hąą.
   CG: hija (hija) 'ųų-nąk-šąną BO: hąą
   CG: there (there) be-POS.NTL-DECL BO: yes

   CG: He was home. BO: Yes.

5. CG: Hegų hija waakewe.
   CG: hegų hija ho<ha>kewe
   CG: that.way there <1E.A>go.inside

   CG: So I went inside.

6. CG: Waxopįnį seep hižąšge hicakoro hiira, 'ee
CG: waxopįnį_seep hižą-šge hicakoro hii-ra 'ee
CG: black.person one-also friend have.kin(SBJ.3SG)-DEF 3EMPH

hakižu mįįnąk 'eeja 'ųųnąkšąną. BO: Hey...
hakižu mįįnąk 'eeja 'ųų-nąąk-šąną BO: hey
be.together sit there do/make-POS.NTL.PL-DECL BO: hey

CG: A black man, who was his friend, they were sitting there together. BO: Hey...

7. CG: Coowexjįkšge karacgą wa'ųnąąkrašge nįįšge
CG: coowexjį-įk-šge ka-racgą wa'ų-nąąk-ra-šge nįį-šge
CG: just.a.little-DIM-also POSS.RFL-drink do/be-POS.NTL.PL-DEF-also 1EMPH-also

jaagu hija hoinąk haanįįsge.
jaagu hija hoinąk_haa-nįįsge
what there begin.task\1E.A-VAGUE

CG: They were drinking a little, so then I started in too.

8. Hegų hija mįąnąknąga. BO: Jaagu hijąhį? CG: Yaa,
hegų hija mįį<ha>nąk-'anąga BO: jaagu hijąhį CG: yaa,
that.way there <1E.A>sit-and BO: what be.different CG: AFFRM

hija hakocąk.
hija hakocąk
there for.a.little.while

CG: I sat down. BO: What else? CG: There, for a little while.

9. CG: Tee hagoreižą seepįkjeega nąąžįanąga hegų
CG: tee hagoreižą seep-įk-jeega nąąžį-'anąga hegų
CG: this sometime be.black-DIM-POS.VERT:DIST stand(SBJ.3SG)-and that.way

kirikere, "Virgil, Virgil, connection!" 'aanąga hegų
kiri-kere Virgil Virgil connection 'ee-'anąga hegų
arrive.back.here-go.back.there Virgil Virgil connection say(SBJ.3SG)-and that.way

hagi hihinąpšąną.
hagi hihinąp-šąną
get.to.a.point go.outside(SBJ.3SG)-DECL

CG: At some point that black man stood up and walked by, "Virgil, Virgil, connection!" he said and he went out the door.

10. CG: "Hąą, yaa, hanįcakje," Virgilga 'ee.
CG: hąą yaa ha<nįį>ca-kje Virgil-ga 'ee
CG: yes AFFRM <1&2>see\1E.A-FUT Virgil-PROP say(SBJ.3SG)

CG: "Okay, I'll see you," Virgil said to him.

11. CG: Virgilga waanąkšąną, "'Hakerekjane.' 'ee
CG: Virgil-ga wee-nąk-šąną ha-kere-kjane 'ee
CG: Virgil-PROP talk(SBJ.3SG)-POS.NTL-DECL 1E.A-go.back.there-FUT 3EMPH

waakšąną." BO: (conne) connection.
wee-ak-šąną BO: (conne) connection
talk-POS.HOR-DECL BO: (conne) connection

CG: Virgil was saying, "He's saying, 'I'm going home.'" BO: Connection.

12. CG: Hąą, žeesge hihajee "connection, connection."
CG: hąą žeesge hihe-jee connection connection
CG: yes thus say\1E.A-POS.VERT connection connection

CG: Yes, that's what I say now "connection, connection."

13. "Hakerekjane," 'ee waakšąną.
ha-kere-kjane 'ee wee-ak-šąną
1E.A-go.back.there-FUT 3EMPH talk(SBJ.3SG)-POS.HOR-DECL

He was saying "I'm going home."

14. Žeegų kiira.
hegų kira
that.way only

That's it.

7.2 The complete Hocąk text without analysis

[1]CG: Mąąnąąpe hakį hahiregi... BO: Hąą. CG: Mąą (mąą) šaagowįnįįsge ha'ųanįhera, hagaira higi hakiri waawešųnų. [2]CG: Virgilga, Virgil Pettibonega Minneapolis 'eeja ciišųnų. [3]BO: Hąą. CG: Hagoreižą 'eejašge hakirira 'eeja hipuša. [4]CG: Hija (hija) 'ųųnąkšąną. BO: Hąą. [5]CG: Hegų hija waakewe. [6]CG: Waxopįnį seep hižąšge hicakoro hiira, 'ee hakižu mįįnąk 'eeja 'ųųnąkšąną. BO: Hey... [7]CG: Coowexjįkšge karacgą wa'ųnąąkrašge nįįšge jaagu hija hoinąk haanįįsge. [8]Hegų hija mįąnąknąga. BO: Jaagu hijąhį? CG: Yaa, hija hakocąk. [9]CG: Tee hagoreižą seepįkjeega nąąžįanąga hegų kirikere, "Virgil, Virgil, connection!" 'aanąga hegų hagi hihinąpšąną. [10]CG: "Hąą, yaa, hanįcakje," Virgilga 'ee. [11]CG: Virgilga waanąkšąną, "'Hakerekjane.' 'ee waakšąną." BO: (Conne) connection. [12]CG: Hąą, žeesge hihajee "connection, connection." [13]"Hakerekjane," 'ee waakšąną. [14]Žeegų kiira.

7.3 The complete English translation

[1]CG: When I was in the military... BO: Yes. CG: I was in (there) for around seven years, I used to come back through here every once in a while. [2]Virgil Pettibone used to live in Minneapolis. [3]BO: Yes. CG: At one time when I came back there, I stopped in there. [4]CG: He was home. BO: Yes. [5]CG: So I went inside. [6]CG: A black man, who was his friend, they were sitting there together. BO: Hey... [7]CG: They were drinking a little, so then I started in too. [8]CG: I sat down. BO: What else? CG: There, for a little while. [9]CG: At some point that black man stood up and walked by, "Virgil, Virgil, connection!" he said and he went out the door. [10]CG: "Okay, I'll see you," Virgil said to him. [11]CG: CG: Virgil was saying, "He's saying, 'I'm going home.'" BO: Connection. [12]CG: Yes, that's what I say now "connection, connection." [13]He was saying "I'm going home." [14]That's it.

8 Buffalo Hunt (Chloris Lowe Sr.) (CD 2 track 3)

8.1 Text with analysis and translation

1.

Hihą	'eegi	wažąįžą	honįįgitakikjanawi:
hihą	'eegi	wažą-ižą	ho<nįį-gi>tak-i-kjene-wi
INTJ	and.then	something-one	<1&2-APPL.BEN>tell\1E.A-0-FUT-PL

ceexjįnąągrešge	Hoocąkrašge	woonį	hahirešųnų.
ceexjį-nąągre-šge	Hoocąk-ra-šge	wa-honį	ha-hii-ire-šųnų
buffalo-POS.NTL.PL:PROX-also	Hocak-DEF-also	OBJ.3PL-hunt	COLL-arrive.there-SBJ.3PL-HAB

Okay then, I'm going to tell you something: these buffalo, the Hocąks used to go hunt them.

2.

Aahm	'ųųsge	Nįoxete	'aakra	'eeja
aahm	'ųųsge	nįoxete	'ee-'ak-ra	'eeja
HESIT	something:HESIT	Mississippi	say-POS.HOR-DEF	there

howaharairešųnų	'ee.
howe-ha-ree-ire-šųnų	'ee
go.about-COLL-go.there-SBJ.3PL-HAB	say(SBJ.3SG)

Aahm, the big river (= the Mississippi) they called it, they would go there, he said.

3.

Ceek	(ceek)	'ųųsge	'ųųharairekjanegi,	šųųkxete
ceek	(ceek)	'ųųsge	'ųų-ha-ree-ire-kjane-gi	šųųkxete
first/new	(first/new)	something:HESIT	do/make-COLL-go.there-SBJ.3PL-FUT-TOP	horse

saagrera	'ee	hąąke	wawi'ųįňanįšųnų
saagre-ra	'ee	hąąke	wa-hi-'ųų-ire-nį-šųnų
be.fast-DEF	3EMPH	NEG.IN	OBJ.3PL-APPL.INST-do/make-SBJ.3PL-NEG.FIN-HAB

'ee,	hiraakjįňą	nųųpahą	waruxairešųnų.
'ee,	hiraak-jį-ra	nųųp-ahą	wa-ruxe-ire-šųnų
say(SBJ.3SG)	be.last-INTS-DEF	two-times	OBJ.3PL-chase-SBJ.3PL-HAB

When they were first going to go, they would not use their fast horses, he said, at the last they would chase them twice.

4.

Ceek	'eeja,	šųųkxete	wii'ųįňera	ceek
ceek	'eeja	šųųkxete	wa-hi-'ųų-ire-ra	ceek
first/new	there	horse	OBJ.3PL-APPL.INST-do/make-SBJ.3PL-DEF	first/new

wii'ųįňera	ğereįkra	žee	'ee,
wa-hi-'ųų-ire-ra	ğere-įg-ra	žee	'ee
OBJ.3PL-APPL.INST-do/make-SBJ.3PL-DEF	be.slow-DIM-DEF	that	say(SBJ.3SG)

wawi'ųįňešųnų.
wa-hi-'ųų-ire-šųnų
OBJ.3PL-APPL.INST-do/make-SBJ.3PL-HAB

At first, they used to use the slow horses, that's what he said, they used them.

5.

Cooka	'eera	hųųgirakšųnų.
cooka	'ee-ra	ho<hį-gi>rak-šųnų
grandfather	have.kin\1E.A-DEF	<1E.U-APPL.BEN>tell(SBJ.3SG)-HAB

My grandfather used to tell me.

6.

Hegųąnąga	hąąp	'eeja	wii'eirega,	šųųkxete	hoinįge
hegų-'anąga	hąąp	'eeja	wa-hi'e-ire-ra	šųųkxete	hoinįge
that.way-and	day	there	OBJ.3PL-find-SBJ.3PL-DEF	horse	ordinary

nąąka	wii'ųįňenąga	waruxaire'anąga
nąąka	wa-hi-'ųų-ire-nąga	wa-ruxe-ire-'anąga
POS.NTL.PL:DIST	OBJ.3PL-APPL.INST-do/make-SBJ.3PL-and	OBJ.3PL-chase-SBJ.3PL-and

hąąke	waguciranį,	(wii'ų)	hąąke	wii'ų
hąąke	wa-guuc-ire-nį	(wii'ų)	hąąke	wii'ų
NEG.IN	OBJ.3PL-shoot-SBJ.3PL-NEG.FIN	bullet	NEG.IN	bullet

hi'ųįňanį,	mąącgu	hi'ųįňeže
hi-'ųų-ire-nį	mąącgu	hi-'ųų-ire-že
APPL.INST-do/make-SBJ.3PL-NEG.FIN	bow	APPL.INST-do/make-SBJ.3PL-QUOT

'aire.
'ee-ire
say-SBJ.3PL

That day, when they found them they'd use an ordinary horse, they would chase them, but they wouldn't shoot them, they wouldn't shoot them with bullets, they would use bow and arrow, it is said.

7.

'Eeja	wooğe	xete	hiiregi,	jaagu
'eeja	wooğe	xete	hii-ire-gi	jaagu
there	noise	be.big	make/CAUS-SBJ.3PL-TOP	what

nųųgiwąkirekjanegi	'eesge	hąąke	wiižukra
nųų<gi>wąk-ire-kjane-gi	'eesge	hąąke	wiižuk-ra
<APPL.BEN>run-SBJ.3PL-FUT-TOP	thus	NEG.IN	gun-DEF

wawi'ųįňąnįšųnų.
wa-hi-'ųų-ire-nį-šųnų
OBJ.3PL-APPL.INST-do/make-SBJ.3PL-NEG.FIN-HAB

If they made a lot of noise (with the guns), they'd run, that's why they wouldn't use the guns.

8.

'Eesge	ahm	hinųkra	hanąącį	'ųųsge	wanįňą
'eesge	ahm	hinųk-ra	hanąącį	'ųųsge	wanį-ra
thus	HESIT	woman-DEF	all	something:HESIT	meat-DEF

wiikišereire,	jaagu	ruuciregi,	'ee,	'eegi	hinųpahą
wa-hikišere-ire	jaagu	ruuc-ire-gi	'ee	'eegi	hi-nųųp-ahą
OBJ.3PL-deal.with-SBJ.3PL	what	eat-SBJ.3PL-TOP	say(SBJ.3SG)	and.then	ORD-two-times

harairegi,	heejąga	'eeja	šųųkxete	saagrerašge
ha-ree-ire-gi	heejąga	'eeja	šųųkxete	saagre-ra-šge
COLL-go.there-SBJ.3PL-TOP	now	there	horse	be.fast-DEF-also

wii'ųįňeže,	'ee	wawoxaraire'anąga,
wa-hi-'ųų-ire-že	'ee	wa-hoxere-ire-'anąga
OBJ.3PL-APPL.INST-do/make-SBJ.3PL-QUOT	say(SBJ.3SG)	OBJ.3PL-catch.up.to-SBJ.3PL-and

'eeja	heejąga	hige	wagucires'aže.
'eeja	heejąga	hige	wa-guuc-ire-s'a-že
there	now	again	OBJ.3PL-shoot-SBJ.3PL-ITER-QUOT

That's when, ahm, all the women they would prepare the meat, whatever they eat, he said, when they went the second time, then there they would use the fast horses, and they'd catch up to the animals and then they'd shoot them again.

9.

Nųųpahą	kiirašge	wooxaraires'aže	'aire,	'eesge
nųųp-ahą	kiira-šge	wa-hoxere-ire-s'a-že	'ee-ire	'eesge
two-times	only-also	OBJ.3PL-catch.up.to-SBJ.3PL-ITER-QUOT	that's.why	what

jaagu	guuciregi	'eeja	wiikišerere'anąga	'eegi
jaagu	guuc-ire-gi	'eeja	wa-hikišere-ire-'anąga	'eegi
shoot-SBJ.3PL-TOP	say-SBJ.3PL	there	OBJ.3PL-deal.with-SBJ.3PL-and	and.then

haguires'aže	'ee.
ha-guu-ire-s'a-že	'ee
COLL-come.back.here-SBJ.3PL-ITER-QUOT	say(SBJ.3SG)

They said, they would catch them only twice, that's why whatever they shot, there they would prepare them and then they'd head back, he said.

10.

Cooka	'eera	(kaga)	jagu	nįįkjąk	kiira	heregają,
cooka	'ee-ra	(kaga)	jagu	nįįkjąk-ra	kiira	here-gają
grandfather	have.kin\1E.A-DEF	(NEG.IN.never)	and.so	child-DEF	only	be-SEQ

'eeja	nųnįge	hicoke	hiirašge,	hi'ąc	nįįsgerašge,
'eeja	nųnįge	hicoke	hii-ra-šge	hi'ąc	nįįsge-ra-šge
there	nevertheless	grandfather	have.kin(SBJ.3SG)-DEF-also	father	VAGUE-DEF-also

hi'ąc	hiirašge	žee	'eeja	harairas'aže
hi'ąc	hii-ra-šge	žee	'eeja	ha-ree-ire-s'a-že
father	have.kin(SBJ.3SG)-DEF-also	that	there	COLL-go.there-SBJ.3PL-ITER-QUOT

'ee.
'ee
say(SBJ.3SG)

My grandfather he was only a child then, however, his grandfather, sort of his father too, his father too, that's who went (hunting), he said.

11.

Wanįňą	ah	waakaraguiregašge	ah
wanį-ra	ah	wa-ha-kara-guu-ire-ga-šge	ah
meat-DEF	HESIT	OBJ.3PL-COLL-POSS.RFL-come.back.here-SBJ.3PL-CONT-also	HESIT

heguągaira	wąąkšik	hijąhį	hikipaires'aže,	hotašge
hegu-hagaira	wąąkšik	hijąhį	hikipa-ire-s'a-že	hota-šge
that.way-sometimes	Indian/person	be.different	meet-SBJ.3PL-ITER-QUOT	some-also

(wakiki)	wakizairas'ašge,	jagu	wanį	rooguįňeanągašge
(wakiki)	wa-kiza-ire-s'a-šge	jagu	wanį	roogu-ire-'anąga-šge
(SLIP/HESIT)	OBJ.3PL-fight-SBJ.3PL-ITER-also	and.so	meat	want-SBJ.3PL-and-also

wąąkšik	hijąhįnąąka.
wąąkšik	hijąhį-nąąka
Indian/person	be.different-POS.NTL.PL:DIST

When they went back after the meat, once in a while they'd meet people from a different tribe, some of them they fought with, those others Indians, they wanted the meat, too.

12.

'Eesge	'ųųsge	mąąnąąperašge	roohą	hakižu	nįįsge
'eesge	'ųųsge	mąąnąąpe-ra-šge	roohą	hakižu	nįįsge
thus	something:HESIT	soldier-DEF-also	a.lot	be.together	VAGUE

harairas'aže	'aire.
ha-ree-ire-s'a-že	'ee-ire
COLL-go.there-SBJ.3PL-ITER-QUOT	say-SBJ.3PL

That's why they would have many warriors go along with them, it is said.

13.

Hanąąc	mąą	wataknįįsge	wąąkra	že'e	wii'ųįňe'anąga
hanąąc	mąą	watak-nįįsge	wąąk-ra	že'e	wa-hi-'ųų-ire-'anąga
all	arrow	a.few-VAGUE	man-DEF	that	OBJ.3PL-APPL.INST-do/make-SBJ.3PL-and

žee	jaagu	mąąnąąpera	wa'ųnąąkšąną.
žee	jaagu	mąąnąąpe-ra	wa'ų-nąąk-šąną
that	what	soldier-DEF	do/be-POS.NTL.PL-DECL

All of them, the men they would use a small number of arrows, those are the warriors.

14.

'Eesge	nąąjurašge	serec	waakaranįňes'ažešge,
'eesge	nąąju-ra-šge	serec	wa-ha<kara>nį-ire-s'a-že-šge
thus	head.hair-DEF-also	be.long	OBJ.3PL-<POSS.RFL>have.NTL-SBJ.3PL-ITER-QUOT-also

jagu	hegų	hoišip	'aagi	kikizaire	hikorohoiregašge,
jagu	hegų	goišip	'aagi	kii-kiza-ire	hikoroho-ire-ga-šge
and.so	that.way	always	be.ready/nearby	RCP-fight-SBJ.3PL	get.ready-SBJ.3PL-CONT-also

žee	Hoocąkra	wawajairega	nąąjura	serec
žee	Hoocąk-ra	wa-haja-ire-ga	nąąju-ra	serec
that	Hocak-DEF	OBJ.3PL-see-SBJ.3PL-CONT	head.hair-DEF	be.long

hakaranįñega	hąąke	wakiza
ha<kara>nį-ire-ga	hąąke	wa-kiza
<POSS.RFL>have.NTL-SBJ.3PL-CONT	NEG.IN	OBJ.3PL-fight

roogųįñąnįs'aže	jagu	kizara	'aagi	('aagi)
roogų-ire-nį-s'a-že	jagu	kiza-ra	'aagi	('aagi)
want-SBJ.3PL-NEG.FIN-ITER-QUOT	and.so	fight-DEF	be.ready/nearby	(be.ready/nearby)

kiikerenįįsge	wa'ųnąąkšąną.
kii-kere-nįįsge	wa'ų-nąąk-šąną
RFL-put.upright-VAGUE	do/be-POS.NTL.PL-DECL

That's why they would wear their hair long, they were always prepared for a fight, when they were getting ready, when they saw the Hocąks and their hair is kept long, they didn't want to fight them, they were getting ready to fight, that's how they hold themselves.

15.

Hoocąkra	'eegi	naajurašge	(ke)	waixewekiregašge
Hoocąk-ra	'eegi	nąąju-ra-šge	(ke)	wa-gixewek-ire-ga-šge
Hocak-DEF	and.then	head.hair-DEF-also	(NEG.IN)	OBJ.3PL-comb-SBJ.3PL-CONT-also

hąąke	žeeži	jagu,	wakiza	roogųįñąnį	'ųųsge	žee
hąąke	žee-ži	jagu	wa-kiza	roogų-ire-nį	'ųųsge	žee
NEG.IN	that-FOC	and.so	OBJ.3PL-fight	want-SBJ.3PL-NEG.FIN	something:HESIT	that

'eesge	hiraire,	heesge	žeegųkiira	hųųgirakšųnų.
'eesge	hire-ire	heesge	žeegų-kira	ho<hį-gi>rak-šųnų
that's.why	think-SBJ.3PL	that's.why	thus-only	<1E.U-APPL.BEN>tell(SBJ.3SG)-HAB

When the Hocąks combed their hair, they didn't think they wanted to fight them, that's all he used tell me.

16.

Hegų	kiirašge	yaaperesnąga,	wahajee.
hegų	kiira-šge	hi<ha>peres nąga	wahe-jee
that.way	only-also	<1E.A>know-and	talk\1E.A-POS.VERT

That's all I know, I'm saying.

17.

Wanįñąšge	'aas	wa'ųnąąk	heesge.
wanį-ra-šge	'aas	wa'ų-nąąk	heesge
meat-DEF-also	be.tasty	do/be-POS.NTL.PL	that's.why

Also the meat is tasty.

18.

Hegų	kiira	yaaperesšąną,	heesge	hegų	taašjąkjene.
hegų	kiira	hi<ha>peres-šąną	heesge	hegų	taašją-kjene
that.way	only	<1E.A>know-DECL	that's.why	that.way	end.speech\1E.A-FUT

That's all I know, so I will quit talking from here.

8.2 The complete Hocąk text without analysis

[1]Hihą 'eegi wažąįžą honįįgitakikjanawi: ceexjįnąągrešge Hoocąkrašge woonį hahirešųnų. [2]Aahm 'ųųsge Nįoxete 'aakra 'eeja howaharairešųnų 'ee. [3]Ceek (ceek) 'ųųsge 'ųųharairekjanegi, šųųkxete saagrera 'ee hąąke wawi'ųįňąnįšųnų 'ee, hiraakjįňą nųųpahą waruxairešųnų. [4]Ceek 'eeja, šųųkxete wii'ųįňera ceek wii'ųįňera ğereįkra žee 'ee, wawi'ųįňešųnų. [5]Cooka 'eera hųųgirakšųnų. [6]Hegųąnąga hąąp 'eeja wii'eirega, šųųkxete hoinįge nąąka wii'ųįňenąga waruxaire'anąga hąąke waguciranį, (wii'ų) hąąke wii'ų hi'ųįňanį, mąącgu hi'ųįňeže 'aire. [7]'Eeja wooğe xete hiiregi, jaagu nųųgiwąkirekjanegi 'eesge hąąke wiižukra wawi'ųįňąnįšųnų. [8]'Eesge ahm hinųkra hanąącį 'ųųsge wanįňą wiikišereire, jaagu ruuciregi, 'ee, 'eegi hinųpahą harairegi, heejąga 'eeja šųųkxete saagrerašge wii'ųįňeže, 'ee wawoxaraire'anąga, 'eeja heejąga hige wagucires'aže. [9]Nųųpahą kiirašge wooxaraires'aže 'aire, 'eesge jaagu guuciregi 'eeja wiikišerere'anąga 'eegi haguires'aže 'ee. [10]Cooka 'eera (kaga) jagu nįįkjąk kiira heregają, 'eeja nųnįge hicoke hiirašge, hi'ąc nįįsgerašge, hi'ąc hiirašge žee 'eeja harairas'aže 'ee. [11]Wanįňą ah waakaraguiregašge ah hegųągaira wąąkšik hijąhį hikipaires'aže, hotašge (wakiki) wakizairas'ašge, jagu wanį roogųįňeanągašge wąąkšik hijąhįnąąka. [12]'Eesge 'ųųsge mąąnąąperašge roohą hakižu nįįsge harairas'aže 'aire. [13]Hanąąc mąą wataknįįsge wąąkra že'e wii'ųįňe'anąga žee jaagu mąąnąąpera wa'ųnąąkšąną. [14]'Eesge nąąjurašge serec waakaranįňes'ažešge, jagu hegų hoišip 'aagi kikizaire hikorohoiregašge, žee Hoocąkra wawajairega nąąjura serec hakaranįňega hąąke wakiza roogųįňąnįs'aže jagu kizara 'aagi ('aagi) kiikerenįįsge wa'ųnąąkšąną. [15]Hoocąkra 'eegi naajurašge (ke) waixewekiregašge hąąke žeeži jagu, wakiza roogųįňąnį 'ųųsge žee 'eesge hiraire, heesge žeegųkiira hųųgirakšųnų. [16]Hegų kiirašge yaaperesnąga, wahajee. [17]Wanįňąšge 'aas wa'ųnąąk heesge. [18]Hegų kiira yaaperesšąną, heesge hegų taašjąkjene.

8.3 The complete English translation

[1]Okay then, I'm going to tell you something: these buffalo, the Hocąks used to go hunt them. [2]Aahm, the big river (= the Mississippi) they called it, they would go there, he said. [3]When they were first going to go, they would not use their fast horses, he said, at the last they would chase them twice. [4]At first, they used to use the slow horses, that's what he said, they used them. [5]My grandfather used to tell me. [6]That day, when they found them they'd use an ordinary horse, they would chase them, but they wouldn't shoot them, they wouldn't shoot them with bullets, they would use bow and arrow, it is said. [7]If they made a lot of noise (with the guns), they'd run, that's why they wouldn't use the guns. [8]That's when, ahm, all the women they would prepare the meat, whatever they eat, he said, when they went the second time, then there they would use the fast horses, and they'd catch up to the animals and then they'd shoot them again. [9]They said, they would catch them only twice, that's why whatever they shot, there they would prepare them and then they'd head back, he said. [10]My grandfather he was only a child then, however, his grandfather, sort of his father too, his father too, that's who went (hunting), he said. [11]When they went back after the meat, once in a while they'd meet people from a different tribe, some of them they fought with, those others Indians, they wanted the meat, too. [12]That's why they would have many warriors go along with them, it is said. [13]All of them, the men they would use a small number of arrows, those are the warriors. [14]That's why they would wear their hair long, they were always prepared for a fight, when they were getting ready, when they saw the Hocąks and their hair is kept long, they didn't want to fight them, they were getting ready to fight, that's how they hold themselves. [15]When the Hocąks combed their hair, they didn't think they wanted to fight them, that's all he used tell me. [16]That's all I know, I'm saying. [17]Also the meat is tasty. [18]That's all I know, so I will quit talking from here.

9 Stealing watermelons (Ed Lonetree) (CD 2 track 4)

9.1 Text with analysis and translation

1.

Wažątire	hižą	hatucapra	hegų	'eejaxjį	mąą	kerepąną
wažątire	hižą	hatucap-ra	hegų	'eejaxjį	mąą	kerepąną
car	one	grab(OBJ.3SG)\1E.A-DEF	that.way	about.there	year	ten

nąga	hakewe	'eejaxjį	haanįgųnį.
nąga	hakewe	'eejaxjį	ha<ha>nį-gųnį
and	six	about.there	<1E.A>have.NTL-DUB

I got a car and I must have been around 16 at the time.

2.

'Eegi	jaanąga	'aašge	hocįcį	ciirera	(žee)	žee
'eegi	jaanąga	'aašge	hocįcį	cii-ire-ra	(žee)	žee
and.then	how.many	closeby	boy	live-SBJ.3PL-DEF	(that)	that

waatutianąga	wicąwą sake	mąąnų	hahiwišųnų.
wa-hatuti-'anąga	wicąwą_sake	mąąnų	ha-hii-wi-šųnų
OBJ.3PL-bring.along\1E.A-and	watermelon	steal	1E.A-arrive.there-PL-HAB

And the boys that lived nearby, I would take them along and we used to go and steal watermelons.

3.

'Eegi	(mąąx hagici)	(mąąx hagici)	mąąx hagicinąka	xeeižą	'eeja
'eegi	(mąąx_hagici)	(mąąx_hagici)	mąąx_hagici-nąka	xee-ižą	'eeja
and.then	(farm)	(farm)	farm-POS.NTL:DIST	hill-one	there

mįįnąkšąną,	'eegi	nąągura	cooweeja	hogiwe,	'eegi	xee
mįįnąk-šąną	'eegi	nąągu-ra	coowe-'eeja	hogiwe	'eegi	xee
sit(SBJ.3SG)-DECL	and.then	road-DEF	in.front-there	pathway	and.then	hill

kųųhąija	nąągura	bocgux	nąąžį,	'eeja	hirokinų.
kųųhą-ija	nąągu-ra	boocgux	nąąžį	'eeja	hirokinų
underneath-there	road-DEF	cut.across	stand(SBJ.3SG)	there	be.out.of.sight

And that farm, there was a hill there and the road ran along the front, and there at bottom there was a crossroads, it was there on the other side (hidden by the hill).

4.

'Eesge	hąąheregi	hija	hahiwinągi,	hatažara
'eesge	hąąhe-regi	hija	ha-hii-wi-nąk-gi	hataža-ra
that's.why	night-SIM/LOC	there	1E.A-arrive.there-PL-POS.NTL-TOP	light-DEF

tuusepwianąga,	wažątirera	tuusepwianąga	hija
tuusep-wi-'anąga	wažątire-ra	tuusep-wi-'anąga	hija
turn.off\1E.A-PL-and	car-DEF	turn.off\1E.A-PL-and	there

hahiwinąkı	hikųhe	hegų	hat'ąphanąkwiną.
ha-hii-wi-nąk-gi	hikųhe	hegų	ha-t'ąąp-ha-nąk-wi-ną
1E.A-arrive.there-PL-POS.NTL-TOP	hurry	that.way	1E.A-get.down-1E.A-POS.NTL-PL-DECL

That's why we'd go there at night, and we turned the lights off and then we turned the car off, and when we got there, we would jump out of the car quickly.

5. 'Eeja nąąwacakra mąijaagre 'eeja, hatucawinąga
`eeja nąąwacak-ra mąą-hija-`agre `eeja hatuce-wi-`anąga
there fence-DEF earth-there-POS.HOR:PROX there cross\1E.A-PL-and

wicąwą sake hižąšąną haanįwianąga 'eeja, hiraati
wicąwą_sake hižą-šąną ha<ha>nį-wi-`anąga 'eeja hiraati
watermelon one-only <1E.A>have.NTL-PL-and there wagon/car

homįanąkwi, 'eegi hegų hąąke (tii) tiire
ho-mįį<ha>nąk-wi `eegi hegų hąąke (tii) tiire
APPL.INESS-<1E.A>sit-PL and.then that.way NEG.IN (HESIT) move

haawinį, hegų howanąregi hegų hahi (xee) xee
haa-wi-nį hegų howaną-regi hegų hahi (xee) xee
make/CAUS\1E.A-PL-NEG.FIN that.way roll-SIM/LOC that.way finally (hill) hill

kųhąija 'eeja hahi wažątire jiikere.
kųųhą-ija 'eeja hahi wažątire jiikere
underneath-there there finally car be.started

There was a fence on the ground there, we crossed there and each of us had a watermelon and we'd get back into the car but we didn't start it, we were letting it roll, and down the hill that's where the car would start.

6. 'Eegi hąąke hegų hųųwesįwįiranįkje
'eegi hegų hąąke hį-howesįwį-ire-nį-kje
and.then that.way NEG.IN 1E.U-notice-SBJ.3PL-NEG.FIN-FUT

waagi'ųhanąkwi.
wa<ha-gi>'ų-ha-nąk-wi
<1E.A-APPL.BEN>do/be-1E.A-POS.NTL-PL

We were doing this so they wouldn't notice us.

7. Hegų hagoreižą jagu hižąšąną ha'ųhajawi'ų hegų
hegų hagoreižą jaagu hižą-šąną ha-`ųų-ha-jee-wi-`ų hegų
that.way sometime what one-only 1E.A-do/make-1E.A-POS.VERT-PL-SIM that.way

hahi waagitupįwi, hegų.
hahi wa<ha-gi>tupį-wi hegų
finally <1E.A-APPL.BEN>know.how.to(manually)\1E.A-PL that.way

At one time, as each of us were doing this, we became good at it.

8. Wicąwą sake hižąšąną haanįwianąga hegų wažątire 'eeja
wicąwą_sake hižą-šąną ha<ha>nį-wi-`anąga hegų wažątire 'eeja
watermelon one-only <1E.A>have.NTL-PL-and that.way car there

hagi homįanąkwi hegų higųąną nįge hegų
ha-gii ho-mįį<ha>nąk-wi hegų higųąną nįge hegų
1E.A-arrive.back.there APPL.INESS-<1E.A>sit-PL that.way right.now somewhere that.way

howaakarawišų̧nų̧.
howe-ha-kere-wi-šų̧nų̧
go.about-1E.A-go.back.there-PL-HAB

We would each have a watermelon, we would get right back into the car, and we'd head back right away.

9.

Ho'ų̧	te'e	hagoreižą̧,	hižą̧	kaga	hija
ho'ų̧	te'e	hagoreižą̧	hižą̧	kaga	hija
time	this	sometime	one	NEG.IN.never	there

hiinį̧šų̧nų̧ra,	žee	hatuti	hahiwi.
hii-nį̧-šų̧nų̧-ra	žee	hatuti	ha-hii-wi
arrive.there(SBJ.3SG)-NEG.FIN-HAB-DEF	that	bring.along\1E.A	1E.A-arrive.there-PL

This one time, someone who'd never gone along with us, we took him along.

10.

Wažą̧tire	'eeja	hagi	hegų̧	wesį̧wį̧nąąkšą̧ną̧,	žee
wažą̧tire	'eeja	hagi	hegų̧	wesį̧wį̧-nąąk-šą̧ną̧	žee
car	there	get.to.a.point	that.way	study(OBJ.3SG)-POS.NTL.PL-DECL	that

jaagu	'ų̧ąkgają̧,	hąąke	(ke)	kirinį̧
jaagu	'ų̧ų̧-'ąk-gają̧	hąąke	(ke)	kiri-nį̧
what	do/make(SBJ.3SG)-POS.HOR-SEQ	NEG.IN	(REP)	arrive.back.here(SBJ.3SG)-NEG.FIN

hajanąąk(šą̧ną̧).
haja-nąąk-šą̧ną̧
see-POS.NTL.PL-DECL

They were watching him from the car, whatever he was doing, he didn't return to the car, they saw him.

11.

Hegų̧	hanąąc	warucgacgajee,	'aanąąkšą̧ną̧.
hegų̧	hanąąc	wa-rucga-cga-jee	'ee-nąąk-šą̧ną̧
that.way	all	OBJ.3PL-feel.for(SBJ.3SG)-RDP:INTS-POS.VERT	say-POS.NTL.PL-DECL

He was feeling all of them, they said.

12.

Xapge	hiigi	pį̧į̧gają̧	hegų̧	yaarawi,	hagoreižą̧
xapge	hii-gi	pį̧į̧-gają̧	hegų̧	hi<ha>re-wi	hagoreižą̧
shortly	arrive.there(SBJ.3SG)-TOP	be.good-SEQ	that.way	<1E.A>think-PL	sometime

'ų̧ų̧ja'ų̧,	guu.
'ų̧ų̧-jee-'ų̧	guu
do/make-POS.VERT-SIM	come.back.here(SBJ.3SG)

If he hurried up that would be good, we thought, and finally he came back.

13. | Warukšira, | hacįįja | nąąwacakra | mąijaagre | žee | hąąke |
|---|---|---|---|---|---|
| warukši-ra | hacįįja | nąąwacak-ra | mąą-ija-'agre | žee | hąąke |
| be.unfortunate-DEF | where | fence-DEF | earth-there-POS.HOR:PROX | that | NEG.IN |

'eeja	caawanįną.
'eeja	caawe-nį-ną
there	approach(SBJ.3SG&OBJ.3SG)-NEG.FIN-DECL

Unfortunately, he didn't go to where the fence was on the ground.

14. | Nąąwacakra | hajinąknąga | haxara | hokąre | hegų |
|---|---|---|---|---|
| nąąwacak-ra | hajinąk-'anąga | haxara | hokąre | hegų |
| fence-DEF | run.into(SBJ.3SG&OBJ.3SG)-and | on.back | fall.into(OBJ.3SG) | that.way |

gixuxux	'eegi	wažok	hanį
gixuxux	'eegi	wažok	hanį
smash(SBJ.3SG&OBJ.3SG)	and.then	land&smash(SBJ.3SG&OBJ.3SG)	have.NTL

kįnįpšgųnį	'eejaxjį,	horaknąąkšąną.
kįnįp-šgųnį	'eejaxjį	horak-nąąk-šąną
land(SBJ.3SG)-DUB	about.there	tell(OBJ.3SG)-POS.NTL.PL-DECL

He ran into the fence and fell backwards, he landed and squashed the watermelon, they told it kinda that way.

15. | Nąąwacakra | hajinąkšąną. |
|---|---|
| nąąwacak-ra | hajinąk-šąną |
| fence-DEF | run.into(SBJ.3SG&OBJ.3SG)-DECL |

He ran into the fence.

16. | 'Eesge, | hegų | žige | xapge | hiigi | pįįgają. |
|---|---|---|---|---|---|
| 'eesge | hegų | žige | xapge | hii-gi | pįį-gają |
| that—s.why | that.way | again | shortly | arrive.there(SBJ.3SG)-TOP | be.good-SEQ |

It would be good if he came back quickly.

17. | Hegų | žige | haakja | hija | honį | ree. |
|---|---|---|---|---|---|
| hegų | žige | haakja | hija | honį | ree. |
| that.way | again | back(wards) | there | seek | go.there(SBJ.3SG) |

He went back to look (for another watermelon).

18. | 'Įį'įį | te'e | jaagu | 'ųgają | xapge | hiigi | pįįgają. |
|---|---|---|---|---|---|---|
| 'įį'įį | te'e | jaagu | 'ųų-gają | xapge | hii-gi | pįį-gają |
| carefully | this | what | do/make-SEQ | shortly | arrive.there(SBJ.3SG)-TOP | be.good-SEQ |

He was careful, whatever he was doing, it would be good if he hurried up.

19.

Hegų	žige	hižą	honį	ree.
hegų	žige	hižą	honį	ree
that.way	again	one	seek	go.there(SBJ.3SG)

Then he went to look for another one.

20.

Hegų	žige	warucgajee.
hegų	žige	wa-rucga-jee
that.way	again	OBJ.3PL-feel.for(SBJ.3SG)-POS.VERT

He was feeling them again.

21.

Hagoreižą	hacįįja	hokewera	'eeja	kiri,	hegų
hagoreižą	hacįįja	hokewe-ra	'eeja	kiri	hegų
sometime	where	go.inside-DEF	there	arrive.back.here(SBJ.3SG)	that.way

wažątire	'eeja	kiri	homįnąkra	hegų	hanąącį
wažątire	'eeja	kiri	ho-mįįnąk-ra	hegų	hanąącį
car	there	arrive.back.here	APPL.INESS-sit-DEF	that.way	all

nąąc hisginąąkšąną	'anąga	hegų	hųųxarairawi	'eegi
nąąc_hisgi-nąąk-šąną	'anąga	hegų	hį-hoxere-ire-wi	'eegi
scold(OBJ.3SG)-POS.NTL.PL-DECL	and	that.way	1E.U-catch.up.to-SBJ.3PL-PL	and.then

nąąkewe	waa'ųhanąkwi.
nąąkewe	wa<ha>'ų-ha-nąk-wi
be.afraid	<1E.A>do/be-1E.A-POS.NTL-PL

He finally went back to where he had entered, and he came back to the car, and they were all scolding him, we were afraid of being caught.

22.

Hegų	wažątire	'eeja	homįnąknaga,	hakarawi	hegų,
hegų	wažątire	'eeja	ho-mįįnąk nąga	ha-kere-wi	hegų
that.way	car	there	APPL.INESS-sit-and	1E.A-go.back.there-PL	that.way

'iiružaknąkšąną,	"'ao,	'ao,"	hirarexjįįk	hiira
'iiružak-nąk-šąną	'ao	'ao	hirarexjį-įk	hii-ra
make.noise-POS.NTL-DECL	ow	ow	after.a.while-DIM	make/CAUS(SBJ.3SG)-DEF

wažątire	rook	'eeja	"hatažanąka	hija	hi'ų"	'ee.
wažątire	rook	'eeja	hataža-nąka	hija	hi'ų	'ee
car	inside	there	light-POS.NTL:DIST	there	use	say(SBJ.3SG)

He got back into the car and we headed back, he was making noises: "ow, ow," after a little while, inside the car, he said "turn the lights on."

23.

Heesge	hija	yaa'ųwigają,	te'e	wicąwą sake,	wicąwą,
heesge	hija	hi<ha>'ų-wi-gają	te'e	wicąwą_sake	wicąwą
that's.why	there	<1E.A>use(OBJ.3SG)-PL-SEQ	this	watermelon	squash

wicąwą zii	xetexjįžą	ru'ąnąkšąną.
wicąwą_zii	xete-xjį-hižą	ru'ą-nąk-šąną
pumpkin	be.big-INTS-one	lift/carry(SBJ.3SG&OBJ.3SG)-POS.NTL-DECL

So we turned it on, the watermelon, the squash, he was carrying a huge pumpkin.

24.

Jaagu	wicąwą sake	waagi'ų	hahiiwira,	hegų
jaagu	wicąwą_sake	wa<ha-gi>'ų	ha-hii-wi-ra	hegų
what	watermelon	<1E.A-APPL.BEN>do/make	1E.A-arrive.there-PL-DEF	that.way

hąąkešge	nįge	hižą	hok'ųiranįkjane.
hąąke-šge	nįge	hižą	hok'ų-ire-nį-kjane
NEG.IN-also	somewhere	one	give(OBJ.3SG)-SBJ.3PL-NEG.FIN-FUT

We went for watermelons, and they weren't going to give him any.

25.

(ka)	Hąkaga	hinųpahąra	hatuti
(ka)	hąkaga	hi-nųųp-ahą-ra	hatuti
(HESIT)	NEG.IN.never	ORD-two-times-DEF	bring.along(OBJ.3SG)\1E.A

hahiwinįgųnį	yaare.
ha-hii-wi-nį-gųnį	hii<ha>re
1E.A-arrive.there-PL-NEG.FIN-DUB	<1E.A>think

I think we never took him again.

9.2 The complete Hocąk text without analysis

[1]Wažątire hižą hatucapra hegų 'eejaxjį mąą kerepąną nąga hakewe 'eejaxjį haanįgųnį. [2]'Eegi jaanąga 'aašge hocįcį ciirera (žee) žee waatutianąga wicąwą sake mąąnų hahiwišųnų. [3]'Eegi (mąąx hagici) (mąąx hagici) mąąx hagicinąka xeeižą 'eeja mįįnąkšąną, 'eegi nąągura cooweeja hogiwe, 'eegi xee kųųhąija nąągura bocgux nąąžį, 'eeja hirokinų. [4]'Eesge hąąheregi hija hahiwinągi, hatažara tuusepwianąga, wažątirera tuusepwianąga hija hahiwinąki hikųhe hegų hat'ąphanąkwiną. [5]'Eeja nąąwacakra mąijaagre 'eeja, hatucawinąga wicąwą sake hižąšąną haanįwianąga 'eeja, hiraati homįanąkwi, 'eegi hegų hąąke (tii) tiire haawinį, hegų howanąregi hegų hahi (xee) xee kųhąija 'eeja hahi wažątire jiikere. [6]'Eegi hąąke hegų hųųwesįwįiranįkje waagi'ųhanąkwi. [7]Hegų hagoreižą jagu hižąšąną ha'ųhajawi'ų hegų hahi waagitupįwi, hegų. [8]Wicąwą sake hižąšąną haanįwianąga hegų wažątire 'eeja hagi homįanąkwi hegų higųąną nįge hegų howaakarawišųnų. [9]Ho'ų te'e hagoreižą, hižą kaga hija hiinįšųnųra, žee hatuti hahiwi. [10]Wažątire 'eeja hagi hegų wesįwįnąąkšąną, žee jaagu 'ųąkgają, hąąke (ke) kirinį hajanąąk(šąną). [11]Hegų hanąąc warucgacgajee, 'aanąąkšąną. [12]Xapge hiigi pįįgają hegų yaarawi, hagoreižą 'ųųja'ų, guu. [13]Warukšira, hacįįja nąąwacakra mąijaagre žee hąąke 'eeja caawanįną. [14]Nąąwacakra hajinąknąga haxara hokąre hegų gixuxux 'eegi wažok hanį kįnįpšgųnį 'eejaxjį, horaknąąkšąną. [15]Nąąwacakra hajinąkšąną. [16]'Eesge, hegų žige xapge hiigi pįįgają. [17]Hegų žige haakja hija honį ree. [18]'Įį'įį te'e jaagu 'ųgają xapge hiigi pįįgają. [19]Hegų žige hižą honį ree. [20]Hegų žige warucgajee. [21]Hagoreižą hacįįja hokewera 'eeja kiri, hegų wažątire 'eeja kiri homįnąkra hegų hanąącį nąąc hisginąąkšąną 'anąga hegų hųųxarairawi 'eegi nąąkewe waa'ųhanąkwi. [22]Hegų wažątire 'eeja homįnąknaga, hakarawi hegų, 'iiružaknąkšąną, "'ao, 'ao," hirarexjįįk hiira wažątire rook 'eeja "hatažanąka hija hi'ų" 'ee. [23]Heesge hija yaa'ųwigają, te'e wicąwą sake, wicąwą, wicąwą zii xetexjįžą ru'ąnąkšąną. [24]Jaagu wicąwą sake waagi'ų hahiiwira, hegų hąąkešge nįge hižą hok'ųiranįkjane. [25](ka) Hąkaga hinųpahąra hatuti hahiwinįgųnį yaarc.

9.3 The complete English translation

[1]I got a car and I must have been around 16 at the time. [2]And the boys that lived nearby, I would take them along and we used to go and steal watermelons. [3]And that farm, there was a hill there and the road ran along the front, and there at bottom there was a crossroads, it was there on the other side (hidden by the hill). [4]That's why we'd go there at night, and we turned the lights off and then we turned the car off, and when we got there, we would jump out of the car quickly. [5]There was a fence on the ground there, we crossed there and each of us had a watermelon and we'd get back into the car but we didn't start it, we were letting it roll, and down the hill that's where the car would start. [6]We were doing this so they wouldn't notice us. [7]At one time, as each of us were doing this, we became good at it. [8]We would each have a watermelon, we would get right back into the car, and we'd head back right away. [9]This one time, someone who'd never gone along with us, we took him along. [10]They were watching him from the car, whatever he was doing, he didn't return to the car, they saw him. [11]He was feeling all of them, they said. [12]If he hurried up that would be good, we thought, and finally he came back. [13]Unfortunately, he didn't go to where the fence was on the ground. [14]He ran into the fence and fell backwards, he landed and squashed the watermelon, they told it kinda that way. [15]He ran into the fence. [16]It would be good if he came back quickly. [17]He went back to look (for another watermelon). [18]He was careful, whatever he was doing, it would be good if he hurried up. [19]Then he went to look for another one. [20]He was feeling them again. [21]He finally went back to where he had entered, and he came back to the car, and they were all scolding him, we were afraid of being caught. [22]He got back into the car and we headed back, he was making noises: "ow, ow," after a little while, inside the car, he said "turn the lights on." [23]So we turned it on, the watermelon, the squash, he was carrying a huge pumpkin. [24]We went for watermelons, and they weren't going to give him any. [25]I think we never took him again.

10 A warrior honor (Richard Mann) (CD 2 track 5)

10.1 Text with analysis and translation

1.

Haho,	hegų	Jąąpgwe	hįįgaire.
haho	hegų	jąąp-guhe	hi<hį>ge-ire
INTJ	that.way	have.open.eyes-be.coming.back.here	<1E.U>say.to-SBJ.3PL

Hello, my name is Jąąpgwe.

2.

Hagoreižą	'eegi	waagax haja	tuušjągają,	waakiišip	nąga	hegų
hagoreižą	'eegi	waagax_haja	tuušją-gają	ho<ha>kišip	nąga	hegų
sometime	and.then	go.to.school	quit\1E.A-SEQ	<1E.A>finish	and	that.way

mąižą	'eegi	hakocakgįk	hegų	wate.
mąą-ižą	'eegi	hakocąk-įk	hegų	wate
year-one	and.then	for.a.little.while-DIM	that.way	work\1E.A

One day when I finished school, I worked for a little while, for about a year.

3.

Hagoreižą	hegų	š'aak	wahaara	hegų	hąąphokahi
hagoreižą	hegų	š'aak	wa-haa-ra	hegų	hąąp-hokahi
sometime	that.way	be.old	OBJ.3PL-have.kin\1E.A-DEF	that.way	day-every

hegų	hoxjąną	wahacwigi	'eeja	'eeja	Vietnam	hegų
hegų	hoxjąną	wahac-wi-gi	'eeja	'eeja	Vietnam	hegų
that.way	evening	eat.sth\1E.A-PL-TOP	there	there	Vietnam	that.way

ha'e hiirešųnų.
ha'e_hii-ire-šųnų
talk.about(SBJ.3SG)-SBJ.3PL-HAB

One day, my parents, every day when we had our evening meal, they would discuss Vietnam.

4.

Heesgegają	hegų	hagoreižą	hegų	š'aak	wahaara
heesge-gają	hegų	hagoreižą	hegų	š'aak	wa-haa-ra
that's.why-SEQ	that.way	sometime	that.way	be.old	OBJ.3PL-have.kin\1E.A-DEF

heesge	wiakarage	mąąnąąpe	hakį,	raagų,
heesge	wa-hi<ha-kara>ge	mąąnąąpe	ha-kįį	roo<ha>gų
that's.why	OBJ.3PL-<1E.A-POSS.RFL>say.to	soldier	1E.A-act/become	<1E.A>want

wiage.
wa-hi<ha>ge
OBJ.3PL-<1E.A>say.to

That's how it was, then one day I said to my parents that I wanted to join the military.

5.

Heesge	hegų	(pįįnąą)	"pįįraakjene"	hįįgaire.
heesge	hegų	(pįįnąą)	pįį-raa-kjene	hi<hį>ge-ire
that's.why	that.way	(HESIT/SLIP)	be.good-make/CAUS\2.A-FUT	<1E.U>say.to-SBJ.3PL

They told me, "You will do good."

6.

'Eegi	heesge	haanąga	'eegi	mąąnąąpe	hakį.
'eegi	heesge	haa-nąga	'eegi	mąąnąąpe	ha-kįį
and.then	that's.why	make/CAUS\1E.A-and	and.then	soldier	1E.A-act/become

And that's what I did, I became a soldier.

7.

Hegų	jaasge	'eegi	wąąkra	jaasge	hiirešųnųra
hegų	jaasge	'eegi	wąąk-ra	jaasge	hii-ire-šųnų-ra
that.way	how	and.then	man-DEF	how	make/CAUS-SBJ.3PL-HAB-DEF

heesge	'eeja	sii woonąžį	hahi.
heesge	'eeja	sii_woonąžį	ha-hii
that's.why	there	match.steps	1E.A-arrive.there

Whatever the men used to go and do, I followed in their footsteps.

8.

Heesgegają	'eegi,	hagoreižą	'eegi	ha'ų	hanįhe
heesge-gają	'eegi	hagoreižą	'eegi	ha-'ųų	ha-nįhe
that's.why-SEQ	and.then	sometime	and.then	1E.A-do/make	1E.A-be/PROG

hajigają,	hegų	Vietnam	'eeja	hahi.
ha-jii-gają	hegų	Vietnam	'eeja	ha-hii
1E.A-arrive.here-SEQ	that.way	Vietnam	there	1E.A-arrive.there

That way, one day I was doing just that, and I went to Vietnam.

9.

'Eeja	(mąija)	mąižą	'eeja	ha'ų.
'eeja	(mąija)	mąą-ižą	'eeja	ha-'ųų
there	(HESIT/SLIP)	year-one	there	1E.A-do/make

I spent one year there.

10.

'Eeja	hagoreižą	'eeja	waakiišipgają	'eeja	žige	'eegi	mąą
'eeja	hagoreižą	'eeja	ho<ha>kišip-gają	'eeja	žige	'eegi	mąą
there	sometime	there	<1E.A>finish-SEQ	there	again	and.then	earth

teegi	hakiri.
teegi	ha-kiri
right.here	1E.A-arrive.back.here

Then one day when I finished there, I came back to this country.

11.

Hakirigają	hegų	'eegi	hi'ąc	haara	hegų	žige
ha-kiri-gają	hegų	'eegi	hi'ąc	haa-ra	hegų	žige
1E.A-arrive.back.here-SEQ	that.way	and.then	father	have.kin\1E.A-DEF	that.way	again

'eeja	hųųkarakit'eanąga	hegų,	'eegi	"woorera	hisge
'eeja	ho<hį-kara>kit'e-nąga	hegų	'eegi	woore-ra	hisge
there	<1E.U-POSS.RFL>talk.to(SBJ.3SG)-and	that.way	and.then	work-DEF	some

nįcųųkjene,”	hįįkarage.
nį-cųų-kjene	hi<hį-kara>ge
2.U-have.much-FUT	<1E.U-POSS.RFL>say.to(SBJ.3SG)

When I came back my father talked to me again, “You’re going to have a lot of work,” he told me.

12.

’Eegi	žige	’eegi	’eegi	mąąšųnąągre	heesgešge	’eegi
’eegi	žige	’eegi	’eegi	mąąšų-nąągre	heesge-šge	’eegi
and.then	again	and.then	and.then	feather-POS.NTL.PL:PROX	that’s.why-also	and.then

ha’e hii.
ha’e_hii
talk.about(SBJ.3SG&OBJ.3SG)

Then again he talked about these feathers.

13.

’Eegi	hagoreižą	’eegi	’eegi	koreesge	’eegi	šawaši
’eegi	hagoreižą	’eegi	’eegi	koreesge	’eegi	ša-waši
and.then	sometime	and.then	and.then	maybe	and.then	2.A-dance

rooragųgiži	hižą	’eeja,	hošawağukną,	nee	rakiikuruxurukjį
roo<ra>gų-giži	hižą	’eeja	ho<ša>wağuk-ną	nee	ra-kiikuruxuruk-jį
<2.A>want-TOP]	one	there	<2.A>wear-POT	2EMPH	2.A-earn(OBJ.3SG)-INTS

nįįsge,	hįįkarage.
nįįsge	hi<hį-kara>ge
VAGUE	<1E.U-POSS.RFL>say.to(SBJ.3SG)

Perhaps some time, if you want to dance, you can wear one, because you (sort of) have definitely proven yourself, he told me.

14.

’Eegi	žige	hinųk	caap	waašįnįňą	žige	hicųųwį
’eegi	žige	hinųk	caap	wa-ha<šį>nį-ra	žige	hicųųwį
and.then	again	woman	kin	OBJ.3PL-<2.A>have.NTL-DEF	again	aunt

waraaga,	hi’ųnį	waraga,	hinųknąągre
wa-raa-ga	hi’ųnį	wa-raa-ga	hinųk-nąągre
OBJ.3PL-have.kin\2.A-PROP	mother	OBJ.3PL-have.kin\2.A-PROP	woman-POS.NTL.PL:PROX

hanąąc	koreesgešge	’eegi	’eegi	wašiiregiži,	’eegi	teegi
hanąąc	koreesge-šge	’eegi	’eegi	waši-ire-giži	’eegi	teegi
all	maybe-also	and.then	and.then	dance-SBJ.3PL-TOP	and.then	right.here

mąąšų	howağuk	roogųiňegiži	heesge	raaną,
mąąšų	howağuk	roogų-ire-giži	heesge	raa-nąą
feather	wear	want-SBJ.3PL-TOP	that’s.why	make/CAUS\2.A-POT

hįįkarage.
hi<hį-kara>ge
<1E.U-POSS.RFL>say.to(SBJ.3SG)

And again your sisters, your aunts and your mothers, all these women, maybe they will dance and if they want to wear a feather, you can do that, he told me.

15.

’Eegi	’eegi	hojišąnąňe	nįįsge	’eegi	te’egi	mąąnąąpe
'eegi	'eegi	hojišąną-re	nįįsge	'eegi	te'egi	mąąnąąpe
and.then	and.then	recently-DEM.PROX	VAGUE	and.then	right.here	soldier

hakįgają,	hąąke	wažą	heesgešge	hakarakjąpnį
ha-kįį-gają	hąąke	hegų	heesge-šge	ha-karakjąp-nį
1E.A-act/become-SEQ	NEG.IN	that.way	that's.why-also	1E.A-expect(OBJ.3SG)-NEG.FIN

’anąga	’eegi,	žige	jaagu	te’egi	’eegi	hi’ąc	haara
'anąga	'eegi	žige	jaagu	te'egi	'eegi	[hi'ąc	haa-ra
and	and.then	again	what	right.here	and.then	[father	have.kin\1E.A-DEF

waajegųnį	yaaraanąga.
wee-jee-gųnį	hii<ha>re-nąga
talk(SBJ.3SG)-POS.VERT-DUB	<1E.A>think(OBJ.3SG)-and

And well, a little while ago, I had become a soldier, I wasn't expecting any of this, I was thinking, why is he telling me this.

16.

’Eegi	hakirigają	’eegi	žige	hakocąki	’eegi
'eegi	ha-kiri-gają	'eegi	žige	hakocąk-gi	'eegi
and.then	1E.A-arrive.back.here-SEQ	'and.then	again	for.a.little.while-TOP	here

ha’ų	hanįhegają	’eegi,	hicųwį	haara	žige
ha-'ųų	ha-nįhe-gają	'eegi	hicųųwį	haa-ra	žige
1E.A-do/make	1E.A-be/PROG-SEQ	and.then	aunt	have.kin\1E.A-DEF	again

heesgešge	hįįkarage,	hegų,	“cųųšgeįk
heesge-šge	hi<hį-kara>ge	hegų	cųųšge-įk
that's.why-also	<1E.U-POSS.RFL>say.to(SBJ.3SG)	that.way	maternal.nephew-DIM

haaxjį,	’eegi	’eegi	mąąšų	’eegi	raagųanąga
haa-xjį	'eegi	'eegi	mąąšų	'eegi	roo<ha>gų-'anąga
have.kin\1E.A-INTS	and.then	and.then	feather	and.then	<1E.A>want-and

wahajee,”	hįįkarage.
wahe-jee	hi<hį-kara>ge
talk\1E.A-POS.VERT	<1E.U-POSS.RFL>say.to(SBJ.3SG)

And when I came back here, I was here for a little while, and my aunt she talked to me about that (the feathers), “My nephew, I want a feather, that's what I am saying,” she said to me.

17.

Hegų	(hi’ąc	hiira)	hi’ąc	haara
hegų	(hi'ąc	hiira)	hi'ąc	haa-ra
that.way	(father	have.kin-DEF)	father	have.kin\1E.A-DEF

wakaragitakgają	“Heesgešge	hegų	yaa	hegų
ho<ha-kara-gi>tak-gają	heesge-šge	hegų	yaa	hegų
<1E.A-POSS.RFL-APPL.BEN>tell\1E.A-SEQ	that's.why-also	that.way	AFFRM	that.way

heesge	raanąą,”	hįįkarage,	hegų	’eegi
heesge	raa-nąą	hi<hį-kara>ge	hegų	'eegi
that's.why	make/CAUS\2.A-POT	<1E.U-POSS.RFL>say.to(SBJ.3SG)	that.way	and.then

nųnįge	'eegi	jaasge	hįhikjanawigi	hegų
nųnįge	'eegi	jaasge	hį-hii-kjane-wi-gi	hegų
nevertheless	and.then	how	1PL.A-make/CAUS-FUT-PL-TOP	that.way

honįgitakikje	hįįkarage.
ho<nįį-gi>tak-i-kje	hi<hį-kara>ge
<1&2-APPL.BEN>tell\1E.A-0-FUT	<1E.U-POSS.RFL>say.to(SBJ.3SG)

And when I told my father (what she said), "Yes, you should do that." he told me, here however, I will tell you how we are going to do it, he told me.

18.

'Eegi	hagoreižą	'eegi	'eegi	wąąk	kiikuruxuruknąągre	'eegi
'eegi	hagoreižą	'eegi	'eegi	wąąk	kiikuruxuruk-nąągre	'eegi
and.then	sometime	and.then	and.then	man	earn-POS.NTL.PL:PROX	and.then

heesgešge	hiirešųnųgają,	'eegi	'eegi	jaagu	'eegi
heesge-šge	hii-ire-šųnų-gają	'eegi	'eegi	jaagu	'eegi
that's.why-also	make/CAUS-SBJ.3PL-HAB-SEQ	and.then	and.then	what	here

'ųįňekjanegiži,	'eegi	'ee	ha'e hiirešųnųgają	'eegi,
'ųų-ire-kjane-giži	'eegi	'ee	ha'e_hii-ire-šųnų-gają	'eegi
do/make-SBJ.3PL-FUT-TOP	and.then	3EMPH	talk.about-SBJ.3PL-HAB-SEQ	and.then

'eegi	(te'egi)	wąąk	kiikuruxuruknąągre	'eegi	'eegi
'eegi	(te'egi)	wąąk	kiikuruxuruk-nąągre	'eegi	'eegi
and.then	(right.here)	man	earn-POS.NTL.PL:PROX	and.then	and.then

hakiriiregiži,	'eegi	wažąpįxjį	roohąxjį
ha-kiri-ire-giži	'eegi	wažą-pįį-xjį	roohą-xjį
COLL-arrive.back.here-SBJ.3PL-TOP	and.then	something-be.good-INTS	a.lot-INTS

hanįhakiriire,	(woore)	woorera	cųų	nįįsge	hegų
hanį-ha-kiri-ire	(woore)	woore-ra	cųų	nįįsge	hegų
have.NTL-COLL-arrive.back.here-SBJ.3PL	(work)	work-DEF	have.much	VAGUE	that.way

wa'ųnąąkgają.
wa'ų nąąk-gają
do/be-POS.NTL-SEQ

And one day these men that proved themselves used to do what they were going to do here, and they would talk about that, and

19.

Hegų	heesgešge	hiiregają,	'eegi	kiikuruxurukiregiži
hegų	heesge-šge	hii-ire-gają	'eegi	kiikuruxuruk-ire-giži
that.way	that's.why-also	make/CAUS-SBJ.3PL-SEQ	and.then	earn-SBJ.3PL-TOP

heesgešge	'eegi	wawikaragairegają	žige.
heesge-šge	'eegi	wa-hi<kara>ge-ire-gają	zige
that's.why-also	and.then	OBJ.3PL-<POSS.RFL>say.to-SBJ.3PL-SEQ	again

And that's what they did, they were told that they had proven themselves, again.

20.

Jaasge	hikiikarac	wa'ųnąąkgiži	hanąąc	nįįsge	wažą
jaasge	hikikarac	wa'ų-nąąk-giži	hanąąc	nįįsge	wažą
how	have.clan.membership	do/be-POS.NTL.PL-TOP	all	VAGUE	something

hijąhį	nįįsge	wawokaragiraknąga	wa'ųnąąk.
hijąhį	nįįsge	wa-ho<kara-gi>rak-nąga	wa'ų-nąąk
be.different	VAGUE	OBJ.3PL-<POSS.RFL-APPL.BEN>tell-and	do/be-POS.NTL.PL

Whatever Clan they belong to, they have been told different things.

21.

Nųnįge	'eegi	heerušga	'eegi	'aanąągre,	heesge
nųnįge	'eegi	heerušga	'eegi	'ee-nąągre	heesge
nevertheless	and.then	all.around.guy	and.then	say-POS.NTL.PL:PROX	that's.why

heesgešge	hegų	woošgą	hižą	hiiregają;	'eegi,	'eegi
heesge-šge	hegų	woošgą	hižą	hii-ire-gają	'eegi	'eegi
that's.why-also	that.way	way/practice	one	make/CAUS-SBJ.3PL-SEQ	and.then	and.then

tee	heesgešge	'eegi	wawikaragairegają	'eegi,	'eegi
tee	heesge-šge	'eegi	wa-hi<kara>ge-ire-gają	'eegi	'eegi
this	that's.why-also	and.then	OBJ.3PL-<POSS.RFL>say.to-SBJ.3PL-SEQ	and.then	and.then

heerušga	'eegi	woošgąižą	heregiži,	'eegi	žige	hacįįja
heerušga	'eegi	woošgą-ižą	here-giži	'eegi	žige	hacįįja
all.around.guy	and.then	way/practice-one	be(SBJ.3SG)-TOP	and.then	again	where

nįįsge	'eegi	wiirorakra	'eegi	hižą	'eeja	kąnąkireanąga
nįįsge	'eegi	wiirorak-ra	'eegi	hižą	'eeja	kąnąk-ire-'anąga
VAGUE	and.then	used.to.demonstrate-DEF	and.then	one	there	place-SBJ.3PL-and

'eegi	wąąk nąąwą	hija	'ųųnąąkgiži	'eegi	hirowagįx
'eegi	wąąk_nąąwą	hija	'ųų-nąąk-giži	'eegi	hirowagįx
and.then	singer	there	do/make-POS.NTL.PL-TOP	and.then	circumvent

nįįsge	'eeja,	'eegi	wąąk	kiikuruxuruknąągre	'eegi	'eegi
nįįsge	'eeja	'eegi	wąąk	kiikuruxuruk-nąągre	'eegi	'eegi
VAGUE	there	and.then	man	earn-POS.NTL.PL:PROX	and.then	and.then

jaasge	'eegi	hirogųįňegi	heesgešge	hiireną
jaasge	'eegi	hi-roogų-ire-gi	heesge-šge	hii-ire-ną
how	and.then	APPL.INST-want-SBJ.3PL-TOP	that's.why-also	make/CAUS-SBJ.3PL-POT

'eegi	wawigaire.
'eegi	wa-hige-ire
and.then	OBJ.3PL-say.to-SBJ.3PL

When they say Herushga, they're talking about a way of life; and thus they were told this, and the Herushga is a way of life, wherever they place a public address system, if they have singers there, and these warrios, who have prooven themselves, and what is wanted of them, they can do this, and they have been told this.

22.

'Ee	'ee	kiikuruxurukireanąga	wa'ųnąąkgają.
'ee	'ee	kiikuruxuruk-ire-'anąga	wa'ų-nąąk-gają
3EMPH	3EMPH	earn-SBJ.3PL-and	do/be-POS.NTL.PL-SEQ

They have proven themselves.

23.

Jaasge	'eegi	jaagu	howağuk	roogųiňegiži	heesgešge	'eegi
jaasge	'eegi	jaagu	howağuk	roogų-ire-giži	heesge-šge	'eegi
how	and.then	what	wear	want-SBJ.3PL-TOP	that's.why-also	and.then

'ųiňaną.
'ųų-ire-ną
do/make-SBJ.3PL-POT

Whatever they want to wear, they can do it.

24.

'Eegi	žige	'eegi	'eegi	mąąšųnąągre	'eegi	wažąxjį
'eegi	žige	'eegi	'eegi	mąąšų-nąągre	'eegi	wažą-xjį
and.then	again	and.then	and.then	feather-POS.NTL.PL:PROX	and.then	something-INTS

'eegi	jaasge	hiiregiži	heesgešge	woowağukirekjenegi,
'eegi	jaasge	hii-ire-giži	heesge-šge	wa-howağuk-ire-kjene-gi
and.then	how	make/CAUS-SBJ.3PL-TOP	that's.why-also	OBJ.3PL-wear-SBJ.3PL-FUT-TOP

'eegi	'eegi	wawigiirekjene,	tee	'eegi	wąąk
'eegi	'eegi	wa-higi-ire-kjene	tee	'eegi	wąąk
and.then	and.then	OBJ.3PL-recognize-SBJ.3PL-FUT	this	and.then	man

kiikuruxuruk	wa'ųnąąkgiži,
kiikuruxuruk	wa'ų-nąąk-giži
earn	do/be-POS.NTL.PL-TOP

And again these feathers, they're considered very sacred, and whatever they do, and if they're going to wear these feathers, they will be thought of this way, if they have proven themselves.

25.

Heesge	hiireanąga	'eegi	'eegi	koreesgešge	'eegi
heesge	hii-ire-'anąga	'eegi	'eegi	koreesge-šge	'eegi
that's.why	make/CAUS-SBJ.3PL-and	and.then	and.then	maybe-also	and.then

hiinųcaap	wahiirera	wažą	wahiirera
hiinų-caap	wa-hii-ire-ra	wažą	wa-hii-ire-ra
older.sister-kin	OBJ.3PL-have.kin-SBJ.3PL-DEF	something	OBJ.3PL-have.kin-SBJ.3PL-DEF

'eegi,	koreesgešge	'eegi	'eeja	waši	roogųiňegiži,	'eegi	'eegi
'eegi	koreesge-šge	'eegi	'eeja	waši	roogų-ire-gi	'eegi	'eegi
and.then	maybe-also	and.then	there	dance	want-SBJ.3PL-TOP	and.then	and.then

mąąšų	'eegi	'eegi	wagikereiregiži	'eegi	'eegi
mąąšų	'eegi	'eegi	wa-gi-kere-ire-giži	'eegi	'eegi
feather	here	and.then	OBJ.3PL-APPL.BEN-put.upright-SBJ.3PL-TOP	and.then	and.then

horoğocra	hiraicera	nįįsge	pįį	nįįsgairegųnį	hirairanąga
horoğoc-ra	hiraicera	nįįsge	pįį	nįįsge-ire-gųnį	hire-ire-nąga
look.at-DEF	more	VAGUE	be.good	VAGUE-SBJ.3PL-DUB	think-SBJ.3PL-and

heesge	'eegi	'eeja	howajii	nįįsge	'eegi	'eegi	hicųųwį
heesge	'eegi	'eeja	howajii	nįįsge	'eegi	'eegi	hicųųwį
that's.why	and.then	there	come.from	VAGUE	and.then	and.then	aunt

haara	heesge	(rookara)	roogų.
haa-ra	heesge	(rookara)	roogų
have.kin\1E.A-DEF	that's.why	(SLIP/HESIT)	want(SBJ.3SG&OBJ.3SG)

And along with this, perhaps their female relatives, their relatives, maybe if they want to dance there, and if they placed feathers on them, they do this because they think that this makes them look better, and coming from that, my aunt wanted a feather.

26.

Hegų	heesgešge	hagigi,	'eegi	mąąšų
hegų	heesge-šge	ha-gigi	'eegi	mąąšų
that.way	that's.why-also	1E.A-let/cause	and.then	feather

hagikere	'anąga	'eegi,	'eegi	žige	'eegi
ha-gi-kere	'anąga	'eegi	'eegi	žige	'eegi
1E.A-APPL.BEN-put.upright(OBJ.3SG)	and	and.then	and.then	again	and.then

(ną)	'eegi	hocįcįra	'eegi	žige	'eegi	nąąwąireanąga	'eeja,
(ną)	'eegi	hocįcį-ra	'eegi	žige	'eegi	nąąwą-ire-'anąga	'eeja
(SLIP)	and.then	boy-DEF	and.then	again	and.then	sing-SBJ.3PL-and	there

paašiwi.
paaši-wi
dance\1E.A-PL

And that's what I did for her, I placed this feather on her, and the boys sang there, and we danced.

27.

'Eegi	nųnįge	neexjį	'eegi	waa'ųnągre
'eegi	nųnįge	nee-xjį	'eegi	wa<ha>'ų-nąągre
and.then	nevertheless	1EMPH-INTS	and.then	<1E.A>do/be-POS.NTL.PL:PROX

hąąkešge	jaasge	hiiregiži	kaga	heesgešge	heesge
hąąke-šge	jaasge	hii-ire-giži	kaga	heesge-šge	heesge
NEG.IN-also	how	make/CAUS-SBJ.3PL-TOP	NEG.IN.never	that's.why-also	that's.why

'eeja	waacanį	haanąga	'eegi,	'eegi
'eeja	wa-haca-nį	haa-anąga	'eegi	'eegi
there	OBJ.3PL-see\1E.A-NEG.FIN	make/CAUS\1.EA-and	and.then	and.then

nįįkjąkxųnų	hanįhera	hegų	'eegi	hįwoowąkšųnųgają.
nįįkjąk-xųnų	ha-nįhe-ra	hegų	'eegi	hį-woowąk-šųnų-gają
child-be.small	1E.A-be/PROG-DEF	that.way	and.then	1E.U-be.naughty-HAB-SEQ

However, as for myself, I'd never seen them do that, and while I was a youngster, I used to be naughty.

28.

Hegų	ke	'eeja	wažą	'eeja	'eeja	hapahi	'eeja
Hegų	hąąke	'eeja	wažą	'eeja	'eeja	hapahi	'eeja
that.way	NEG.IN	there	something	there	there	go.toward(SBJ.3SG)	there

waacanįšųnų	hegų,	'eegi	'eegi	nųnįge	wąąknųįkra
wa-haca-nį-šųnų	hegų	'eegi	'eegi	nųnįge	wąąknųįk-ra
OBJ.3PL-see\1E.A-NEG.FIN-HAB	that.way	and.then	and.then	nevertheless	old.man-DEF

hąąkešge	hįįkaraganį	tee	nee	woorera	nee
hąąke-šge	hi<hį-kara>ge-nį	tee	nee	woore-ra	nee
NEG.IN-also	<1E.U-POSS.RFL>say.to-NEG.FIN	this	1EMPH	work-DEF	1EMPH

hįįnį,	nee	hašįnį.
hį-hanį	nee	ha<šį>nį
1DI.A-have.NTL	2EMPH	<2.A>have.NTL

I never saw anything of that, however, the old men, they never said anything, this is our job, it is yours.

29.

’Eegi	heesgešge	hįkarageanąga	hegų	’eegi
’eegi	heesge-šge	hi<hį-kara>ge-’anąga	hegų	’eegi
and.then	that’s.why-also	<1E.U-POSS.RFL>say.to(SBJ.3SG)-and	that.way	and.then

yaa’ųjaxjį	’anąga	’eegi,	’eegi	ceekjį	ha’ųgają	hąąke
hi<ha>’ųja-xjį	’anąga	’eegi	’eegi	ceek-jį	ha-’ųų-gają	hąąke
<1E.A>try-INTS	and	and.then	and.then	first/new-INTS	1E.A-do/make-SEQ	NEG.IN

’eegi	jaasge	haakjanegiži	hąąke	yaaperesnį.
’eegi	jaasge	haa-kjane-gi	hąąke	hi<ha>peres-nį
and.then	how	make/CAUS\1E.A-FUT-TOP	NEG.IN	<1E.A>know(OBJ.3SG)-NEG.FIN

And he told me that, and I’m trying really hard, when at first, when I did it, I didn’t know how to do it.

30.

’Eegi	žige	wąąknųįkra	žige	heesgešge	’eegi	’eegi
’eegi	žige	wąąknųįk-ra	žige	heesge-šge	’eegi	’eegi
and.then	again	old.man-DEF	again	that’s.why-also	and.then	and.then

heesgešge	hįįkaragegają	’eegi	“Hinįk	haaxjį,
heesge-šge	hi<hį-kara>ge-gają	’eegi	hinįk	haa-xjį
that’s.why-also	<1E.U-POSS.RFL>say.to(SBJ.3SG)-SEQ	and.then	son	have.kin\1E.A-INTS

’eegi	’eegi	tee	heesgekjenegiži	’eegi	’eegi
’eegi	’eegi	tee	heesge-kjene-giži	’eegi	’eegi
and.then	and.then	this	that’s.why-FUT-TOP	and.then	and.then

woorakarakgikje	heesge	jaasge	wąąk	hižą	mąįja
wa-ho<ra-ka>rak-i-kje	heesge	jaasge	wąąk	hižą	mąą-hija
OBJ.3PL-<2.A-POSS.RFL>tell-0-OBL.IN	OBL.FIN	how	man	one	earth-there

rat’ųpgiži.
ra-t’ųųp-gi
2.A-put.down(OBJ.3SG)-TOP

And the old men old me, “My son, if it’s going to be this way, you have to tell your story, however you put a man down (killed a man).

31.

Hicakoro,	hicakoro	hija	hahiire;	hisge	'eegi,	hižą
hicakoro	hicakoro	hija	ha-hii-ire	hisge	'eegi	hižą
friend	friend	there	COLL-arrive.there-SBJ.3PL	some	here	one

'eeja	mąija	rat'ųpgiži"	(horašo)
'eeja	mąą-hija	ra-t'ųųp-giži	(horašo)
there	earth-there	2.A-put.down(OBJ.3SG)-TOP	(SLIP/HESIT)

My warrior friends they've been there; and some of them, if you have put down an enemy soldier, you must tell this."

32.

Heesge	hįįkarage	'anąga	'eegi	'eegi	yaa'ųca
heesge	hi<hį-kara>ge	'anąga	'eegi	'eegi	hi<ha>'ųja
that's.why	<1E.U-POSS.RFL>say.to(SBJ.3SG)	and	and.then	and.then	<1E.A>try

ha'ų	hanįhe.
ha-'ųų	ha-nįhe
1E.A-do/make	1E.A-be/PROG

He told me this and so I've been trying to do this.

33.

'Eegi	Hoocąkra	hocįcįňa	roohą	hija	'eeja	hahiire,
'eegi	Hoocąk-ra	hocįcį-ra	roohą	hija	'eeja	ha-hii-ire
and.then	Hocak-DEF	boy-DEF	a.lot	there	there	COLL-arrive.there-SBJ.3PL

'eegi	hąąpte'e	žige	heesgešge	hiire,	'ųųnąąkgają
'eegi	hąąp-te'e	žige	heesge-šge	hii-ire	'ųų-nąąk-gają
and.then	day-this	again	that's.why-also	make/CAUS-SBJ.3PL	do/make-POS.NTL.PL-SEQ

hegų,	'eeja	hinųk	caap	wahiirera	hegų	heesgešge
hegų	'eeja	hinųk	caap	wa-hii-ire-ra	hegų	heesge-šge
that.way	there	woman	kin	OBJ.3PL-have.kin-SBJ.3PL-DEF	that.way	that's.why-also

'eegi,	'eegi	s'iirejąšge	heesgešge	hiperesiregają.
'eegi	'eegi	s'iireją-šge	heesge-šge	hiperes-ire-gają
here	and.then	long.time.ago-also	that's.why-also	know-SBJ.3PL-SEQ

And many Hocąk boys have been there, and today they're doing this, while they're there, their female relatives, they have been doing this, and they knew of this a long time ago.

34.

'Eegi	hąąke	'eegi	mąąšų	hegų	hegų	'eeja	(n)eexjį
'eegi	hąąke	'eegi	mąąšų	hegų	hegų	'eeja	'ee-xjį
and.then	NEG.IN	and.then	feather	that.way	that.way	there	3EMPH-INTS

'eegi	(wakikara)	wakiikereirekje	heesge(nį)	'eeja
'eegi	(wakikara)	wa-kii-kere-ire-kje	heesge-nį	'eeja
and.then	(SLIP)	OBJ.3PL-RFL-put.upright-SBJ.3PL-OBL.IN	OBL.FIN-NEG.FIN	there

'aire.
'ee-ire
say-SBJ.3PL

It is said that a person cannot just personally place a feather.

35.

'Eegi	'ee	nųnįge	hąąpte'e	'eegi	'eegi	hijąhįxjį
'eegi	'ee	nųnįge	hąąp-te'e	'eegi	'eegi	hijąhį-xjį
and.then	3EMPH	nevertheless	day-this	and.then	and.then	elsewhere-INTS

nįįsgeakgają	'eegi,	hegų	woorohą	'eegi,	'eegi
nįįsge-'ak-gają	'eegi	hegų	wa-ho-roohą	'eegi	'eegi
VAGUE-POS.HOR-SEQ	ant.then	that.way	OBJ.3PL-APPL.INESS-a.lot	here	and.then

wąąkšiknąągre	hąąke	Hoocąk	hirenįnąga,	neexjį
wąąkšik-nąągre	hąąke	Hoocąk	hire-nį-nąga	nee-xjį
Indian/person-POS.NTL.PL:PROX	NEG.IN	Hocak	SBJ.3PL-NEG.FIN-and	1EMPH-INTS

'eegi	waaganįnąkgają,	hegų	hanąącį	nįįsge	woošgą
'eegi	wa<ha>ge-nį-nąk-gają	hegų	hanąącį	nįįsge	woošgą
and.then	<1E.A>mean-NEG.FIN-POS.NTL-SEQ	that.way	all	VAGUE	way/practice

hanį	wa'ųnąąkgają.
hanį	wa'ų-nąąk-gają
have.NTL	do/be-POS.NTL.PL-SEQ

But it seems to be very different these days, most of these Indians, they don't think Hocąk, I don't mean myself, they all have their own way of life.

36.

Hegų	nųnįge	jaagu	hųųgirak	hanįhairera
hegų	nųnįge	jaagu	ho<hį-gi>rak	ha-nįhe-ire-ra
that.way	nevertheless	what	<1E.U-APPL.BEN>tell	COLL-be/PROG-SBJ.3PL-DEF

'eegi	hotoğocgają	heesgešge	hiinąąkgają	hegų.
'eegi	hotoğoc-gają	heesge-šge	hii-nąąk-gają	hegų
and.then	look.at\1E.A-SEQ	that's.why-also	make/CAUS-POS.NTL.PL-SEQ	that.way

However, what they've been telling me, as I look at this, that's what they're doing (what's happening).

37.

Hegų	koreesgešge	'eegi	hąąkešge	'eegi	wažą	'eeja	'eeja
hegų	koreesge-šge	'eegi	hąąke-šge	'eegi	wažą	'eeja	'eeja
that.way	maybe-also	and.then	NEG.IN-also	and.then	something	there	there

ruxurukirenįanąga	'eegi	nųnįge	'eegi	mąąšų	'eeja
ruxuruk-ire-nį-'anąga	'eegi	nųnįge	'eegi	mąąšų	'eeja
accomplish-SBJ.3PL-NEG.FIN-and	and.then	nevertheless	and.then	feather	there

howağuknąąkšąną;	hišge	'eegi	hinųknąąkašge	heesgešge
howağuk-nąąk-šąną	hisge	'eegi	hinųk-nąąka	heesge-šge
wear-POS.NTL.PL-DECL	some	and.then	woman-POS.NTL.PL:DIST	that's.why-also

hiireanąga.
hii-ire-'anąga
make/CAUS(OBJ.3SG)-SBJ.3PL-and

And maybe there is nothing, they didn't do anything to earn that but they were wearing a feather; and these women are doing it.

38. ’Eegi hąąpte’e ’eegi jaasge ’eegi š’aak hįwahiwira
’eegi hąąp-te’e ’eegi jaasge ’eegi š’aak hį-wa-hii-wi-ra
and.then day-this and.then how and.then be.old 1PL.A-OBJ.3PL-have.kin-PL-DEF

’eegi woošgą ’eegi hanį hajirera žee
’eegi woošgą ’eegi hanį ha-jii-ire-ra žee
and.then way/practice and.then have.NTL COLL-arrive.here-SBJ.3PL-DEF that

wooroh ą hąąke hiperesiranį.
wa-ho-roohą hąąke hiperes-ire-nį
OBJ.3PL-APPL.INESS-a.lot NEG.IN know-SBJ.3PL-NEG.FIN

And today, our elders, who brought this way of life forward to here, that, a lot of people don’t know.

39. Nųnįge hąąke (n)ee wa’ųiňanįgają ’eegi, kaga
nųnįge hąąke ’ee wa’ų-ire-nį-gają ’eegi kaga
nevertheless NEG.IN 3EMPH do/be-SBJ.3PL-NEG.FIN-SEQ and.then NEG.IN.never

’eeja heesge ’eeja wogirakiranįgiži jaasgegają
’eeja heesge ’eeja wa-ho<gi>rak-hire-nį jaasge-gają
there that’s.why there OBJ.3PL-<APPL.BEN>tell-SBJ.3PL-NEG.FIN how-SEQ

hiperesirekjanegają.
hiperes-ire-kjane-gają
know-SBJ.3PL-FUT-SEQ

But they didn’t do this, if they’ve never been told this, how were they supposed to know.

40. ’Eegi nųnįge ’eegi jaagu ’eegi š’aak wahaara
’eegi nųnįge ’eegi jaagu ’eegi š’aak wa-haa-ra
and.then nevertheless and.then what and.then be.old OBJ.3PL-have.kin\1E.A-DEF

’eegi ’aahanįhairera heesgešge hįįkarage.
’eegi ’ee-ha-nįhe-ire-ra heesge-šge hi<hį-kara>ge
and.then say-COLL-be/PROG-SBJ.3PL-DEF that’s.why-also <1E.U-POSS.RFL>say.to

However, my elders, what they’ve been saying, that’s what he told me.

41. Hegų hagoreižą ’eegi nįt’ųųňąwįgiži, ’eegi wažąňą
hegų hagoreižą ’eegi nį-t’ųųnee-wi-giži ’eegi wažą-ra
that.way sometime and.then 2.U-leave.behind(SBJ.3SG)-PL-TOP and.then something-DEF

’eegi ’eegi hijąhįxjį nįįsgekjane.
’eegi ’eegi hijąhį-xjį nįįsge-xjį-kjane]
and.then and.then be.different-INTS VAGUE-INTS-FUT]

One of these times, when I leave you all, things will be sort of very different then.

42.

Nųnįge	jaagu	'eegi	hašjagiži	jaagu	'eegi
nųnįge	jaagu	'eegi	ha<š>ja-giži	jaagu	'eegi
nevertheless	what	and.then	<2.A>see-TOP	what	and.then

hanąňąxgųgiži	hegų	kiira	š'ųųkjawi	heesge.
hanąą<ra>xgų-giži	hegų	kira	š-'ųų-kje-wį	heesge
<2.A>listen/understand-TOP	that.way	only	2.A-do/make-OBL.IN-PL	OBL.FIN

But whatever you see here and whatever you hear, that's all you're all supposed to do.

43.

Heesgešge	'eegi	hįįkaragaireanąga	waa'ųnąkgają.
heesge-šge	'eegi	hi<hį-kara>ge-ire-'anąga	wa<ha>'ų-nąk-gają
that's.why-also	and.then	<1E.U-POSS.RFL>say.to-SBJ.3PL-and	<1E.A>do/be-POS.NTL-SEQ

This is what they told me.

44.

Hąąke	neexjį	waa'ųnągre	hąąke	wažąįžą
hąąke	nee-xjį	wa<ha>'ų-nągre	hąąke	wažą-įžą
NEG.IN	1EMPH-INTS	<1E.A>do/be-POS.NTL:PROX	NEG.IN	something-one

waa'ųnįnąk,	nųnįge	'eegi	'eegi	jaagu	'eegi
wa<ha>'ų-nį-nąk	nųnįge	'eegi	'eegi	jaagu	'eegi
<1E.A>do/be-NEG.FIN-POS.NTL	nevertheless	and.then	and.then	and.then	what

x'ookeįk	waanįňą	'eegi	hųųgirakire
x'ooke-įk	wa-ha<ha>nį-ra	'eegi	ho<hį-gi>rak-ire
parent-DIM	OBJ.3PL-<1E.A>have.NTL-DEF	and.then	<1E.U-APPL.BEN>tell-SBJ.3PL

hanįhairera	hegų	kiira	nįįsge	'eegi	yaa'ųja	nįįsge
ha-nįhe-ire-ra	hegų	kiira	nįįsge	'eegi	hi<ha>'ųja	nįįsge
COLL-be/PROG-SBJ.3PL-DEF	that.way	only	VAGUE	and.then	<1E.A>try	VAGUE

waa'ųnąkgają.
wa<ha>'ų-nąk-gają
<1E.A>do/be-POS.NTL-SEQ

I, myself, I am nothing, whatever my parents had been telling me, that's all I am sort of trying to do.

45.

'Eegi	hąąke	tee	'eegi	goosgeįk	wahanįnąkšąną.
'eegi	hąąke	tee	'eegi	goosge-įk	wahe-nį-nąk-šąną
and.then	NEG.IN	this	and.then	for.no.reason-DIM	talk\1E.A-NEG.FIN-POS.NTL-DECL

hižą	'eegi	'eegi	hinųkįkižą	'eegi	jianąga	'eegi
hižą	'eegi	'eegi	hinųk-įk-įžą	'eegi	jii-'anąga	'eegi
one	and.then	and.then	woman-DIM-one	and.then	arrive.here(SBJ.3SG)-and	here

teeją	'aakcja	howajiianąga	'eegi,	'eegi	tee	koreesgešge
teeją	'aak-'eeja	howajii-'anąga	'eegi	'eegi	tee	koreesge-šge
ocean	POS.HOR-there	come.from(SBJ.3SG)-and	and.then	and.then	this	maybe-also

hakocąkįk	nįįsge	'eegi	wažą	'eegi	waagitakgiži,
hakocąk-įk	nįįsge	'eegi	wažą	'eegi	ho<ha-gi>tak-giži
for.a.little.while-DIM	VAGUE	and.then	something	and.then	<1E.A-APPL.BEN>tell\1E.A-TOP

’eegi,	’eegi	haną̨xgųňą,	wą̨ąk	wa’ųną̨ąkgiži,	heesgešge
’eegi	’eegi	hanąxgų-ra	wąąk	wa’ų-nąąk-giži	heesge-šge
and.then	and.then	listen/understand-DEF	man	do/be-POS.NTL.PL-TOP]	that’s.why-also

’eegi	yaa’ųca	nįįsge,	wahanąkšąną.
’eegi	hi<ha>’ųja	nįįsge	wahe-nąk-šąną
and.then	<1E.A>try	VAGUE	talk\1E.A-POS.NTL-DECL

I am not saying this for nothing, a little girl, when she came here, she came from across the ocean, and maybe for a little while, if I tell her something, if the listeners are men, that’s what I’m trying to do, that’s what I am saying.

46.

’Eegi,	haho,	’eegi	waakiišipikjane.
’eegi	haho	’eegi	ho<ha>kišip-i-kjane
and.then	INTJ	and.then	<1E.A>finish-0-FUT

Finally, I am going to finish.

10.2 The complete Hocąk text without analysis

[1]Haho, hegų Jąąpgwe hįįgaire. [2]Hagoreižą 'eegi waagax haja tuušjągają, waakiišip nąga hegų mąižą 'eegi hakocakgįk hegų wate. [3]Hagoreižą hegų š'aak wahaara hegų hąąphokahi hegų hoxjąną wahacwigi 'eeja 'eeja Vietnam hegų ha'e hiirešųnų. [4]Heesgegają hegų hagoreižą hegų š'aak wahaara heesge wiakarage mąąnąąpe hakį, raagų, wiage. [5]Heesge hegų (pįįnąą) "pįįraakjene" hįįgaire. [6]'Eegi heesge haanąga 'eegi mąąnąąpe hakį. [7]Hegų jaasge 'eegi wąąkra jaasge hiirešųnųra heesge 'eeja sii woonąžį hahi. [8]Heesgegają 'eegi, hagoreižą 'eegi ha'ų hanįhe hajigają, hegų Vietnam 'eeja hahi. [9]'Eeja (mąija) mąižą 'eeja ha'ų. [10]'Eeja hagoreižą 'eeja waakiišipgają 'eeja žige 'eegi mąą teegi hakiri. [11]Hakirigają hegų 'eegi hi'ąc haara hegų žige 'eeja hųųkarakit'eanąga hegų, 'eegi "woorera hisge nįcųųkjene," hįįkarage. [12]'Eegi žige 'eegi 'eegi mąąšųnąągre heesgešge 'eegi ha'e hii. [13]'Eegi hagoreižą 'eegi 'eegi koreesge 'eegi šawaši rooragųgiži hižą 'eeja, hošawağukną, nee rakiikuruxurukjį nįįsge, hįįkarage. [14]'Eegi žige hinųk caap waašįnįňą žige hicųųwį waraaga, hi'ųnį waraga, hinųknąągre hanąąc koreesgešge 'eegi 'eegi wašiiregiži, 'eegi teegi mąąšų howağuk roogųiňegiži heesge raaną, hįįkarage. [15]'Eegi 'eegi hojišąnąňe nįįsge 'eegi te'egi mąąnąąpe hakįgają, hąąke wažą heesgešge hakarakjąpnį 'anąga 'eegi, žige jaagu te'egi 'eegi hi'ąc haara waajegųnį yaaraanąga. [16]'Eegi hakirigają 'eegi žige hakocąki 'eegi ha'ų hanįhegają 'eegi, hicųwį haara žige heesgešge hįįkarage, hegų, "cųųšgeįk haaxjį, 'eegi 'eegi mąąšų 'eegi raagųanąga wahajee," hįįkarage. [17]Hegų (hi'ąc hiira) hi'ąc haara wakaragitakgają "Heesgešge hegų yaa hegų heesge raanąą," hįįkarage, hegų 'eegi nųnįge 'eegi jaasge hįhikjanawigi hegų honįgitakikje hįįkarage. [18]'Eegi hagoreižą 'eegi 'eegi wąąk kiikuruxuruknąągre 'eegi heesgešge hiirešųnųgają, 'eegi 'eegi jaagu 'eegi 'ųįňekjanegiži, 'eegi 'ee ha'e hiirešųnųgają 'eegi, 'eegi (te'egi) wąąk kiikuruxuruknąągre 'eegi 'eegi hakiriiregiži, 'eegi wažąpįxjį roohąxjį hanįhakiriire, (woore) woorera cųų nįįsge hegų wa'ųnąąkgają. [19]Hegų heesgešge hiiregają, 'eegi kiikuruxurukiregiži heesgešge 'eegi wawikaragairegają žige. [20]Jaasge hikiikarac wa'ųnąąkgiži hanąąc nįįsge wažą hijąhį nįįsge wawokaragiraknąga wa'ųnąąk. [21]Nųnįge 'eegi heerušga 'eegi 'aanąągre, heesge heesgešge hegų woošgą hižą hiiregają; 'eegi, 'eegi tee heesgešge 'eegi wawikaragairegają 'eegi, 'eegi heerušga 'eegi woošgąižą heregiži, 'eegi žige hacįįja nįįsge 'eegi wiirorakra 'eegi hižą 'eeja kąnąkireanąga 'eegi wąąk nąąwą hija 'ųųnąąkgiži 'eegi hirowagįx nįįsge 'eeja, 'eegi wąąk kiikuruxuruknąągre 'eegi 'eegi jaasge 'eegi hirogųiňegi heesgešge hiireną 'eegi wawigaire. [22]'Ee 'ee kiikuruxurukireanąga wa'ųnąąkgają. [23]Jaasge 'eegi jaagu howağuk roogųiňegiži heesgešge 'eegi 'ųiňaną. [24]'Eegi žige 'eegi 'eegi mąąšųnąągre 'eegi wažąxjį 'eegi jaasge hiiregiži heesgešge woowağukirekjenegi, 'eegi 'eegi wawigiirekjene, tee 'eegi wąąk kiikuruxuruk wa'ųnąąkgiži, [25]Heesge hiireanąga 'eegi 'eegi koreesgešge 'eegi hiinųcaap wahiirerą wažą wahiirera 'eegi, koreesgešge 'eegi 'eeja waši roogųiňegiži, 'eegi 'eegi mąąšų 'eegi 'eegi wagikereiregiži 'eegi 'eegi horoğocra hiraicera nįįsge pįį nįįsgairegųnį hirairanąga heesge 'eegi 'eeja howajii nįįsge 'eegi 'eegi hicųųwį haara heesge (rookara) roogų. [26]Hegų heesgešge hagigi, 'eegi mąąšų hagikere 'anąga 'eegi, 'eegi žige 'eegi (ną) 'eegi hocįcįra 'eegi

žige 'eegi nąąwąireanąga 'eeja, paašiwi. [27]'Eegi nųnįge neexjį 'eegi waa'ųnągre hąąkešge jaasge hiiregiži kaga heesge heesge 'eeja waacanį haanąga 'eegi, 'eegi nįįkjąkxųnų hanįhera hegų 'eegi hįwoowąkšųnųgają. [28]Hegų ke 'eeja wažą 'eeja 'eeja hapahi 'eeja waacanįšųnų hegų, 'eegi 'eegi nųnįge wąąknųįkra hąąkešge hįįkaraganį tee nee woorera nee hįįnį, nee hašįnį. [29]'Eegi heesgešge hįkarageanąga hegų 'eegi yaa'ųjaxjį 'anąga 'eegi, 'eegi ceekjį ha'ųgają hąąke 'eegi jaasge haakjanegiži hąąke yaaperesnį. [30]'Eegi žige wąąknųįkra žige heesgešge 'eegi 'eegi heesgešge hįįkaragegają 'eegi "hinįk haaxjį, 'eegi 'eegi tee heesgekjenegiži 'eegi 'eegi woorakarakgikje heesge jaasge wąąk hižą mąįja rat'ųpgiži. [31]Hicakoro, hicakoro hija hahiire; hisge 'eegi, hižą 'eeja mąija rat'ųpgiži" (horašo) [32]Heesge hįįkarage 'anąga 'eegi 'eegi yaa'ųca ha'ų hanįhe. [33]'Eegi Hoocąkra hocįcįňa roohą hija 'eeja hahiire, 'eegi hąąpte'e žige heesgešge hiire, 'ųųnąąkgają hegų, 'eeja hinųk caap wahiirera hegų heesgešge 'eegi, 'eegi s'iirejąšge heesgešge hiperesiregają. [34]'Eegi hąąke 'eegi mąąšų hegų hegų 'eeja (n)eexjį 'eegi (wakikara) wakiikereirekje heesge(nį) 'eeja 'aire. [35]'Eegi 'ee nųnįge hąąpte'e 'eegi 'eegi hijąhįxjį nįįsgeakgają 'eegi, hegų woorohą 'eegi, 'eegi wąąkšiknąągre hąąke Hoocąk hirenįnąga, neexjį 'eegi waaganįnąkgają, hegų hanąącį nįįsge woošgą hanį wa'ųnąąkgają. [36]Hegų nųnįge jaagu hųųgirak hanįhairera 'eegi hotoğocgają heesgešge hiinąąkgają hegų. [37]Hegų koreesgešge 'eegi hąąkešge 'eegi wažą 'eeja 'eeja ruxurukirenįanąga 'eegi nųnįge 'eegi mąąšų 'eeja howağuknąąkšąną; hišge 'eegi hinųknąąkašge heesgešge hiireanąga. [38]'Eegi hąąpte'e 'eegi jaasge 'eegi š'aak hįwahiwira 'eegi woošgą 'eegi hanį hajirera žee woorohą hąąke hiperesiranį. [39]Nųnįge hąąke (n)ee wa'ųiňanįgają 'eegi, kaga 'eeja heesge 'eeja wogirakiranįgiži jaasgegają hiperesirekjanegają. [40]'Eegi nųnįge 'eegi jaagu 'eegi š'aak wahaara 'eegi 'aahanįhairera heesgešge hįįkarage. [41]Hegų hagoreižą 'eegi nįt'ųųňąwįgiži, 'eegi wažąňą 'eegi 'eegi hijąhįxjį nįįsgekjane. [42]Nųnįge jaagu 'eegi hašjagiži jaagu 'eegi hanąňąxgųgiži hegų kiira š'ųųkjawi heesge. [43]Heesgešge 'eegi hįįkaragaireanąga waa'ųnąkgają. [44]Hąąke neexjį waa'ųnągre hąąke wažaįžą waa'ųnįnąk, nųnįge 'eegi 'eegi jaagu 'eegi x'ookeįk waanįňą 'eegi hųųgirakire hanįhairera hegų kiira nįįsge 'eegi yaa'ųja nįįsge waa'ųnąkgają. [45]'Eegi hąąke tee 'eegi goosgeįk wahanįnąkšąną. hižą 'eegi 'eegi hinųkįkižą 'eegi jianąga 'eegi teeją 'aakeja howajiianąga 'eegi, 'eegi tee koreesgešge hakocąkįk nįįsge 'eegi wažą 'eegi waagitakgiži, 'eegi, 'eegi hanąxgųňą, wąąk wa'ųnąąkgiži, heesgešge 'eegi yaa'ųca nįįsge, wahanąkšąną. [46]'Eegi, haho, 'eegi waakiišipikjane.

10.3 The complete English translation

[1]Hello, my name is Ją̧pgwe. [2]One day when I finished school, I worked for a little while, for about a year. [3]One day, my parents, every day when we had our evening meal, they would discuss Vietnam. [4]That's how it was, then one day I said to my parents that I wanted to join the military. [5]They told me, "You will do good." [6]And that's what I did, I became a soldier. [7]Whatever the men used to go and do, I followed in their footsteps. [8]That way, one day I was doing just that, and I went to Vietnam. [9]I spent one year there. [10]Then one day when I finished there, I came back to this country. [11]When I came back my father talked to me again, "You're going to have a lot of work," he told me. [12]Then again he talked about these feathers. [13]Perhaps some time, if you want to dance, you can wear one, because you (sort of) have definitely proven yourself, he told me. [14]And again your sisters, your aunts and your mothers, all these women, maybe they will dance and if they want to wear a feather, you can do that, he told me. [15]And well, a little while ago, I had become a soldier, I wasn't expecting any of this, I was thinking, why is he telling me this. [16]And when I came back here, I was here for a little while, and my aunt she talked to me about that (the feathers), "My nephew, I want a feather, that's what I am saying," she said to me. [17]And when I told my father (what she said), "Yes, you should do that." he told me, here however, I will tell you how we are going to do it, he told me. [18]And one day these men that proved themselves used to do what they were going to do here, and they would talk about that, and [19]And that's what they did, they were told that they had proven themselves, again. [20]Whatever clan they belong to, they have been told different things. [21]When they say Herushga, they're talking about a way of life; and thus they were told this, and the Herushga is a way of life, wherever they place a public address system, if they have singers there, and these warrios, who have prooven themselves, and what is wanted of them, they can do this, and they have been told this. [22]They have proven themselves. [23]Whatever they want to wear, they can do it. [24]And again these feathers, they're considered very sacred, and whatever they do, and if they're going to wear these feathers, they will be thought of this way, if they have proven themselves. [25]And along with this, perhaps their female relatives, their relatives, maybe if they want to dance there, and if they placed feathers on them, they do this because they think that this makes them look better, and coming from that, my aunt wanted a feather. [26]And that's what I did for her, I placed this feather on her, and the boys sang there, and we danced. [27]However, as for myself, I'd never seen them do that, and while I was a youngster, I used to be naughty. [28]I never saw anything of that, however, the old men, they never said anything, this is our job, it is yours. [29]And he told me that, and I'm trying really hard, when at first, when I did it, I didn't know how to do it. [30]And the old men old me, "My son, if it's going to be this way, you have to tell your story, however you put a man down (killed a man). [31]My warrior friends they've been there; and some of them, if you have put down an enemy soldier, you must tell this." [32]He told me this and so I've been trying to do this. [33]And many Hocąk boys have been there, and today they're doing this, while they're

there, their female relatives, they have been doing this, and they knew of this a long time ago. [34]It is said that a person cannot just personally place a feather. [35]But it seems to be very different these days, most of these Indians, they don't think Hocąk, I don't mean myself, they all have their own way of life. [36]However, what they've been telling me, as I look at this, that's what they're doing (what's happening). [37]And maybe there is nothing, they didn't do anything to earn that but they were wearing a feather; and these women are doing it. [38]And today, our elders, who brought this way of life forward to here, that, a lot of people don't know. [39]But they didn't do this, if they've never been told this, how were they supposed to know. [40]However, my elders, what they've been saying, that's what he told me. [41]One of these times, when I leave you all, things will be sort of very different then. [42]But whatever you see here and whatever you hear, that's all you're all supposed to do. [43]This is what they told me. [44]I, myself, I am nothing, whatever my parents had been telling me, that's all I am sort of trying to do. [45]I am not saying this for nothing, a little girl, when she came here, she came from across the ocean, and maybe for a little while, if I tell her something, if the listeners are men, that's what I'm trying to do, that's what I am saying. [46]Finally, I am going to finish.

11 Picking cherries (Richard Mann) (CD 2 track 6)

11.1 Text with analysis and translation

1.

Hagoreižą	hegų	nįįkjąknįk	hanįhe	hegų	hikorokeįk
hagoreižą	hegų	nįįkjąk-nįk	ha-nįhe	hegų	hikoroke-įk
sometime	that.way	child-DIM	1E.A-be/PROG	that.way	grandmother-DIM

haara	haakaraikižu	'eegi	nąąpak	hagihi
haa-ra	ha<ha-kara-gi>kižu	'eegi	nąąpak	ha-gihi
have.kin\1E.A-DEF	<1E.A-POSS.RFL-APPL.BEN>be.together	and.then	cherry	1E.A-pick

hahiwišųnų.
ha-hii-wi-šųnų
1E.A-arrive.there-HAB

Once when I was a child, with my grandmother we used to go cherry picking.

2.

'Eeja	wąąkšikra	roohą	'eeja	hiišųnų.
'eeja	wąąkšik-ra	roohą	'eeja	hii-šųnų
there	Indian/person-DEF	a.lot	there	arrive.there-HAB

A lot of Indians used to go there.

3.

'Eegi	tookregi	hegų	'eeja	haciwianąga	hegų	jaagu
'eegi	took-regi	hegų	'eeja	ha-cii-wi-'anąga	hegų	jaagu
and.then	summer-SIM/LOC	that.way	there	1E.A-live-PL-and	that.way	what

hagoreižąšge	'eeja	hahiiwigająšge	'eegi	'eeja	wagigoire.
hagoreižą-šge	'eeja	ha-hii-wi-gają-šge	'eegi	'eeja	wagigo-ire
sometime-also	there	1E.A-arrive.there-PL-also	and.then	there	give.feast-SBJ.3PL

In the summertime we used to live there, and what else, at one time when we went there, they had a feast.

4.

Hegų	'eegi	gipįesgešųnų.
hegų	'eegi	gipįesge-šųnų
that.way	and.then	be.enjoyable(OBJ.3SG)-HAB

It used to be enjoyable.

5.

Hegų	wąąkšikxetera	roohąxjį	'eeja	'ųųšųnų	nąga	hegų
hegų	wąąkšik-xete-ra	roohą-xjį	'eeja	'ųų-šųnų	nąga	hegų
that.way	Indian/person-be.big-DEF	a.lot-INTS	there	be-HAB	and	that.way

'eeja	ha'ųanįhawigają	hegų	hoišip	hegų	Hoocąk
'eeja	ha-'ųų-ha-nįhe-wi-gają	hegų	hoišip	hegų	Hoocąk
there	1E.A-be-1E.A-be/PROG-PL-SEQ	that.way	always	that.way	Hocak

hit’et’era	hanąąnąxgųšųnų.
hit’et’e-ra	haną<ha>xgų-šųnų
talk-DEF	<1E.A>listen/understand-HAB

There used to be a lot of elders there, and as we were living there, I would always hear the Hocąk language.

6.

Hegų	gipįesgeanąga	hegų	hąąheregiži	’eegi	Egg	Harbor
hegų	gipįesge-’anąga	hegų	hąąhe-regi-giži	’eegi	Egg	Harbor
that.way	be.enjoyable-and	that.way	night-SIM/LOC-TOP	and.then	Egg	Harbor

’aanąąkre	’eeja	hahiwišųnų,	’eeja	’eegi	wąąkšikižą
’ee-nąągre	’eeja	ha-hii-wi-šųnų	’eeja	’eegi	wąąkšik-iżą
say-POS.NTL.PL:PROX	there	1E.A-arrive.there-PL-HAB	there	and.then	Indian/person-one

’eeja	Trading	Postnįįsge	’aanąąkre	woruwį hocikereanąga	’eeja
’eeja	Trading	Post-nįįsge	’ee-nąąkre	woruwį_hocikere-’anąga	’eeja
there	Trading	Post-VAGUE	say-POS.NTL.PL:PROX	store.clerk-and	there

paašiwišųnų.
paaši-wi-šųnų
dance\1E.A-PL-HAB

It was enjoyable and at night we used to go to a place they called Egg Harbor, there was a person who ran what they called the trading post there, we used to dance there.

7.

Hegų	šawašiwigiži	hegų	žuura	hegų	silver	dollar
hegų	ša-waši-wi-giži	hegų	žuura	hegų	silver	dollar
that.way	2.A-dance-PL-TOP	that.way	money	that.way	silver	dollar

’aanąąkre	heesgeižą	honįk’ųįňeną.
’ee-nąąkre	heesge-ižą	ho<nį>k’ų-ire-ną
say-POS.NTL.PL:PROX	that’s.why-one	<2.U>give-SBJ.3PL-DECL

And if you danced there, they would give you what is called a silver dollar.

8.

Hegų	heesgešge	haawišųnųnąga	’eegi	hegų	hagairašge
hegų	heesge-šge	haa-wi-šųnų-’anąga	’eegi	hegų	hagaira-šge
that.way	that’s.why-also	make/CAUS\1E.A-PL-HAB-and	and.then	that.way	sometimes-also

hegų	hegų	nįįňą	sįnįgają	hegų	teexete	nįįsge
hegų	hegų	nįį-ra	sįnį-gają	hegų	tee-xete	nįįsge
that.way	that.way	water-DEF	feel.cold-SEQ	that.way	lake-be.big(OBJ.3SG)	VAGUE

wa’ųnąkgają	’eeja	(hahita)	hahira	hahiiwišųnų.
wa’ų-nąk-gają	’eeja	(ha-hiira)	ha-hiira	ha-hii-wi-šųnų
do/be-POS.NTL-SEQ	there	(1E.A-bathe)	1E.A-bathe	1E.A-arrive.there-PL-HAB

We used to do that and sometimes the water was cold in the big lake, we used to go bathe there.

9\. Hegų hegų hakocąkįk 'eeja hahiwi 'anąga hegų
hegų hegų hakocąk-įk 'eeja ha-hii-wi 'anąga hegų
that.way that.way for.a.little.while-DIM there 1E.A-arrive.there-PL and that.way

'eeja tuušjąwigiži 'eegi haakja nįįsge 'eeja 'eegi (cii)
'eeja tuušją-wi-giži 'eegi haakja nįįsge 'eeja 'eegi (cii)
there quit\1E.A-PL-TOP and.then backwards VAGUE there and.then (live)

hacįįja hikorokeįk haara 'eeja ciišųnų, 'eeja
hacįįja hikoroke-įk haa-ra 'eeja cii-šųnų 'eeja
where grandmother-DIM have.kin\1E.A-DEF there live(SBJ.3SG)-HAB there

haakja 'eeja caawawišųnų.
haakja 'eeja caa<ha>we-wi-šųnų
backwards there <1E.A>approach-PL-HAB

For a little while we'd go there and when we were finished there, we would head back towards where my grandmother was living.

10\. Hegų hihanąkgają 'eeja wąąkšikxete roohą hii
hegų hihe-nąk-gają 'eeja wąąkšik-xete roohą hii
that.way say\1E.A-POS.NTL-SEQ there Indian/person-be.big a.lot arrive.there

'anąga hegų 'eegi žige nįįkjąknįkra roohą 'eeja hegų
'anąga hegų 'eegi žige nįįkjąk-nįk-ra roohą 'eeja hegų
and that.way and.then again child-DIM-DEF a.lot there that.way

gipįesgešųnų, hegų.
gipįesge-šųnų hegų
be.enjoyable-HAB that.way

As I'm saying, there were many elders that were there, and then also the small kids, it used to be enjoyable.

11\. Hegų hagaira 'eeja wažąįžą honįgirakire 'anąga
hegų hagaira 'eeja wažą-įžą ho<nį-gi>rak-ire 'anąga
that.way sometimes there something-one <2.U-APPL.BEN>tell-SBJ.3PL and

hegų hąįnįxjį hiirakį 'anaga 'eegi nąąpak ragihiwi
hegų hąįnį-xjį hii<ra>kį 'anąga 'eegi nąąpak ra-gihi-wi
that.way morning-INTS <2.A>wake.up and and.then cherry 2.A-pick-PL

hii 'anąga nųnįge xųnųįk waa'ųajegają hegų
hii 'anąga nųnįge xųnų-įk wa<ha>'ų-ha-jee-gają hegų
arrive.there and nevertheless be.small-DIM <1E.A>do/be-1E.A-POS.VERT-SEQ that.way

hąąkešge hąąpserecnįįsge hegų nąąpak hagihinįšųnų, hegų
hąąke-šge hąąp-serec-nįįsge hegų nąąpak ha-gihi-nį-šųnų hegų
NEG.IN-also day-be.long-VAGUE that.way cherry 1E.A-pick-NEG.FIN-HAB that.way

hakocąkįk nįįsge waagihi 'anąga hegų žige 'eegi
hakocąk-įk nįįsge wa-ha-gihi 'anąga hegų žige 'eegi
for.a.little.while-DIM VAGUE OBJ.3PL-1E.A-pick and that.way again and.then

hakirikerešųnų.
ha-kiri-kere-šųnų
1E.A-arrive.back.here-go.back.there-HAB

Once in a while, they would tell you something, and you would wake up very early, and you went to pick cherries, however, because I was little and I wouldn't pick cherries all day long, I would pick for a little while and then I would leave.

12. Hihąą, hegų kiira.
hihą hegų kiira
INTERJ that.way only

Ok, that's all.

11.2 The complete Hocąk text without analysis

[1]Hagoreižą hegų nįįkjąknįk hanįhe hegų hikorokeįk haara haakaraikižu 'eegi nąąpak hagihi hahiwišųnų. [2]'Eeja wąąkšikra roohą 'eeja hiišųnų. [3]'Eegi tookregi hegų 'eeja haciwianąga hegų jaagu hagoreižąšge 'eeja hahiiwigająšge 'eegi 'eeja wagigoire. [4]Hegų 'eegi gipįesgešųnų. [5]Hegų wąąkšikxetera roohąxjį 'eeja 'ųųšųnų nąga hegų 'eeja ha'ųanįhawigają hegų hoišip hegų Hoocąk hit'et'era hanąąnąxgųšųnų. [6]Hegų gipįesgeanąga hegų hąąheregiži 'eegi Egg Harbor 'aanąąkre 'eeja hahiwišųnų, 'eeja 'eegi wąąkšikižą 'eeja Trading Postnįįsge 'aanąąkre woruwį hocikereanąga 'eeja paašiwišųnų. [7]Hegų šawašiwigiži hegų žuura hegų silver dollar 'aanąąkre heesgeižą honįk'ųįňeną. [8]Hegų heesgešge haawišųnųnąga 'eegi hegų hagairašge hegų hegų nįįňą sįnįgają hegų teexete nįįsge wa'ųnąkgają 'eeja (hahita) hahira hahiiwišųnų. [9]Hegų hegų hakocąkįk 'eeja hahiwi 'anąga hegų 'eeja tuušjąwigiži 'eegi haakja nįįsge 'eeja 'eegi (cii) hacįįja hikorokeįk haara 'eeja ciišųnų, 'eeja haakja 'eeja caawawišųnų. [10]Hegų hihanąkgają 'eeja wąąkšikxete roohą hii 'anąga hegų 'eegi žige nįįkjąknįkra roohą 'eeja hegų gipįesgešųnų, hegų. [11]Hegų hagaira 'eeja wažąįžą honįgirakire 'anąga hegų hąįnįxjį hiirakį 'anaga 'eegi nąąpak ragihiwi hii 'anąga nųnįge xųnųįk waa'ųajegają hegų hąąkešge hąąpserecnįįsge hegų nąąpak hagihinįšųnų, hegų hakocąkįk nįįsge waagihi 'anąga hegų žige 'eegi hakirikerešųnų. [12]Hihąą, hegų kiira.

11.3 The complete English translation

[1]Once when I was a child, with my grandmother we used to go cherry picking. [2]A lot of Indians used to go there. [3]In the summertime we used to live there, and what else, at one time when we went there, they had a feast. [4]It used to be enjoyable. [5]There used to be a lot of elders there, and as we were living there, I would always hear the Hocąk language. [6]It was enjoyable and at night we used to go to a place they called Egg Harbor, there was a person who ran what they called the trading post there, we used to dance there. [7]And if you danced there, they would give you what is called a silver dollar. [8]We used to do that and sometimes the water was cold in the big lake, we used to go bathe there. [9]For a little while we'd go there and when we were finished there, we would head back towards where my grandmother was living. [10]As I'm saying, there were many elders that were there, and then also the small kids, it used to be enjoyable. [11]Once in a while, they would tell you something, and you would wake up very early, and you went to pick cherries, however, because I was little and I wouldn't pick cherries all day long, I would pick for a little while and then I would leave. [12]Ok, that's all.